ADDRESSING THE LETTER:

Italian Women Writers' Epistolary Fiction

Italian women writers have reinvigorated the modern epistolary novel through their refashioning of the genre as a tool for examining women's roles and experiences. *Addressing the Letter* argues that many of these authors purposely tie narrative structure to thematic content, creating in the process powerful texts that reflect and challenge literary and socio-cultural norms.

Laura A. Salsini considers how the epistolary works of many nineteenth- and twentieth-century Italian women authors, including the Marchesa Colombi, Sibilla Aleramo, Gianna Manzini, Natalia Ginzburg, Dacia Mariani, and Oriana Fallaci, highlight such issues as love, the loss of ideals, lack of communication and connection, and feminist ideology. She also analyses what may be the first woman-authored example of Italian epistolary fiction: Orintia Romagnuoli Sacrati's *Lettere di Giulia Willet* (1818). In their reworking of the genre, Italian women writers challenged dominant assumptions about female behaviours, roles, relationships, and sexuality in modern Italy.

LAURA A. SALSINI is an associate professor in the Department of Foreign Languages and Literatures at the University of Delaware.

LAURA A. SALSINI

Addressing the Letter

Italian Women Writers' Epistolary Fiction

UNIVERSITY OF TORONTO PRESS
Toronto Buffalo London

© University of Toronto Press 2010
Toronto Buffalo London
utorontopress.com

Reprinted in paperback 2022

ISBN 978-1-4426-4165-5 (cloth)
ISBN 978-1-4875-2627-6 (paper)

Toronto Italian Studies

Library and Archives Canada Cataloguing in Publication

Title: Addressing the letter : Italian women writers' epistolary fiction / Laura A.
    Salsini.
Names: Salsini, Laura A. (Laura Anne), author.
Series: Toronto Italian studies.
Description: Series statement: Toronto Italian studies | Includes some text in
    Italian.
Identifiers: Canadiana 20210384271 | ISBN 9781487526276 (softcover)
Subjects: LCSH: Epistolary fiction, Italian – History and criticism. | LCSH:
    Italian fiction – Women authors – History and criticism. | LCSH: Italian
    fiction – 19th century – History and criticism. | LCSH: Italian fiction – 20th
    century – History and criticism. | LCSH: Sex role in literature. | LCSH:
    Women in literature. | LCSH: Gender identity in literature. | LCSH: Women
    and literature – Italy – History – 19th century. | LCSH: Women and literature
    – Italy – History – 20th century.
Classification: LCC PQ4181.E65 S25 2021 | DDC 853.009/9287–dc23

We wish to acknowledge the land on which the University of Toronto Press
operates. This land is the traditional territory of the Wendat, the Anishnaabeg,
the Haudenosaunee, the Métis, and the Mississaugas of the Credit First Nation.

This book has been published with the aid of a grant from the University of
Delaware.

University of Toronto Press acknowledges the financial support of the Government of Canada, the Canada Council for the Arts, and the Ontario Arts Council,
an agency of the Government of Ontario, for its publishing activities.

**Canada Council   Conseil des Arts
for the Arts   du Canada**

**ONTARIO ARTS COUNCIL
CONSEIL DES ARTS DE L'ONTARIO**
an Ontario government agency
un organisme du gouvernement de l'Ontario

Funded by the   Financé par le
  Government   gouvernement
  of Canada   du Canada

To my parents, Paul and Barbara Salsini,
and in memory of Nancy Tobias

Contents

Acknowledgments

This book was a joy to write, and not just because it allowed me to spend a few years reading other people's mail. I was fortunate to have both institutional and personal support throughout the researching and writing of this project.

A University of Delaware General Research Grant provided funds to begin my exploration of Italian women writers and their epistolary production. Dr Richard Zipser, Chair of the Foreign Languages and Literatures Department at UD, has been a staunch champion of this project from its inception.

Portions of this book have appeared in other publications, in modified forms. 'Rewriting the Risorgimento: Isabella Bossi Fedrigotti's *Amore mio uccidi Garibaldi*' appeared in *Forum Italicum* in 2008 (vol. 42) and 'Maraini Addresses Tarmaro: Revising the Epistolary Novel' was published in volume 78 of *Italica* in 2001. I am grateful to these periodicals for allowing me to reprint this material.

Ron Schoeffel at the University of Toronto Press has been a gracious and supportive editor. Other colleagues at UD, particularly Gretchen Bauer, Giuseppina Fazzone, Gabriella Finizio, Susan Goodman, Roberta Morrione, Vincenza Pastecchi, Riccarda Saggese, Monika Shafi, and Deborah Steinberger, have given me practical and personal assistance over the years. I thank Larry Baldassaro for his unwavering confidence in my work. Meredith Ray has been a wonderful sounding board for all matters epistolary.

Susan McKenna, Annette Giesecke, and Cindy Schmidt-Cruz are the best LWL ever; they never fail to inspire and energize me. Virginia Picchietti has read every word of this book at least twice and has offered advice ranging from the literary to the sisterly – *tante tante grazie*. My parents, Paul and Barbara Salsini, also applied their journalistic skills to drafts of the manuscript; for that, and for their never-ending faith in me, I am so grateful. To Doug and John, who bring such joy to my life, I give you all my love.

ADDRESSING THE LETTER:
ITALIAN WOMEN WRITERS' EPISTOLARY FICTION

Introduction

Italian women writers have reinvigorated the modern epistolary novel, fashioning it as a site for examinations of female roles and experiences. The intersection between the epistolary structure and the discussion of the female figure generates trenchant social analysis of contemporary mores. This study analyses, for the first time, how these authors deployed the letter text to rigorously critique the assumptions – literary or social – governing female behaviours.

A study of the centuries-old epistolary narrative may seem an anomaly in our technology-driven world. Certainly the ever-greater use of electronic mail, text messages, and cell phones has changed the way we speak and write to each other. Indeed, John L. Brown writes that in the midst of these innovations the epistolary novel 'perishes, unwept, unhonored, unsung, and largely unnoticed by the world at large' (220). But it is precisely in the midst of this communication revolution that other, older forms of interaction begin to seem especially intriguing. Despite periodic predictions that the epistolary novel is obsolete, no longer suitable in a society where written interactions are both instantaneous and incessant, it continues to thrive.[1] Cultural and literary critics are studying this phenomenon by looking at both fictional and real epistolary exchanges, seeking in them a means to better understand contemporary concerns through the letters of those often left out of traditional historical accounts.

Several recent projects in Italy attempt to incorporate these lost voices into the national consciousness. Since 1984 the Archivio Nazionale of Pieve Santo Stefano in Arezzo has published diaries, memoirs, and unedited correspondences in order to create 'una specie di banca della memoria' (*Emilia: Le parole nascoste*, 10) ['a type of memory bank'].[2] It recently published the letters of a certain Emilia, an unhappily married Milanese woman, to Federico, a young soldier, written from September 1872 to October 1881. The letters describe their affair, their separation, and finally his suicide. In addition, the epistles examine, albeit briefly, the post-unification, pre-emigration struggles of Italy. Saverio Tutino, the editor of *Emilia: Le parole nascoste* (*Emilia: The Hidden Words*), suggests that these older epistolary works – fictional or real – can make connections with our contemporary lives: '[A]nche le cose di un secolo addietro si legano direttamente alla nostra vita' (10) ['Even the things from a century ago tie directly to our lives']. The epistolary builds bridges, as it were, to different political and historical moments.

Another epistolary project, taken from the same archive, focuses more specifically on female correspondents and their world. *La finestra, l'attesa, la scrittura: ragnatele del sé in epistolari femminili dell'800* (*The Window, the Waiting, the Writing: Webs of the Self in Female Epistolaries of the 1800s*), edited by Clotilde Barbarulli and others, is a collection of letters four women wrote to their betrothed or husbands between 1844 and 1903. These letters revolve around the traditional feminine concerns of that era: husband, children, and home. In these letters, female roles, culturally prescribed and confined to 'sorella-figlia-moglie-madre' (sister-daughter-wife-mother) were defined strictly in relation to others (80). But while these letters often espoused traditional roles, they also served as a means of creating an identity for the female correspondents: '[L]e donne comuni possono trovare, nella lettera amorosa, sia pure in mezzo a dubbi ed incertezze, l'unica possibilità di lasciare sulla carta e non solo nella trama dei ricami la dichiarazione: io esiste' (10) ['Women can find in the love letter, even in the midst of doubt and uncertainty, the only possibility of leaving behind on paper, and not just in their embroidery stitches, the declaration: I exist']. These letters were not intended for publication, but the very act of writing them served as a vehicle for self-expression, allowing their authors to articulate their own concerns and desires. By employing the presumably innocuous genre of the love letter, these women fashioned their own voices in a culture and an era that did not value female expression. In rescuing these texts from the dusty trunks of family attics, the editors of *La finestra* liberate these otherwise unknown women from anonymity. In the process, the socio-cultural fabric of late nineteenth-century Italy must be reconstructed to embrace the heretofore silenced voices recording female experiences.[3]

My examination of nineteenth- and twentieth-century epistolary fiction by Italian women writers is triggered by this same desire to bear witness to these lost voices, and to see in these texts a connection between the literary codes and social injunctions that inform – and enforce – female roles and behaviours. The works I discuss demonstrate how these authors used the letter novel as a vehicle to illustrate, and often challenge, literary and social perceptions of women. The narrative structure becomes an integral part of this process, for through epistolary tenets – or a revision of them – these authors were able to communicate the poetics of their works to their readers through the connections inherent to the genre. Although some of the authors and texts studied here have received critical attention, my study is the first to systematically analyse the crossroads of genre and content in the works of these writers. Why did these women authors make use of this narrative structure, and how did they refashion it for their own female (if not always feminist) poetics?

Epistolary fiction has had a long and fruitful history across national literatures, illustrating the narrative structure's capacity to adapt throughout centuries of literary, socio-cultural, and political transformations. Perhaps the most famous early practitioner was Samuel Richardson, whose portrayals of persecuted heroines in *Pamela, or Virtue Rewarded* (1740) and *Clarissa* (1747–8) set the tone for future letter novels.[4] In France, *Letters of a Portuguese Nun* (1669) with its mysterious origins was followed by Choderlos de Laclos's *Dangerous Liaisons* in 1782. Examples of early epistolary fiction by women include Aphra Behn's three-volume *Love Letters between a Nobleman and His Sister* (1684–7), Françoise de Graffigny's *Lettres d'une Péruvienne* (1747), and Jane Austen's *Lady Susan* (published posthumously in 1871). Contemporary texts focus less on the traditional romantic plot and more on an exploration of female identity. Works such as Alice Walker's *The Color Purple* (1982), Margaret Atwood's *The Handmaid's Tale* (1986), and Jane Gardam's *The Queen of the Tambourine* (1991) recast the traditional format into a vehicle for a subjective female voice.

In Italy, the modern epistolary text has not received the same critical and systemic evaluation as in England, France, Germany, and the United States.[5] Rather, much work has been done on the rise of epistolary expression during the late medieval and Renaissance periods. During this time, such noted figures as St Catherine of Siena, Alessandra Macinghi Strozzi, and Arcangela Tarabotti used letters to discuss political, religious, and socio-cultural affairs. Other authors, including Vittoria

Colonna, Veronica Franca, and Isabella Andreini, examine in their letters familial, sentimental, and literary matters. Epistolary production for these women served as a valuable means of entering into a literary discourse with their male cohorts.

The focus of this study, however, is the epistolary *novel*, a tradition begun later in Italy than in other European countries. Thomas Beebee, in his study of the letter text in Europe from 1500 to 1850, has identified Ferrante Pallavicino's 1644 novel *Il Corriere svaligiato* (*The Ransacked Courier*) as the first fictional epistolary text written by an Italian.[6] There were a few other such Italian novels in the years that followed, but we must make a rather large leap to 1802 before the next successful epistolary novel is published: Ugo Foscolo's *Le ultime lettere di Jacopo Ortis* (*The Last Letters of Jacopo Ortis*), modelled in part on Johann Wolfgang von Goethe's *The Letters of Young Werther* (1774) and *Julie, or The New Heloise* (1761), by Jean-Jacques Rousseau. But while other national literatures heavily featured epistolary production in the first half of the 1800s, Italian authors favoured instead historical novels, and only turned to other narrative structures in the later part of the century.[7]

As with other European countries, both male and female authors in Italy produced epistolary fiction. Giovanni Verga's 1871 novel *Storia di una capinera* (*Sparrow*) features a virtuous heroine who narrates, through her letters, a tale of forbidden love and forced enclosure within a convent. In Guido Piovene's modern response to Verga's novel, *Lettera di una novizia* (*Confessions of a Novice*) (1941), his protagonist is also forced to take religious vows, although she is decidedly an anti-heroine. More recently, Antonio Tabucchi's *Si sta facendo sempre più tardi: Romanzo in forma di lettera* (*It's Getting Later All the Time*) (2001) uses the epistolary format to unhinge 'le categorie del genere letterario e [altera] la divisione tra mondo reale e mondo fittizio' (Brizio-Skov, 668) ['the categories of literary genres and alter the division between the real world and the fictitious world']. Certainly a thorough examination of these and other texts would reveal how male authors interpret the letter novel and offer a rich contribution to our understanding of literary styles and canon formation.

The focus of this study is the modern epistolary text by Italian women writers. Despite the popular and critical success of letter novels by well-known male authors in Italy and other countries, the genre has historically been considered a 'female' genre, practised by and most suitable for women authors.[8] The letter novel did stem in part from the tradition of letter writing, a practice that began, after all, as an intimate and often anti-literary expression of self – in other words, a practice that needed no particular or specialized education, as Ruth Perry points out. Because female letter writing historically revolved around matters of the heart, the male literary establishment posited that woman's very nature was inherently drawn to this practice. Women, then, were encouraged to participate in letter writing (as opposed to more challenging literary forms) since 'letter-writing had always been thought of as an accomplishment rather than an art' (Perry, 17). But when letter writing evolved into letter fiction, an interesting shift in critical assessment took place. Although early female-authored epistolary novels were often a popular success, they were speedily dispatched to a literary graveyard, for when the male critical establishment coupled women's writing with the epistolary mode it soon became devalued as a genre. Katharine Jensen, in her study of letter novels by French women writers, offers a succinct description of how perceptions of gender play into canon formation: the epistolary tradition 'fatally equates women's writing with letters; women's letters with unselfconsciousness, disorderly emotion; women's disorderly emotion with amorous suffering; and women's letters of suffering with nonliterary writing' (85).[9] Beebee also comments on this dichotomy: 'The letter is at once the most prominent and often-used literary genre considered suitable for women's voices and experience, and a sub-literary form to which they are condemned by the hierarchy of the genre' (105). What many of the critics condemning the epistolary format – and by extension, its practitioners – failed to recognize was how these women innovated the novel through their revision of the genre.

This book explores what these women writers did *within* the epistolary genre to challenge literary and social conventions, to find a voice or sense of identity, and to create an alternative to the male-constructed national canon. I take as my touchstone the work of Joanne Frye, who, while not studying specifically the epistolary text, does examine modern female-authored works written in the first person, a technique certainly analogous to the letter novel. She posits that an analysis of the parameters of the novel can lead to a radical reworking of both narrative and cultural conventions. Indeed, she writes, authors concerned with genre revisions do more than just challenge literary conventions, for 'to alter literary form is to participate in the process of altering women's lives' (33). The epistolary novels studied in the following chapters, with their open discussions of female experiences, encourage such a process as they question hegemonic institutions and traditions in Italy.

Feminist literary criticism provides the theoretical foundation upon which I constructed my analyses of the modern epistolary texts, although not all the works in this study are feminist in approach or tone. In the larger sense, feminism is predicated on some of the same tenets of epistolarity: a commitment to dialogue and collaboration (among women) and an emphasis on self-expression. This common ground was highlighted in the 1999 text *Letters of Intent: Women Cross the Generations to Talk about Family, Work, Sex, Love and the Future of Feminism*. Here, the chapters are set up as conversations between two women, one an established figure within the women's movement and a second, younger one. In the introduction, the two editors also write letters to one another, reinforcing the notion that 'positive relationships across generations are possible and fruitful' (Bondoc and Daly, 1). One, Meg Daly, describes how the project benefited her personally: 'Our friendship has deepened considerably through our collaboration, which is a testament to the importance of female friendship, correspondence, and collaboration' (2). The other editor, Anna Bondoc, points to the inherently complex, impassioned, and often ambiguous nature of the epistolary text when she notes its correlation with feminism: 'After reading our manuscript for the umpteenth time, I am struck by a kind of beauty about the unruly, unwieldy, nonhomogeneous nature of the book' (7).[10]

Feminist criticism also allows us to shift the focus of the traditional narrative presentation of woman from object to subject, both intra- and extra-textually. As Rodica Diaconescu-Blumenfeld points out in her essay on Dacia Maraini, 'Engaged in various representational strategies, from a subject position, women writers are rewriting the classic patriarchal masterplots, are transforming the rules of genre. Their chosen narratives, bound up with social identities and ideologies, are acts of resistance and of creativity' (9). While Diaconescu-Blumenfeld speaks specifically of the literary works produced during the Italian feminist movement of the 1970s and 1980s, Anna Santoro believes the evolution of a distinct female point of view began in the nineteenth century. Those writers, she points out, introduced 'nella narrativa italiana una grossa novità, e cioè che la voce narrante è quella di una donna. Semplicemente. Portano esse le loro scrittura come portano il volto, il corpo, che è corpo e volto di donna' (11) ['into Italian narrative an important innovation, and, put simply, that was the narrating voice of a woman. They wear their writing as they wear their face, their body, which is the body and face of a woman'].

Chapter 1 begins with the first female practitioners of the modern letter novel in Italy, examining the traditional epistolary narrative, centred on the love plot. The Marchesa Colombi, Matilde Serao, and Sibilla Aleramo all wrote sentimental letter novels that simultaneously incorporated conventional epistolary tropes and challenged both narrative and genre expectations. I include as well a discussion of the first modern Italian epistolary novel published by a woman: Orintia Romagnuoli Sacrati's 1818 *Lettere di Giulia Willet* (*The Letters of Giulia Willet*).

Chapter 2 examines how Aleramo, Benedetta Cappa Marinetti, and Gianna Manzini used the letter novel to explore important literary debates in twentieth-century Italy. In the process, the issue of canon formation is challenged, as these authors deployed the epistolary as a means for significant literary experimentation.

Chapter 3 focuses on how Natalia Ginzburg and Alba de Céspedes address the ethos of post-war Italy. Here, the correspondences contained in the epistolary novel lead to discussions on personal and socio-political commitment and communication. Both Ginzburg and de Céspedes deploy the letter text as a means to counter what they saw as a culture of widespread and debilitating personal and social alienation.

The final chapter looks at overtly feminist texts published during the height of the women's movement in Italy. Here Oriana Fallaci and Dacia Maraini energize the epistolary text by using it as a forum to discuss the cultural and political goals of the feminist movement. In contrast, Susanna Tamaro returns to a more conservative position, both in her novel's structure and in its poetics. Finally, Isabella Bossi Fedrigotti's epistolary historical novel reimagines a female voice within the male-centred chronicle of the Risorgimento.

Narrative structure was a fundamental component in the literary production of all of these authors. If we look at their works, we see an astonishing variety of genres: novels (feminist, Gothic, sentimental, *verista*, autobiographical, historical), short stories, poetry, critical essays, journalism pieces, travel writings, children's literature, diaries, memoirs, dramas, screenplays, and even visual art. They deliberately chose the narrative format that would best illustrate a particular thematic concern, whether it is the choral structure of de Céspedes's *Nessuno torna indietro* (*There's No Turning Back*) to reveal both female solidarity and the individual stories of young schoolgirls or Maraini's monologue-play *Dialogo di una prostituta con un suo cliente* (*Dialogue between a*

Prostitute and Her Client), which allows a marginalized figure her own space and voice. As this study demonstrates, the epistolary framework itself allowed these artists to focus on gender and genre.

Although these authors were (and in some cases continue to be) successful, productive writers, because of their sex, their works were often relegated to a secondary status among their contemporaries. The earlier, nineteenth-century writers such as the Marchesa Colombi and Serao were typically compared to each other, or to other 'lady authors' of their time, despite their active involvement in the literary and journalistic milieu and their vast literary production. Aleramo, who flouted both literary and social conventions, faced criticism that focused more on her amorous liaisons than on her works. The writers of the 1960s and 1970s, on the other hand, were generally grouped together under the label 'feminist,' despite often significant differences in style and content. Manzini generally escaped being pigeonholed as a 'woman' writer, perhaps because there were few women writing the *prose d'arte* for which she became known. Ginzburg, too, perhaps because of her firm disavowal of being categorized as a woman writer, was typically judged on her merits alone.

In this work, I, too, weigh these authors and their works against each other. But my approach is not to further banish them to a literary ghetto, reducing their achievements to a chapter – at best – in surveys of Italian literature.[11] Instead, by reading them *through* each other and in a rough chronological order, we can recognize more clearly their role in the creation of a literary genealogy. By examining how these women authors revised and revitalized the epistolary novel,we can finally acknowledge and pay tribute to their unique contribution to the world of letters.

Before delving into the works themselves, a discussion of the nature of letter novels is in order. Pinning down the specific characteristics of an epistolary text is an elusive process, especially in modern works. Ana Castillo, for example, in her *The Mixquiahuala Letters* (1986), completely destabilizes narrative structure in the epistolary by inviting readers to craft their own texts by selecting from three different tables of contents. Castillo's work points to the predicament of discussing an epistolary text: how to define it. Structurally, it is a work revolving around letters, but that basic framework includes much variation. An epistolary text can be composed of a one-, two-, or multi-sided correspondence.

Some such works are made up completely of letters; others may contain straight narrative as well. For the purposes of this study, a narrative is considered an epistolary work if it is in a fundamental way stimulated or affected by letters. The use of letters to drive the plot is the primary feature in an epistolary work, but other elements, both in structure and content, help distinguish this literary subgenre. Indeed, the connection *between* the structural and thematic components of letter novels serves to distinguish it from other forms. I focus my analyses on this connection, on how these authors deployed specific structural tenets of the epistolary to achieve particular thematic positions.

Because the central mode of communication among protagonists is written rather than oral, some measure of separation must exist to give rise to the letter writing within the text. This separation may consist of many years and many miles, or it may be a matter of a few brief hours apart. The point, however, is that the protagonists must rely on epistles to share their feelings and experiences. This creates a distinct sense of suspension in the epistolary text, for often the protagonists never meet, or do so rarely. As Janet Gurkin Altman points out, 'As an instrument of communication between sender and receiver, the letter straddles the gulf between presence and absence; the two persons who "meet" through the letter are neither totally separated nor totally united' (42-3). This space between the sender and the receiver of a letter is filled by the novel's reader, who, because the epistles call for both inter-textual and extra-textual responses, observes the creation of the narrative. In other words, because the epistolary allows for, and indeed insists on, an unusually engaged audience, the reader joins in the process of crafting the story.

The reader, then, plays an integral part in interpreting the missives sent to and from the protagonists. Often the external reader is represented by a figure who provides a framework that encloses the epistles and moves the narrative beyond the story contained within the correspondence. This figure has typically 'stumbled' across the correspondence in an attic or some such place, and serves as a guide as he or she introduces (and often concludes) the protagonists' story. This framework, absent from more modern letter novels, allows for commentary from an outside source, creating then an extra-textual interpretive stance.

The reliance on letters to transmit information and sentiment creates a particular temporal mood in these works: typically, the epistles use the present tense, although past events are often discussed and the future reunion of the separated protagonists is always uppermost in mind. But because events described in the missives have already taken place when the letters are read, and future events have usually been experienced, the concept of time plays a strikingly important role in epistolary texts. As Ronald Rosbottom points out, 'Letters are an attempt at arresting time, at controlling it, and in the epistolary work, time is shortened, lengthened, intensified through the processes of memory and anticipation' (289). The awareness of time is paralleled by an attentiveness to the marking of time; that is, to highlighting specific temporal elements within the letters. Missives are often dated, with attention given not only to day and year, but often to the hour in which they were written. The sense of immediacy that underpins all epistolary texts anchors them firmly to a recognition of the fleetingness of time, an element that often proves significant in the progression of the protagonists' relationship.

The awareness of time is mirrored by an awareness of self, an element fostered by the use of a first-person narrator. Indeed, the letter often becomes an opportunity for what Rosbottom calls 'themes of self-analysis, self-justification, and self-awareness in the narrative' (292). Protagonists, as they describe and interpret their lives, often come away from the process of letter writing with a greater understanding of themselves. This becomes especially important for female-authored texts, for heroines who are allowed a voice through their epistles are often more aware of their role within the text proper and the world in general. Feminist works in particular explore the connection between the epistolary first person and the development of self, although texts written before the women's movement also revealed an equally strong, if less explicit, discussion of this connection.

The first-person narrator's ability to analyse herself is facilitated by her separation from other characters, a necessary condition for the correspondence to exist. Heroines, especially in more traditional epistolary works, were often isolated from others in these novels: literally shut up in convents, sent to lonely country homes, or otherwise physically removed from the scene. Even though this seclusion was often involuntary, it could provide the stimulus needed for an honest and thorough examination of self. As Ruth Perry writes, 'The isolation of the characters is essential to the epistolary formula because it throws the characters back into themselves, to probe their own thoughts, their own feelings' (117). The structural element of isolation common to most epistolary novels serves to underline their focus on self-awareness and development.

Finally, although epistolary texts can be political, psychological, or historical in nature and intent, the traditional letter novel is typically categorized as either sentimental or educative. The first such type encompasses the erotic narrative, and involves the separation of two lovers and the unfolding of their relationship. The latter type embraces instead a narrative in which the protagonist is guided through social or cultural expectations to reach some level of maturity. Both approaches are critical to an understanding of female roles and experiences, within the text itself and within a socio-literary context.

For many modern epistolary texts, these generic conventions may exist in altered forms. Indeed, the elusiveness of epistolary tenets has perhaps allowed for the genre's survival, as Linda S. Kauffman points out: '[T]he very looseness of its conventions has made it resilient, adaptable, and relevant in diverse historical epochs' (*Special Delivery*, xiv). My study looks at how these Italian women writers have adopted the letter novel – in all its variations – as a means to redefine both literary and social expectations of female experiences.

1 Love Letters

The epistolary text traditionally pivots on a romantic entanglement; indeed, the lovers' separation is the catalyst for the exchange of letters. Because of the genre's emphasis on a romance narrative, it was often dismissed by critics as too sentimental and lacking in the cultural or social analysis found in those literary genres considered more substantial, such as the historical novel or the *bildungsroman*. However, these critics failed to see that many of the novels produced by women were indeed quite radical in their interpretations of the traditional love plot and of the very structure of the epistolary text. Indeed, I would argue that many of these authors chose the framework of the letter novel deliberately, as a means of deflecting critical attention from both their creative and thematic intentions.

The romantic letter novel is unique in offering a forum for social intercourse between unmarried men and women. While Ann Hallamore Caesar rightly asserts that 'the novel of courtship is rare' in eighteenth- and nineteenth-century Italy, due in part to the rigid social rules that kept the sexes separated until marriage, the epistolary text often undermined those conventions (29). In these works, this enforced separation actually sets up the conditions necessary for epistolary relationships. If unmarried men and women could socialize freely, there would be little need for an exchange of letters. The texts examined in this chapter focus primarily on couples who typically would not be allowed to interact; only through their letters are they able to bare their souls and their hearts. These exchanges often became the forum for the characters – and the authors – to directly challenge the social and cultural conventions of their times, from the codes of behaviour established for women (and men) to the attributes assigned to various female roles.

The letter text's predication on private correspondence allows for such challenges, for the authors are often able to conceal more subversive ideas in the compellingly intimate details that enliven and propel the relationship between lovers.

The authors examined in this chapter, Orintia Romagnuoli Sacrati,[1] Matilde Serao, the Marchesa Colombi (penname of Maria Antonietta Torriani), and Sibilla Aleramo, all produced letter fiction that, while relying heavily on traditional literary tropes, succeeded in confounding expectations about both narrative and genre. These women were part of the growing professional class of nineteenth-century writers, respected – and remunerated – for their work. This group of women, including Neera, Emma Perodi, Contessa Lara, and Vittoria Aganoor, were the literary grandmothers of later generations of female authors, paving the way for the more overtly feminist texts of the twentieth century. According to Antonia Arslan, these 'nonne' (grandmothers) were not afraid of confrontation with the male-dominated literary establishment: 'combattevano la buona battaglia delle idee, fra loro e con i colleghi maschi, in una sostanziale parità di trattamento da parte degli editori, che allora come oggi badavano al successo' ('L'opera della Marchesa Colombi,' 21) ['they fought the good fight of ideas, among themselves and with their male colleagues, in a substantial equality of treatment on the part of their editors, who then like today paid attention to success']. But being accepted by the literary establishment did not ensure inclusion in it, and many of these authors exhibited a generalized anxiety of authorship that influenced how explicitly they attempted to revise or confront canonic strictures.[2] Certainly, one would look in vain among their texts for undisguised challenges to entrenched literary models. But the authors under study here do reveal a growing awareness of how literary models – and the socio-cultural expectations in which they are rooted – position women in both fictional texts and in the real world.

Significantly, all four of the women discussed in this chapter periodically engaged in revising genre and literary conventions. They did this in part by employing a variety of genres, including novels, dramas, short stories, journalistic essays, poetry, children's literature, diaries, and travel books.[3] In many of these works, the writers struggled to create new archetypes that moved beyond the traditional portrayals of female experience. But all were handicapped by what Lucienne Kroha calls, in her description of the Marchesa Colombi's endeavour to script alternative narratives of (and for) women, 'a lack of both prestigious feminine role models for herself, as a woman engaged in an unusual activity, and of solid feminine literary models for her own experience as a woman' (49). These authors were limited in a very large part by the expectations of their particular time and place: nineteenth-century, conservative, Catholic Italy. However, it is precisely with the use of the epistolary text, with its implication of benign and propitiating narratives, that these authors were able to subtly subvert the conventions of the genre in meaningful ways. Indeed, careful readings of these works reveal that these women created a type of meta-text that focused as much on the creation of the letter novel as it did on the sentimental narrative contained within it.

I argue in this chapter that several Italian women employed the epistolary genre in order to question expectations – social, cultural, or literary – about female behaviour. The genre itself created a seemingly innocuous and non-threatening forum from which to incorporate potentially heretical ideas. Indeed, many of these works are very conventional in structure and tone. None of the works in this chapter come close to the proto-feminist agenda of Aleramo's 1906 novel *Una donna* (*A Woman*), for example, with its powerful message of female empowerment. But the very focus of the epistolary text is the domestic, the sentimental, the familial. If revolutions begin at home, then what better place for women writers to begin the slow march to liberation than through an examination of these quintessentially female sites?[4]

I begin with Orintia Romagnuoli Sacrati (1762–1834), a novelist, playwright, and short-story writer from Cenese. Despite a frustrating lack of information about her life or her work, it appears that she was the first modern Italian woman to have published an epistolary novel.[5] The 1818 *Lettere di Giulia Willet* (*The Letters of Giulia Willet*) employs many of the themes found in typical eighteenth- and nineteenth-century letter novels written by women in Italy and other European countries. These texts were often based in the domestic sphere and revealed a vision of women as either heroines or victims. The private realm, however, can become a rich and productive site of cultural analysis, and I believe that the authors discussed here intended to use their sentimental story lines as a vehicle for probing social criticism.

Certainly that is the case with *Lettere di Giulia Willet*, for Sacrati creates a text that eventually silences the female protagonist, a significant strategy for a genre predicated on the creation of a literary voice – that of the letter writer. By doing so, the author turns the emphasis away from the romantic plot, offering in its place piercing criticism of the cultural and social restrictions faced by women. Like the other authors in this study, Sacrati aims a reproachful eye at the conventions regulating a woman's life. She is concerned in particular with the proscriptions against social intercourse and financial independence for women in early nineteenth-century Italy, limitations that will see very little change during the course of the 1800s.

The theme of woman's lack of autonomy is reflected in two extratextual notes found at the beginning and end of the novel. The first is the dedication to the Prince of Saxe Gotha, who, the author hopes, will act as a sort of literary godfather to her fictional creation. 'Ognuno crederà, che io abbia in Voi ricercato un Protettore all'opera mia, e lo sareste, se per tale io v'invocassi,' she writes (iii) ['Everyone will believe that I have sought in You a Protector of my work, and you would be it if I asked that of you']. Here, she does more than just reveal the relationship between a female writer and the male protector and legitimator of her work. By using the hypothetical construction and emphasizing that the text comes from her hand, Sacrati also challenges that relationship, and, on a more profound level, the history of women writers forced to hide behind male pseudonyms in order to gain acceptance from the critical establishment. She then singles out one of the novel's characters in particular need of protection: 'La mia Giulietta avrebbe avuto in Voi Serenissimo Principe, un Protettore, un appoggio, se realmente più che un essere immaginato fosse pur stata un individuo nella società' (iv) ['My Giulietta would have in you most Serene Prince, a protector, a support, if such an imaginary being actually existed in society']. In her opening epistle, Sacrati neatly conflates the genuine and the fictional, moving the plight of her female protagonist into the realm of the real world.

At the end of the text is a second short note, this one apparently written by the publisher or editor, rather than the author herself. Here, the text is declared free of immoral material and is therefore approved for publication by Catholic authorities. The two notes serve to contextualize the novel itself, for they reveal a society and a literary generation at the mercy of political and religious institutions. The defencelessness of Sacrati's protagonist, then, is underscored at the text's opening and conclusion, a reminder of the constraints faced by women and enforced by two institutions. Artists – and perhaps female writers in particular – had to craft texts that appealed both to their reading public and to those authorities without whose blessing the works could not be published.

These extra-textual notes were a commonplace of earlier literary works, stemming from the tradition of capturing the attention, and perhaps the patronage, of the author's audience. However, the tradition becomes conflated with the epistolary practice of introducing and concluding a letter text with a short note from an anonymous editor, explaining how and where these letters – presumably private – came to light. Sacrati's use of this opening note becomes more relevant in light of its function in the epistolary genre. In *Lettere di Giulia Willet*, these explanatory asides are moved out of the text proper and the short note explaining the source of the novel's correspondence becomes more than just a literary commonplace. Instead, it suggests a criticism of the powers-that-be controlling literary production. By shifting the focus of the notes beyond the text, while still linking them to the defenceless condition of her heroine, Sacrati's analysis of those social forces limiting female experiences becomes particularly acute.

These constraints, at least in the case of Giulia, the novel's heroine, are both financial and social. In a series of 116 letters, exchanged by Giulia, her lover Alfredo, and a host of their relatives and friends, the protagonist's piteous situation and poignant fate are gradually revealed. Because Giulia's parents died young, she was raised by a cruel aunt who has designs on the family's fortunes. Giulia, who often bemoans the lack of a mother to guide her entry into womanhood, is able to leave her aunt's house only after receiving part of the family inheritance. But she is painfully aware of her status as an unmarried and unprotected female, turning down Alfredo's request for a visit because she must observe the etiquette required by what she calls 'lo stato mio di fanciulla' (46) ['my status as a maiden']. They can, however, exchange notes, and through these epistles their love grows despite – or perhaps because of – a lack of physical contact. This is, of course, a convention of the epistolary text: Lovers really do find the heart grows fonder through absence. The written word often brings about a true meeting of the minds; more corporeal interactions may then ensue, but they are typically left off the page.

Giulia's awareness of the precarious position of an unmarried woman without family or (much) fortune is a central motif in her letters to Alfredo. Although she finally allows him to call on her in chaperoned visits, she eventually regrets her decision, remarking in one letter that his courtship jeopardizes her reputation: 'Alfredo!' she writes. 'Riflettete che l'onore di una fanciulla è un fiore delicatissimo' (77) ['Reflect that the honour of a maiden is a very delicate flower']. Indeed an unmarried woman can taint even those close to her, as she writes: 'Una fanciulla indipendente è un oggetto singolare ... che ispira timore a chi deve riceverla in casa' (167) ['An independent maiden is a singular object ... who inspires fear in those who must receive her at home']. By the end of the novel, it becomes clear that the preoccupation with the fragility of the heroine's social standing is a means to disrupt the loving bond between Giulia and Alfredo.

But in *Lettere di Giulia Willet*, only a fraction of the letters concerns the amorous relationship. Instead, Sacrati underscores in the other epistles a heroine's tenuous grip on her own narrative. These letters deal with her guardian's legal battles to obtain Giulia's rightful inheritance, her aunt's efforts to besmirch Giulia's name by encouraging several reprobates to publicly pay her court, her friend Luisa's warnings against improper behaviour, and Alfredo's father's concerns about the value (social and financial) of his son's relationship with the young woman.[6] Through these letters we are privy to the ethos of an entire social milieu, in this case the aristocracy and upper class of Torino, an environment in which female behaviour is strictly regulated. It comes as no surprise, then, when Giulia's name does become compromised, both through her own innocent encounters with other men and her aunt's malicious gossiping.

Poor Giulia! She doesn't stand a chance at happiness, quietly sinking instead under the weight of all those expectations and proscriptions. Or at least, that is how Sacrati leaves it, for after many misunderstandings, intercepted messages, and spiteful manoeuvrings on the part of Giulia's aunt, the novel ends with the heroine's death. Giulia ran off to Genova after learning that Alfredo, believing himself jilted, married another woman. After an anguished reunion with her (ex)-lover, Giulia slowly succumbs to heartbreak, dying a week later in Luisa's arms after forgiving the guilt-stricken Alfredo. It is interesting to note that while Alfredo, who has not been entirely straight-forward in his dealings with Giulia or the woman he finally marries, is granted a 'happily ever after,' the female protagonist must pay the price for her tainted reputation. Sacrati's obvious sympathy for her heroine, her insistence on setting Giulia's plight against a discussion of her financial and social situation, and the carefully constructed extra-textual notes all point to a desire to move beyond the love plot and into an examination of those mandates by which all women, and society as a whole, were expected to behave. Because of the multiple viewpoints afforded by the various letter writers, the epistolary text in this case becomes the ideal forum to examine those social codes.

As Giulia becomes the sacrificial lamb, as it were, the archetypal victim of social mores, the use of the epistolary text becomes crucial. While we will see in later epistolary novels a growing sense of self-identity on the part of the female protagonists, in *Lettere di Giulia Willet*, it is the self-effacement of the heroine that is so striking. Twentieth-century epistolary novels by women often explicitly link the protagonists' act of letter writing with artistic creativity and self-expression. Their correspondence – with lovers, friends, and family members – becomes a means to explore by their own hand their development as women. But Giulia, piteously attempting to negotiate alone the expectations of the larger world, finds her voice and her identity effaced by the end of the text. Indeed, her last letters are increasingly erratic and short, reflecting the lack of control she has over her life and the concomitant inability to express herself. Although she is the protagonist of the novel, its final ten letters are not even written by her. Instead, others discuss Giulia and her tragic plight, effectively removing her from the action and reducing her from agent to object. By eradicating the protagonist's contribution to the text's final letters, the author makes clear how social expectations can erase female identity. Certainly the epistolary novel, with its first-person narration and its capacity for privileging some characters over others through the use of letter length and placement, is ideally suited for an examination of the deleterious effects of these expectations on female development. In *Lettere di Giulia Willet*, Sacrati uses the model of the sentimental letter text to forcefully criticize larger issues pertaining to women's identity.

Romantic narratives – and how women figured in them – were also the focus of a large part of the Marchesa Colombi's works. Indeed, her epistolary novel *Prima morire* (*First Die*) examines, as Sacrati did in *Lettere di Giulia Willet*, how literary expectations of female characters prove stifling and even life-threatening. Like other nineteenth-century women writers, Maria Antonietta Torriani (1840–1920) has been recently rediscovered, with conferences and monographs devoted to her works and reprintings of her writings.[7] This interest stems in part from the general undertaking by feminist, literary, and cultural critics intent on uncovering the voices of those whose artistic contributions have been forgotten, ignored, or even denigrated. In the Marchesa Colombi's case, scholars have been intrigued by nuances in her works, including subtexts and stylistic choices that indicate a profound interest in the presentation of female experiences in all levels of society.[8] She is perhaps best known for her novels *In risaia* (1878) (*In the Ricefields*) and *Un matrimonio in provincia*

(1885) (*A Small-Town Marriage*), as well as a lively and at times provocative conduct book titled *La gente per bene* (1877), works Arslan calls 'assolutamente originali nel panorama della letteratura italiana dell'epoca' ('L'opera della Marchesa Colombi,' 16) ['absolutely original in the panorama of Italian literature of that time']. Throughout her literary career, the Marchesa Colombi interrogated canonic strictures, questioning how male-established literary norms could accurately depict female lives.[9]

One narrative strategy in particular that illustrates the Marchesa Colombi's engagement with literary models involves the use of ironic authorial asides, calling on her *lettrici* (female readers) to unearth alternative readings within each text. This was a clever approach on her part, for while the authorial interventions did not overtly challenge entrenched literary codes, they did point to her interest in questioning those codes and in leading her reading public to do the same. Through these messages directed to her readers, the author also created a sisterly bond, solidifying her literary popularity while discreetly disseminating potentially seditious material.[10] She examines, for example, the hardships facing working women, the unhappy marriages of the bourgeoisie, and the hypocrisy of the upper classes.

The subversive relationship she creates with her female readers permeates the Marchesa Colombi's works, even those that do not overtly reference the reader. In her 1887 epistolary novel *Prima morire*, for example, the text's very structure begs to be read with such intent in mind. The direct and immediate invocations found in letter novels – from one letter writer to another – invite the readers to be an active part of this correspondence, in what Janet Altman calls the 'desire for *exchange*' (89). The first-person narration already pulls us in; the letters themselves serve as direct bridges to the reader. As Gail Pool writes, '[L]etter stories don't simply invite, they require participation. The salutation, the personal voice, the immediacy are enticing, and the stories engage us on at least two levels; the tale the letter tells and the tale of the letter itself, the larger context' (2). If romantic novels of the nineteenth century were aimed in particular at a female readership, then those women writers who chose to utilize the epistolary genre did so in part to communicate directly with that public. This becomes even more meaningful when we consider that the 'larger context' to which Pool refers often encompasses the social criticism evident in Sacrati's *Lettere di Giulia Willet* and that which we will uncover in the Marchesa Colombi's work. The result is thus, again, a correspondence between author and readers that mimics the epistolary structure of the text.

The epistolarity of *Prima morire* allows the Marchesa Colombi to address this larger context, for the novel's twin narratives create alternative articulations of female experiences. She is able to exercise her authorial intervention in the form of the letters themselves. Through these letters, the author comments on prevalent literary approaches and their role in creating female archetypes. What is interesting in this letter text, however, is how she disengages the strongest and most innovative female character from the epistolarity of work. This heroine is removed from the letter exchange, a narrative device that in this case ultimately emphasizes a freedom from the more restrictive conventions of romantic fiction. As Sacrati did with *Lettere di Giulia Willet*, the Marchesa Colombi questions the conventions of the letter genre and by extension its role in creating female identity.

The plot itself is doubled, as multiple correspondents carry on in thirty-six letters two separate love narratives, one ending in marriage, the other in death. Eva Malvezzi, married to a kindly but staid Milanese banker, falls in love with Augusto Cato, an impetuous and brilliant young composer who is completing his operatic masterpiece. After months of heroically resisting the lure of their love, they finally run off together to Lugano, but upon hearing that her young daughter is gravely ill, Eva returns home, and Augusto, realizing that their liaison is over, eventually takes his own life. In the second narrative, Augusto's closest friend, Leonardo Giordano, a poor tutor, marries out of pity the seemingly unschooled, unpolished daughter of a pharmacist. Mercede eventually reveals herself to be a beautiful, cultured polyglot, and the two settle down to a marriage based on mutual esteem and affection.

The use of the two disparate narratives, with their opposing thematic paradigms, is striking. Augusto, the musician, represents passion, and his affair with Eva is conducted through the language and rituals of romantic fiction. The young scholar Leonardo, on the other hand, is the epitome of rationality, and his relationship with Mercede, while concluding on a note of contented bliss, is not initiated with any thought of romantic fulfilment. As Leonardo writes to Augusto, '[I]l tuo amore si chiama tempesta, il mio si chiama pace' (174) ['your love is called tempest, mine is called peace'].

Kroha finds embedded within these parallel narratives a commentary on contemporary literary models. The author, she believes, confronts the limitations of both the romantic and the realist narrative (50). In fact, Kroha continues, in *Prima morire* the Marchesa Colombi deliberately criticizes these literary models for their failure to move beyond hackneyed and inaccurate portrayals of female experiences. By confronting contemporary narrative models through these opposing plots, the author 'has expressed her disapproval of these plots and characters by calling attention to their literary nature, and by creating situations which depict ... the distortions and disasters wrought by "unrealistic" literary expectations of life' (54). *Prima morire*, then, becomes a sort of meta-fiction, and its commentary on literature itself is further emphasized by its many references to other authors, including Shakespeare, Dante, Zola, and Foscolo. Even Manzoni is invoked – and then dismissed – with Eva criticizing *I promessi sposi* (*The Betrothed*) as unrealistic and lacking in verisimilitude.

Indeed, the impetus for the initial correspondence between Eva and Augusto is tied directly to a shared passion for literature. Eva accidentally leaves in a library book by Zola a letter to a friend commenting on the novel. Augusto finds the note when he reads the novel, and, intrigued by its author, decides to write to her. Eva's breezy letter to her friend offers a clue as to how this character approaches the art of writing and reading, for she says, '[S]ono certa che la mia lettera ti riuscirà più interessante del romanzo [di Zola]; sembra il principio d'un romanzo anch'essa; ma d'un romanzo vero' (3–4) ['I am certain that my letter will be more interesting to you than Zola's novel; it seems the beginning of a novel, but a real novel']. This is a revealing comment, for it indicates how willing the Marchesa Colombi was to challenge both the literary canon – Zola's novel – and the very notion of genre. Here, a female character equates her own writing – her letter – to that of a renowned novelist. The epistle becomes conflated with the literary, both as an example of great writing and as a narrative structure. Is the Marchesa Colombi also commenting on the literary merits of the epistolary novel? It appears so, for she asks her readers to question those critical standards that traditionally devalued the genres that were more closely associated with female authorship.

While traditional epistolary texts focus almost exclusively on the amorous relationship between the male and female protagonists, the Marchesa Colombi's use of the two liaisons in *Prima morire* involves more significant concerns for this study.[11] First, and in a concrete way, the author examines the limitations faced by two women, who, despite belonging to different socio-economic classes, are both defined and restricted by their female roles. Mercede, for example, is the daughter of a miserly and cruel man, who, because he refuses her a dowry, has effectively destroyed her chances of marriage. Instead, he forces her to enter a convent to avoid paying for her upkeep. She is rescued by Leonardo, who through his 'atto eroico' ['heroic act'] saves her from a lifetime of solitude and poverty (161). Both her wretched circumstances and her eventual salvation come about through her roles as daughter and then as wife. Mercede's forbearance in the face of misfortune does get rewarded, however, but it is not through her own agency. At the end of the text, Leonardo recognizes that she is 'coraggiosa, intelligente, bella, ... superiore a me' (172) ['courageous, intelligent, beautiful ... superior to me']. With this female character, the Marchesa Colombi addresses the cultural and literary convention in post-unification Italy that endowed women with a spiritual superiority, and portrays Mercede as the most principled character of the novel.[12] In Mercede's new role as wife, she will become the perfect helpmeet for Leonardo, a position the author extends to their professional life, for Mercede has a critical mind as sharp as her husband's and will doubtless be involved in his future literary endeavours.

But while the roles of daughter and wife come equipped with their own set of duties and proscriptions, those assigned to a mother outrank them all. The nineteenth century was a critical moment for the institutionalization of motherhood in Italy, for the Catholic Church officially proclaimed the dogma of the Immaculate Conception in 1854, although the cult and glorification of Mary had existed prior to this. The Virgin Mary became the model for all female behaviour, and the mother became the spiritual and emotional centre of the domestic sphere (Amatangelo, 71). *Prima morire* showcases this fateful development, for although Eva, the maternal figure in this text, initially – and selfishly – chooses the affection of a lover over that of her child, she eventually is brought to reason by circumstances designed to appeal to her motherly instincts. Eva aborts her flight with Augusto when she learns that her young daughter is ill with a severe case of measles. When Leonardo, appalled that his friend has broken their vow to lead honest and pure lives, writes to Augusto with news of the girl's illness, he emphasizes the child's fears that Eva has abandoned her.[13] '[L]a mamma non deve voler bene a nessuno più che alla sua bambina,' the child cries (134) ['A mother shouldn't love anyone more than her child'].

By privileging the needs of her child – and in the process sacrificing her own – Eva finally learns to embody nineteenth-century strictures regulating female behaviour. As the editors for the collection of genuine letters mentioned in the Introduction of this study point out, this was an era in which 'il ruolo femminile si conforma quasi sempre in uno stereotipo, fondato sul modello tradizionale della donna che rinuncia alla propria autonomia' (9) ['the female role conforms almost always to a stereotype, founded on the traditional model of the woman who renounces her own autonomy']. When Eva renounces her love for Augusto, she does so at great personal cost. Although she is allowed to return home, it becomes clear that life with her husband and child will be forever marked by the episode with Augusto. By blatantly flouting her roles as wife and mother, she has thoroughly disgraced herself in the domestic and public arena. But, interestingly, it is Augusto who suffers the far harsher fate; in the process of committing suicide he also destroys his music, obliterating any trace of himself, corporeal or artistic. By concluding the tales of Eva and Augusto with renunciation and death, the Marchesa Colombi comments on the perils of passion, a position made even clearer when juxtaposed with the much happier ending scripted for Leonardo and Mercede. While the author may be following the traditional literary trope that punishes women for expressing their sexuality, she also examines how female behaviour was restricted by those very roles engendered by social, cultural, and literary expectations.

In *Prima morire*, the Marchesa Colombi uses the letters between Augusto and Leonardo to address how male characters construct their female counterparts, furthering her examination of how these expectations circumscribed opportunities for women. In this instance, the epistolary text is an ideal forum for such an investigation, for through the deeply intimate and often philosophical correspondence between Augusto and Leonardo, the author reveals contemporary attitudes toward female behaviour. Augusto, an impoverished artist suffering in his cheerless and solitary garret, conforms to and embodies the codes of romantic fiction, revealed by his own pen. In an early letter to Leonardo, Augusto writes of his first view of Eva, a description that turns on a visual dissection of the woman and her feminine attributes. Because of the positioning of his lodgings, Augusto can see into Eva's room as she prepares for her bath. He spies her 'caviglia bianca come di marmo' (13) ['ankle as white as marble'] and then, as she reaches to close the window, sees 'tutto il braccio, la spalla e la rotondità nascente del petto' (14) ['all of her arm, shoulder and the budding roundness of her breast']. Augusto realizes his observations are indiscreet, confessing to Leonardo 'Mi parve di ascoltare ad una porta, di leggere una lettera diretta ad un altro; ne arrossii' (13) ['I felt as if I listened at a door, as if I had read a letter directed to someone else; I blushed for it'].[14] This phrase is significant, for it identifies the letter as a very private form of communication – like a conversation behind closed doors. Augusto also comments on a key taboo in epistolary fiction: the act of reading someone else's correspondence. This first indiscretion symbolized by reading the intimate correspondence of letters paves the way for the more serious transgressions to follow.

The letter, then, becomes the site of forbidden knowledge and, in Augusto's case, the catalyst for his subsequent ardour for Eva. When he sees Eva on her balcony, he notes that she is in fact an ordinary mortal, 'e non ha punto l'apparenza d'una eroina da romanzo' (15) ['and does not at all have the appearance of a heroine from a novel']. But after he discovers and reads Eva's misdirected letter to her friend in the library book, Augusto's initial attraction is rekindled by her description of his musical gifts, which she hears from her balcony. He returns her letter, wrapped in a copy of the musical composition that she had praised in it. While Augusto claims to Leonardo that he is not interested in this woman, the epistolary exchange between Augusto and Eva has clearly laid the foundation for their relationship.

Part of this foundation, at least for Augusto, rests in his desire to create an idealized woman. Both men reveal in their letters to each other their desire to improve their respective lovers. Over the course of their correspondence, we can trace the expectations they share of appropriate female behaviour, and their role in moulding such comportment. Early in their friendship, Augusto enthusiastically takes on the mantle of teacher, instructing Eva first in matters of music and art, but also in how to become a more virtuous person.[15] He attempts to construct, through the language of romantic fiction, the ideal romantic heroine, endowed with all the positive attributes of femininity. Eva is complicit in this metamorphosis, taking Augusto's advice to heart and striving to transform herself from a frivolous bourgeois matron to an altruistic patron of the poor. Of course, Augusto's plan backfires, as it were, for the two eventually fall in love and end up betraying their respective vows to their best friend and husband. Tied to the discourse of romantic literature and bound by its traditions, the couple succeed only in ruining themselves and the lives of those around them.

Leonardo's letters to Augusto also reveal his hope that Mercede will evolve into something other than the 'giovine disillusa, inasprita, e senza la potente attrattiva della bellezza' he had initially observed (158) ['disillusioned, embittered youth, and without the powerful attraction of beauty']. Interestingly, Mercede, who does finally reveal herself to be good, beautiful, intelligent, and passionately in love with her husband, is the only one of the four central characters who is not granted a means of self-expression; in other words, she writes no letters. This is not to suggest that Mercede is mute; almost all the letters of any length contain a fair degree of dialogue, and Leonardo reports his conversations with Mercede verbatim to Augusto. However, she is denied the more formal and immediate means of self-expression granted the other principal characters: the letter.

There is a simple narrative reason for such an omission: we are meant to be surprised (and delighted) to discover at novel's end that Mercede is in fact a literate and discerning individual. But with this narrative strategy, the Marchesa Colombi also comments on the function of letter texts and their role in affirming social and cultural roles of women. The author does this in a subversive way: she denies Mercede the right to participate in the correspondences among the friends and lovers. However, unlike the heroine in Sacrati's *Lettere di Giulia Willet*, whose identity becomes gradually effaced by her withdrawal from the epistolary narrative, Mercede, although seemingly passive, emerges in *Prima morire* as a strong and eloquent character.

The epistolary exchanges between Augusto, Eva, and Leonardo allow them to advance their own plots, and take control to some degree of their own narratives. But they are confined and limited by their roles as exemplars of romantic or realist fiction, as Kroha would have it – roles emphasized by the language and motifs of their letters. As a minor character and one seen only through the letters of her lover, Mercede is unable to shape her own destiny. However, because she exists to a large degree outside of the limitations of literary models or genres, she is free of their attendant expectations of female conduct. She can do this only by defying the conventions of the epistolary genre, by not directly participating in the exchange of letters that specify appropriate female behaviour. The Marchesa Colombi, then, circumvents the traditional structure of the epistolary text to create a heroine who escapes the prescriptions of the genre. In the process, the author comments on literary expressions of female roles.

This concern with the role and depiction of women within well-defined literary genres and approaches is certainly evident as well in the works of Matilde Serao (1856–1927), whose works are often quietly subversive.[16] Serao's examination of female experiences was often played out across a spectrum of diverse genres, including romantic, realist, and

Gothic fiction, as well as journalism pieces, and travel and religious texts.[17] She wrote several works grounded in epistolary fiction, including the 1905 novel *Tre donne*, which concludes with long epistles sent by the three female characters to the man they all love.[18] Serao's articulation of the epistolary plays a significant role in her project to address traditional literary genres, although few critics have chosen to examine her letter texts, especially in the light of their discussion of female experiences. This connection between literary models and their portrayal of female lives, however, is crucial to our understanding of Serao.[19]

What thematic and stylistic conventions was Serao working through when she turned to the epistolary genre? Three of Serao's letter texts, two short stories and a novel, reveal how this prolific author often articulated alternative versions of traditional literary models, creating works that questioned the cultural assumptions on which those genres were founded. The two stories, similar in style and narrative trajectory, can be read against each other, a critical strategy that is especially resonant for epistolary works, for the genre is predicated on an active and perceptive reader response, both within the text proper and beyond the narrative. Reading the two texts in this way – as a dialogue with each other – also allows us to trace the evolution of Serao's exploration of literary conventions.[20]

'Falso in scrittura' ('Falsehood in Writing'), published in 1899, clearly reveals Serao's clever manipulation of the epistolary genre. Briefly, the story consists of three letters written by a young, married woman over the course of her six-month liaison with a certain Cesare. The first epistle is a long response to a love letter sent by Cesare but unseen by the reader. Adriana rebuffs his overture, saying she had never encouraged his advances, and professing her fidelity to her husband, despite their unhappy marriage. Instead, she proposes a fraternal relationship with the young man, declaring that friendship 'è un affetto più grave e più serio di quel che pare' (200) ('is an affection graver and more serious than it appears'). In her second letter, a brief and passionate epistle obviously written in the throes of the affair, she begs Cesare to visit her during an impending four-day absence by her husband. The intensity of her ardour is underlined in the closing words, as she writes: 'Non t'amo, non t'adoro, t'idolatro. Sei il mio Dio' (201) ['I don't love you, I don't adore you, I idolize you. You are my God']. The final letter, again a lengthy one, reveals how Adriana is suffering terribly from guilt. She has decided, despite her enduring love for Cesare, to renounce their relationship and live quietly with her husband, calling herself 'una sposa indegna ma pentita' (202–3) ['an unworthy but repentant wife'].

With this story Serao appears to follow the strictures of the traditional epistolary text focusing on a love narrative: the affair is played out in letters, with the accompanying romantic rhetoric and an appropriately tragic (in this case) or happy ending. Several elements of 'Falso in scrittura,' however, attest to Serao's desire to question some of those very conventions. For example, the catalyst for this particular liaison may have been the male figure's letter, as is conventional. But it appears that it is Adriana who controls the relationship, granting Cesare visits at her convenience (and during her husband's absence, of course), and even determining when to end the affair. Later, Adriana uses as justification for terminating the affair her social position and her duties as wife, writing to Cesare: 'Parla all'anima mia, l'alta voce del dovere' (202) ['The loud voice of duty speaks to my soul']. This is, in fact, the very explanation used by Eva to break off her relationship with Augusto in *Prima morire*. An extramarital intrigue may be all fun and good, but it ultimately takes a back seat to being a wife and mother. These authors indicate that these female roles bring with them an entrenched set of expectations and duties that prove difficult – if not impossible – to ignore.

In 'Falso in scrittura,' then, is Serao arguing that women were restrained to some degree from acting in ways antithetical to the tenets governing their cultural and familial roles? Was she criticizing those restraints, or, given the way the short story concludes with the dissolution of the affair and a return to social order, was she merely remarking on how women *should* act? As always with Serao, the contradictions and ambiguities found in her personal and professional life – and those found within her fictive writings – mean that a definitive interpretation of a specific text is difficult.[21] However, I believe that Serao left clear textual directives here, in the form of an epistolary convention no less, on how to read this tale.

'Falso in scrittura' opens and closes with a short note from an anonymous editor, a traditional practice among epistolary writers. As we saw with Sacrati's *Lettere di Giulia Willet*, these brief notes typically frame the text, explaining the origins of the letters at hand. Serao's use of the anonymous narrator in 'Falso in scrittura' conforms to epistolary conventions, but she is in fact employing the narrative strategy to ponder issues of genre. In the opening letter, the narrator relates in rather lugubrious words that the three letters were found in a small ebony case, buried beneath a thimble and a shred of lace, and forming 'un morto solo, che furono un sol lutto' (197) ['a single death, which was a single mourning']. After reprinting the three letters, the narrator returns with a strangely ambiguous coda. He cannot remember how many years have passed since those letters were written, adding that after much reflection, 'non mi sono mai potuto accertare, in quale delle tre lettere, quella donna mentiva' (204) ['I was never able to ascertain in which of the three letters that woman lied']. It appears clear that this is Cesare writing, for who else would have in his possession three letters directed, long ago, to him? The trinkets in the ebony box can only be souvenirs given to him by Adriana, emblems of their love. Even more telling than these tangible tokens of their relationship, however, is the implication that the letters were false, that Adriana never loved him, or only loved him during part of their tempestuous affair. We can never gauge the authenticity of Adriana's feelings for Cesare, but we can read this tale as a commentary on epistolary fiction, and perhaps even romantic literature in general. The story's title cleverly suggests this itself. Are letters ever sincere, Serao asks? Can a genre that is grounded solidly on a fictional presentation of self-expression ever be anything other than unreliable? Serao does not provide a definitive answer, but by revisiting the conventions of the epistolary genre – and offering alternative textual readings – she points out the limitations in adhering to traditional models. I would argue that Serao is especially concerned with the influence generic conventions have on the construction of female archetypes and experiences, a subtext that runs through all of her works.

Examining a second short story that acts as a mirror image of 'Falso in scrittura' will further illuminate Serao's articulation of the intersection of the epistolary genre and gender. While 'Falso in scrittura' suggests the author is questioning literary conventions – both thematic and structural – 'La vita è così lunga' ('Life Is So Long') is a pointed criticism of romantic fiction and its construction of the female protagonist.[22] 'Falso in scrittura' and the 1918 short story 'La vita è così lunga' can be read as a turn-of-the century version of the modern 'he said/she said' tale; an approach that validates Serao's challenging of the legitimacy of the narrative voice. This approach also allows the reader to participate in a meta-literary epistolary dialogue.

Like 'Falso in scrittura,' 'La vita è così lunga' describes in three letters the evolution of a six-month affair between two members of the upper class. By using a male narrator in this second story, Serao significantly changes the focus of the plot from that of the earlier tale. In 'La vita è così lunga,' Luciano initiates the relationship by writing a long, impassioned epistle to Lillia, his interest piqued by her abrupt departure from a country house where a large group of friends have gathered. She is apparently attracted to him as well – she left with his handkerchief, the epitome of a romantic souvenir – and by the second letter the affair is well under way. The third letter mirrors that of 'Falso in scrittura,' for here, too, the narrator writes to break off the relationship, promising eternal love, but arguing that their numerous social and familial obligations prevent the affair from continuing.

At first glance, then, 'La vita è così lunga' appears to be simply the male rendition of 'Falso in scrittura.' However, a closer reading reveals how Serao is engaged in a larger discussion that revolves around the creation of female characters within the epistolary genre in particular and romantic fiction in general. The most striking element of Luciano's letters is the idealized and eroticized portrait they paint of Lillia. His first letter reduces this woman to a fragmented depiction of her face, with its 'bianchezza della fronte, con la luce vivida degli occhi … con gli angoli delle labbra rialzati che lasciano vedere i denti' (34) ['whiteness of the forehead, with the vivid light in her eyes, with the corners of her mouth raised to reveal her teeth']. Like Augusto in *Prima morire*, Luciano's first description of his future lover rests primarily on a recitation of disconnected body parts. For Luciano, Lillia represents Love itself, a living embodiment of the 'forma più alta dell'amore, la realtà più affascinante di qualunque ideale' (39) ['highest form of love, the most fascinating reality of any ideal']. But she is not lacking in the more sensual attributes of love; indeed, Luciano calls her 'mia tigre innamorata, mia gazzella dagli occhi morenti' (37) ['my enamoured tiger, my gazelle with the dying eyes'].

Even more alarming is how Luciano manipulates the depiction of Lillia so that she is left oddly without any identity of her own. He tells her: 'Non voglio conoscerti. Voglio amarti, misteriosa creatura, o mia sfinge che mi graffii il cuore, ma non voglio sapere la parola del tuo enigma' ['I do not want to know you. I want to love you, mysterious creature, oh my sphinx who scratches my heart, but I do not want to know the answer to your puzzle'], finally ordering her, rather frighteningly, 'Taci.' (39) ['Hush']. When Lillia does appear to reveal genuine feelings – when she no longer acts as an idealized and complacent lover – Luciano ignores or belittles her. In fact, in the final letter, Luciano admits that Lillia's most recent epistle, apparently reacting to his decision to end their affair, reveals that she is still 'agitata, inquieta e febbrile' (40) ['agitated, restless, and feverish']. Rather than address the cause of such feelings, he urges her instead to simply stop crying. He adds, in a particularly cruel coda, 'Forse ci rivedremo presto. Per quel giorno ti raccomando padronanza di te. Dissimula e ridi' (41) ['Perhaps we will see each other soon. On that day I advise you to be in control of yourself. Pretend and laugh']. The female character becomes almost completely effaced in this version of the epistolary text as Luciano succeeds in erasing her role in the relationship. Through this narrative strategy Serao appears to be warning against the genre's capacity to produce, in its use of letters, misleading and even purposely deceptive readings, a theme already highlighted by both the title and ambiguous coda of 'Falso in scrittura.'

But perhaps more indicative of Serao's denunciation of traditional romantic fiction is Luciano's conflation of his lover with Lillia's own text. He refers several times to letters she has written over the course of their affair, although these epistles are not included in the short story itself. While Lillia is denied an authentic portrayal of herself, her letters stand in for her when Luciano writes: 'La tua lettera è veramente una parte di te, l'ho a mente ... l'ho nel cuore' (38–9) ['Your letter is truly a part of you, I have it memorized, I have it in my heart']. Her epistles, in other words, act as metonymic manifestations of the woman herself; her word becomes flesh. If this female character can be reduced to her letters, what, then, is Serao saying about the epistolary novel and its representations of female experiences? What happens when a male character controls the letter text?

Again, I would point to Serao's use of an epistolary staple for directions as how to read both the text proper and the author's subtle interrogation of this genre. As in 'Falso in scrittura,' an anonymous editor relates how the letters fell into his/her hands, although in 'La vita è così lunga' it is clear that the writer is not the original recipient of the love letters. Instead, it is apparently a friend, who has been sent this correspondence from Lillia so that she could 'cancellarne l'ultimo amaro ricordo della sua mente' (33) ['cancel the last bitter memory from her mind']. Lillia no longer loves Luciano; indeed, the editor suspects she would not even recognize the letters from this long-past liaison. At the very end of this explanation, just as in 'Falso in scrittura,' Serao supplies an enigmatic clue to the meaning of the longer narrative itself. 'L'amore è così breve,' writes the editor, 'la vita è così lunga!' (33) ['Love is so brief; life is so long!']. Luciano's construction of Lillia as first an idealized woman and later a pathetic and hysterical ex-lover was merely a fleeting episode in her life. Since then, 'È tanto tempo che la tempesta si è allontanata dal suo cuore; è tanto tempo che ella ha raggiunto la serenità' (33) ['It has been a long time since the storm has left her heart; it has been a long time since she has regained her serenity']. In short, she has succeeded in throwing off the persona manufactured by her lover, choosing instead to construct a self-identity that does not depend on a stereotypical depiction of feminine behaviour.[23] Luciano's interpretation of Lillia's behaviour throughout the text may be rooted in his desire to yoke it to the staples of romantic fiction, but Serao's brief postscript undermines that attempt.[24]

An even more radical reworking of the epistolary convention is the 1914 novel *Ella non rispose* (*She Did Not Reply*), where Serao eschews the anonymous editor and enters directly into the text. This long novel is composed of a fairly lengthy introduction by Serao, ninety letters sent from the protagonist Paolo Ruffo to Diana Sforza, and several concluding chapters that are not in letter form. By taking over the role of the anonymous editor, Serao is able to more directly address the epistolary genre and its close connection with romantic fiction. Indeed, in her opening lines, she implores her readers not to dismiss or denigrate this text simply because it is a 'romanzo d'amore' (v). 'Non ti sorprenda,' she warns her readers, that 'tutta quanta questa storia di amore, compaia nelle lettere di Paolo a Diana … e solo da queste lettere essa palpiti di una vita passionale indomita, nelle sue gioie supreme e nelle sue estreme disperazioni' (vii) ['Do not be surprised that all this love story appears in Paolo's letters to Diana, and only from these letters does [the love story] beat its indomitable and passionate life, in its supreme joys and its extreme despairs'] .[25] She endows the love letter, then, with the ability to generate amorous feelings as well as to create and shape narrative. 'Ah, tu lo sai bene che la lettera d'amore … è tutto l'amore!' she adds (vii) ['Ah, you know well that the love letter … it is all love!']. The love letter's particular power rests partly in its permanence, or as Serao succinctly puts it, *scripta manent*, loosely translated as 'the written word is enduring' (viii). Not only, then, will the letters from Paolo to Diana last forever, but so also, presumably, will this epistolary novel, granting Serao's fiction a lasting position in the annals of romantic literature.

As she continues her introduction, Serao moves from the discussion of the novel's fictive correspondence to an examination of real letters, conflating the fictive with the genuine in a strategy that emphasizes the more realist aspects of *Ella non rispose*. She also underlines the fluidity of genre categories, calling attention specifically to the historical connection between writing letters and writing epistolary novels. Serao does this by discussing the many letters she receives from admirers all over the world after the publication of each of her works. She not only confirms her literary legacy by noting the magnitude and devotion of her reading public, she also emphasizes that she writes specifically for these readers, as opposed to the more critical literary establishment. 'E sempre,' she writes, 'questa lettera mi è bastata, per dire che la mia opera non era stata un vano e sterile esercizio di letteratura: ma qualche cosa di semplice e di schietto, nella sua forza di sentimento' (xii) ['And as always, I only needed this letter to say that my work was not a vain and sterile literary exercise: but something simple and pure in its strength of feeling']. The letter – be it real or fictive – possesses and voices a tremendous authority, and, as we shall see in *Ella non rispose,* even determines issues of life and death. To sum up, Serao's introduction contextualizes the letter text within its earlier incarnation as a love letter, eliding the two modes of expression. By viewing the love letter as agent and creator of narrative, the author validates the letter novel, even if it falls within the realm of conventional romantic fiction.

In *Ella non rispose,* Serao addresses many of the same concerns regarding the construction of female characters and the depiction of female experiences within the epistolary text that we saw in her previous works. The narrative itself mirrors that of traditional epistolary narratives, for the letters from Paolo to Diana follow the familiar trajectory of infatuation to love and finally to abandonment, a course evident in 'Falso in scrittura' and 'La vita è così lunga.' There are several fundamental differences between the short stories and the novel, however, both stylistically and thematically. *Ella non rispose* concludes with several chapters allowing Diana her own voice, for up to this point the character existed only through Paolo's letters. It is in these concluding chapters that Serao again confronts the tenets of epistolary fiction, questioning their sincerity in addressing female experiences.

Despite the one-sided nature of the correspondence, *Ella non rispose* exemplifies the epistolary text's ability to create a rhythm all its own as each letter serves to move the action forward while remaining within the present. This structure serves to underline – through each single letter – the here and now of the narrative while also – through the overarching course of the correspondence – examining more universal literary and social concerns, such as the construction of female identity in a romantic text. Altman believes this narrative strategy is characteristic of the epistolary text: 'This sense of immediacy, of a present that is precarious, can only exist in a world where the future is unknown' (124). These letters are linked carefully together, each one a miniature narrative of its own, often with an open ending that moves easily into the next. This is an important component of the epistolary text, according to Altman. 'Like *tesserae*, each individual letter enters into the composition of the whole without losing its identity as a separate entity with recognizable borders' (167). In *Ella non rispose*, the epistles focus almost exclusively on the sole subject of Paolo's futile attempts to win Diana's love.

A brief summary of the narrative itself reveals how *Ella non rispose* departs from Serao's epistolary short stories. The opening of the novel mirrors *Prima morire*, for the young man writing the first epistle is enchanted by a woman he has never met. In the Marchesa Colombi's work, Augusto wrote about Eva's beautiful ankles and arms after spying her in her bathroom from his neighbouring apartment. In *Ella non rispose*, Paolo hears a young woman singing an aria from Gluck in a nearby villa and immediately writes her a letter detailing how her performance captivated his heart and soul.[26] Like Augusto, Paolo is drawn to a mere fragment of a woman, hardly a person in her own right. This allows him, however, to create his own vision of the woman behind the voice, and sure enough, in his second letter, written the following day, Paolo writes that she exists only in his dreams (9). She is, in fact, a blank slate, someone on whom he can project his desires and his fantasies. Indeed, over the course of the correspondence, Paolo calls Diana a 'fantasma ... dietro un cristallo' (91) ['fantasy ... behind a crystal'], his 'Dama del Silenzio' (142) ['Woman of Silence'] whose face appears in a 'mistica visione' (74) ['mystical vision']. And while their paths eventually do cross, Diana never actually speaks to him. Paolo's unrequited love for Diana is painstakingly detailed in his ninety letters, none of them acknowledged, reciprocated, or even returned, a narrative structure foreshadowed and emphasized by the novel's title.

The variety of letters in this text is certainly a *tour de force* for Serao, and reflects as well the radically different moods offered by epistolary texts. As with most long letter texts, the novel opens with several epistles that are almost pure exposition, depicting how Paolo pieces together Diana's sad tale. The twenty-five-year-old woman was born of noble blood, but after the death of her parents has lived a life contingent on the charity of others. Here, her situation mirrors that of Giulia in Sacrati's text; both are upper-class women whose lack of familial guidance and financial freedom severely circumscribes their life. But, in *Ella non rispose*, Diana follows a different life path from that of Giulia, for Serao's heroine succeeds in finding a protector in the guise of a husband. However, in what is clearly a loveless match, Diana is compelled to marry Sir Randolph Montagu, the English ambassador who is thirty years her senior. After expository letters describing Diana's relationship with Sir Randolph come others, and their diversity is truly astounding. Paolo writes letters of reproach when Diana refuses to acknowledge his gifts of flowers; of jealousy when she briefly appears interested in another man; of ultimatums when he proposes that the two run off together; of sarcasm when she marries, and of mortification when he realizes how bitter and spiteful his sarcastic letter was.

The second part of the novel, appropriately titled 'Pelligrino d'amore' ['Pilgrimage of Love'], becomes a travelogue both of Paolo's attempt to shadow the couple on their honeymoon and of his mental decline as he begins to despair of ever meeting her. He follows them to small towns in Switzerland, to Paris, and finally to Sussex, England, where the couple has decided to settle down. Paolo realizes how ridiculous and perverse this endeavour is, but cannot bring himself to abandon his quest. In a letter he writes after arriving in England, he describes his predicament: 'Diana, da sette mesi vi amo, vi scrivo, vi seguo: da sette mesi non ho più patria, nè casa, nè famiglia, per voi: da sette mesi io sono un pellegrino d'amore: e sono in fondo a un paese ignoto, obbliato, fra gente di un'altra razza, di un'altra lingua, di un'altra fede' (213–14) ['Diana, for seven months I have loved you, I have written to you, I have followed you: for seven months I have no longer had a fatherland, nor a home, nor family, for you: for seven months I have been a pilgrim of love: and after all that I am in an unknown country, forgotten, among people of another race, of another language, of another faith']. But despite not knowing if Diana is even reading his letters, despite his isolation and his desperation, Paolo is compelled to continue. His doomed mission, however, leads to obsession, and Serao deftly reflects Paolo's deteriorating mental condition through a stylistic evolution in his letters. The language in one such epistle borders on the deranged, for he writes warningly after seeing her talking with another man:

[V]oi siete la mia Diana, mia, esclusivamente mia, unicamente mia ed è il mio amore che deve prendervi tutta, e darvi a me, Diana, che solo vi merito, io solo, Diana, io solo, perché vi ho amata unicamente, sovra ogni altra cosa, sovra ogni altra persona, che vi amo unicamente, che sono, per voi, l'amore intenso, profondo ... perché sono l'Amore che tutto abbatte e tutto conquista! (246)

You are my Diana, mine, exclusively mine, uniquely mine and it is my love
that must take all of you, and give you to me, Diana, as only I deserve you,
I alone, Diana, I alone, because I have loved you uniquely, above every
other thing, above every other person, I love you uniquely, I am for you
intense, profound love ... because I am Love which fights and conquers all!

Clearly Paolo's long endeavour to gain Diana's love is endangering
his mental health. He gives her one more opportunity to demonstrate
that she does have feelings for him. Paolo asks her to commemorate
the first anniversary of the evening he heard her sing, the incident that
launched the one-sided affair. But his request is ignored, and he writes
despairingly in a one-sentence letter, 'Inutile veglia, inutile ansia, inutile amore!' (302) ['Useless vigil, useless anxiety, useless love!'].

Paolo does at last abandon his quest for Diana's love, although we
later learn that this lopsided correspondence will indeed have a permanent and fatal effect on the female protagonist. In his final letter, a
seemingly sensible epistle in which he uses her formal title for the first
time, Paolo calmly explains why he no longer loves Diana, primarily
because he has never received encouragement from her. He plans on
leaving Italy forever for parts unknown, travelling with his devoted
sister, and creating a life that no longer revolves around his doomed
love for Diana. Only in the short and desperate coda to this final letter
do we recognize that Paolo will always love Diana, for he writes: 'O voi
che foste la mia Euridice, o Creatura del mio sogno, o Creatura della
mia illusione, o Diana, Diana, o amor mio unico, o amor mio ultimo, o
voi che io non vedrò più mai, coi miei occhi mortali, addio, addio!' (313)
['Oh you who were my Euridice, oh creature of my dreams, oh Creature
of my illusions, oh Diana, Diana, my one love, my last love, oh you
whom I will never see again with my mortal eyes, farewell, farewell!'].
Paolo may not write any more letters, but it seems clear that he is never
going to forget Diana.

The final section of the novel is told through Diana's perspective, the
first time we are able to read between the lines, as it were, of Paolo's
epistles and meet the woman who inspired the fantasy. Diana is now
wintering in Bordighera, accompanied only by her trusted companion,
Miss Annie Ford. Sir Randolph has recently died in a mountain-climb-
ing accident, his demise in frozen circumstances an ironic ending for
a man described as 'glaciale,' 'taciturno,' and 'rigido' (317) ['glacial,'
'taciturn,' and 'rigid']. Ironically, Diana's only occupation is waiting for
the post to arrive each day, although each time she is disappointed as

'*la lettera attesa non era giunta*' (323) ['the awaited letter did not arrive']. Serao's use of italics here emphasizes the importance of Paolo's letters in Diana's life. Although she had refused to return Paolo's love or to even answer his letters, Diana nonetheless remains enmeshed in this relationship. She gradually withdraws from the convivial social scene into a spiritual and emotional isolation soon accompanied by a physical deterioration. Her doctor, stymied by the lack of a physical source of her debilitating illness, can only say, '[P]otrebbe guarire, se volesse ... potrebbe guarire' (321) ['She could recover, if she wanted ... she could recover']. He does not recognize the symptoms: Diana is, in fact, slowly dying of heartbreak.

In her fourth winter at this resort town, with her physical forces ebbing rapidly, Diana finally asks her loyal companion to read aloud Paolo's letters, which are tied with a lilac ribbon embroidered with the words of Gluck's aria: 'Che farò, senza Euridice?' (331) ['What will I do without Euridice?']. This lament formed part of Paolo's first letter to her, an epistle inspired by the melodious sound of her voice singing this aria. This ribbon, then, binds together Paolo's love with Diana's, a love hidden and unspoken up to this point. Over the course of the long cold winter, Miss Ford reads aloud Paolo's letters, tracing the arc of his infatuation, his love, his obsession, and finally, his renunciation. With each letter, Diana's strength fades, until, after the last one, she can only whisper weakly her final instructions to Miss Ford. After Diana's death, her companion must attempt to discover Paolo's whereabouts and tell him that she loved him from the very first letter. Her reason for not complying with Paolo's repeated requests for a letter in return, or giving him a sign that she cared for him, is simple and telling: 'Io non ho voluto peccare. ... Io avevo promesso: io avevo giurato. Ho spezzato il suo cuore: ma anche il mio' (335) ['I did not want to sin ... I had promised: I had vowed. I broke his heart, but also mine']. Diana dies shortly after this declaration, and despite Miss Ford's valiant but failed efforts to trace his whereabouts, Paolo never learns of 'la rivelazione dell'amore, della virtù, del sacrificio mortale di Diana Sforza' (338) ['the revelation of the love, the virtue, the mortal sacrifice of Diana Sforza']. By denying even a posthumous relationship between Paolo and Diana, Serao creates a text weighted in irony and captive to the strictures of the epistolary genre, where love is allowed only within the forum of the actual correspondence.

Diana's rejection of Paolo's love, then, stems from her sense of duty, a duty grounded in her role as Sir Randolph's wife, for, despite her unhappy marriage, she remains faithful to her cold and indifferent husband.[27] Just as Eva renounces her love affair with Augusto to return to her ailing child in *Prima morire*, so does Diana invoke the obligations of a fundamental female role. The pallor of her face, the ivory hue of her increasingly frail hands, and the whiteness of her simple dress in her final days emphasize not only Diana's mortal illness but also the purity of her soul, which has never been stained by a violation of her wifely duty.

In *Ella non rispose*, Serao appears to be underscoring the hypocrisy of the social conventions forcing women into loveless matches based on economic considerations while at the same time binding them to their sacred – and apparently irrevocable – roles of wife and mother. The author returned often to this theme in her works, from the realist short story 'Non più' ('No More') to the romantic novel *Tre donne* (*Three Women*). In both these texts, female characters are compelled to marry men they do not love because they lack financial resources to live independent lives. In *Ella non rispose*, Serao's criticism is even sharper, for Diana literally pays with her life for fulfilling her wifely duties.

While this trenchant appraisal of the perils of proscribed social roles underlines Serao's narrative, I believe that there is even more at stake. Again, we must look at the intersection between gender and genre to examine how subtly Serao revises the traditional epistolary text. For example, how do Paolo's letters, which revolve, after all, around a woman depicted as a 'fantasma,' become conflated with the 'fantasma' herself? In other words, once the love letters have been read a final time, why does Diana die? Serao appears to be saying even more emphatically than she did in 'La vita è così lunga' that the female subject risks being grossly endangered by the conventions of the epistolary text. Without the epistolary novel allowing her a self-generated narrative in the form of corresponding letters, the female protagonist simply ceases to exist. And so, the heroine must create a life outside of the epistolary exchange, either in anonymous introductions ('La vita è così lunga') or in epilogues that portray to some degree how the female protagonist has been a carefully constructed but ultimately unknowable figure in the male-authored letters ('Livia Speri' and *Ella non rispose*). Does Serao then resolve this issue of how traditional generic tenets can work against an authentic depiction of the female character and her experiences? Not satisfactorily, for although Diana's voice is heard in the novel's final section and her motivations are finally revealed, she is ultimately silenced by the closure scripted for her. This somewhat disappointing dénouement is characteristic of Serao, who often challenged literary conventions but failed at creating alternative literary models. Instead, she worked within those models, crafting elegant, fascinating, and occasionally provocative texts that questioned the conventions, rather than the genres themselves. Perhaps more significant for this study, however, is how Serao consistently linked together the idea of female experiences and their depiction through various interpretations of the epistolary text.

While Serao briefly addressed the connection between genuine and fictional love letters in the introduction to *Ella non rispose*, Sibilla Aleramo more concretely revealed the slippage between the two genres in her 1914 novella *Trasfigurazione (Lettera non spedita)* (*Transfiguration [Letter Not Sent]*). Aleramo (1876–1960) is best known for *Una donna* (*A Woman*), the first novel by an Italian woman to explicitly challenge the legal, social, and cultural codes of post-unification Italy. In this text and in many other works, including novels, poetry, journalism essays, and diaries, Aleramo endeavoured to create alternative literary models and archetypes, believing that only by fashioning new literary patterns would women writers – and women in general – be free of both canonic and social restrictions. As Anna Grimaldi Morosoff writes, the author 'consciously set out to pose a challenge to her society and to set the example for future female writers' (3). In Aleramo's case, this meant conflating the real and the fabricated, the autobiographical and the fictional. 'This constant osmosis across the permeable boundaries separating the literal and the invented realm leads inevitably to a blurring of the boundaries of genre as well,' Bernadette Luciano points out. 'Under the guise of novels, her fictions become untransformed accounts of a life: conversely, pages of her diaries and private letters are copied and inserted into fictional works' (97).[28] I do not want to examine Aleramo's work from a purely autobiographical perspective; such an approach, while entertaining, negates the author's creativity and reduces her texts to mere transcriptions of life experiences. Certainly *Trasfigurazione* was inspired by real events in the writer's life, including a brief relationship with the writer Giovanni Papini. Rather than tracing the connection between their affair and its portrayal in the text, I will focus on Aleramo's very personalized articulation of the epistolary genre, for this literary model did evolve in part from the intimate, subjective, and self-expressive practice of letter writing.[29]

Like the other texts examined in this chapter, *Trasfigurazione* revolves around an amorous narrative. However, Aleramo subverts the traditional focus of these romantic narratives, for the text's single long letter is written not from one lover to another, but from a woman to her lover's wife.[30] Aleramo's choice of correspondents represents a significant departure from traditional epistolary fiction, which, when interested third parties – such as spouses – are involved, rarely addressed them directly. In *Trasfigurazione*, the connection between the two women is quickly established in its abrupt opening, with the narrator declaring simply: 'Sono io, sì' (25) ['It is I, yes'].[31] Without further introduction, she finds common ground with her lover's wife, writing: 'Ti do del tu, sì. Da tante settimane non fai mentalmente lo stesso anche tu' (25) ['I will give you the tu, yes. For many weeks haven't you done the same in your head']. She sets up at the very opening of the text a relationship between the two women. The narrator continues throughout the letter to establish this bond 'da sorella a sorella' (26) ['from sister to sister'], even writing, 'Vieni qui, metti un momento la tua mano sulla mia fronte. Siamo due donne, siamo due madri' (40) ['Come here, put your hand on my forehead for a moment. We are two women, we are two mothers']. The two women, connected only through their love for the same man, form their own relationship, grounded in their shared gender and female roles. In fact, the narrator's concluding words emphasize how the wife will no longer be able to forget or ignore the lover's role in her life: 'Metti ancora un momento la tua mano nella mia. D'or innanzi, qualunque cosa accada, vedrai la vita come ti si è mostrata in fondo ai miei occhi. Addio' (53) ['Put your hand in mine for a moment. From now on, whatever happens, you will see life as it unfolds in front of my eyes. Farewell']. Aleramo all but effaces the more traditional relationship in this text, between the two lovers. Instead, she focuses on the 'sisterly' bond between the two women, both dependent on the male character's decision to continue the affair or be faithful to his wife.

As the relationship between the two women slowly develops, the purpose of the letter becomes clear. The couple has recently broken off the liaison, and the narrator writes to ask her lover's wife to renounce their marriage, to allow the man to abandon his wife and children and take up permanently with the other woman. The letter, then, becomes what Rita Guerricchio likens to a military intervention, which has as sole purpose 'la "trasfigurazione," la conversione della corrispondente' (52) ['the "transfiguration," the conversion of the correspondent']. The narrator's persuasive techniques, however, are neither deferential nor diplomatic. Rather, she details why the man would be much more satisfied, intellectually and physically, with his lover than with his wife. He no longer loves his wife romantically, she maintains, but instead regards her as 'una piccola dolce bambina ... una creatura cui si rivolgono parolette senza senso' (37) ['a sweet little girl ... a creature to whom you speak nonsense words']. It is only with his lover that the husband has experienced true passion, she adds, claiming, '[P]er la prima volta dacchè era uomo, per la prima volta, intendi, ha compreso che cos'è l'amore, ha sentito nell'amore esaltare tutto il proprio essere' (36) ['For the first time since he became a man, for the first time, you understand, he understood what love is, he felt his entire being exalt in love']. In short, the two are soul mates, and the wife is committing a great injury to her husband by not freeing him from his marital ties and allowing him a chance at happiness. Interestingly, it is the male character whose actions are prescribed by a sense of duty, for the husband has invoked his responsibilities to his wife and small children as the reason for ending the affair. The narrator takes him to task for this, pointing out that if he stays with his family out of obligation and not true love, he is actually being unfair to his wife and children.

But while the husband/lover may ultimately decide the fate of both his wife and his mistress, the female narrator manipulates the telling of the tale. Unlike the other epistolary texts examined in this chapter, *Trasfigurazione* has an open ending, allowing a multitude of possible 'transfigurations' for the characters contained in the novella. Does the narrator succeed in convincing the wife to release her husband from his marital and paternal responsibilities? Is the husband capable of renouncing these duties? And is the narrator correct when she declares to the wife and her children: 'Io peso quanto voi sulla bilancia' (47) ['I weigh as much as you on the scale']? With this narrative strategy, Aleramo rewrites the connection between the love letter and the letter text, questioning the real and fictional closures of the romance plot. Barbara Zaczek believes Aleramo wrote this tale to offer an 'alternative ending' to her very real and ultimately failed relationship with Papini ('Plotting Letters,' 66). By creating a fictional ending that is inconclusive, Aleramo transforms the genuine event as well, plotting out a different narrative trajectory.

Just as Serao offered extra-textual clues in the introductions to her epistolary works, Aleramo further emphasizes the fictitious nature of the text by including a brief subtitle to the novella: *Trasfigurazione (Lettera non spedita)*. This text then – this unsent letter – radically subverts the validity of the epistolary narrative, which exists only if the letters contained within it are actually read and preferably exchanged. Aleramo instead points to the *fiction*, as it were, inherent to the genre, a fiction in which the readers as well as the actual characters participate. I would argue that with this subtitle Aleramo underscores the evolution of the letter text from the love letter, a movement from the subjective and highly private epistle to a text with all the trappings of this personal correspondence.

Aleramo's reconstruction of the epistolary narrative is concomitant with her presentation of the female narrator, for she frees this character from the static closures of the romantic plot. This stratagem is a remarkable progression in the typical literary narrative of this time, and one that reflects a similar evolution in Aleramo's writing from the 1906 *Una donna* to *Trasfigurazione*, written just a few years later. In this latter work, Anna Meda writes, 'l'esplorazione di sé e la creazione del proprio mito femminile prende forma, non più come in *Una donna* quale reazione e ribellione al potere tirannico della cultura patriarcale, ma per la prima volta come ricerca autonoma e libera della propria identità femminile non più *all'interno* del sistema patriarcale ma *fuori* di esso' (50) ['the exploration of self and the creation of her own female myth takes form, no longer as reaction and rebellion to the tyrannical power of the patriarchal culture as in *A Woman*, but for the first time as an autonomous and free search into her own female identity no longer within the patriarchal system but outside of it']. But although Aleramo creates decidedly non-traditional elements in her epistolary work, including an unusual correspondent and an open ending, the female characters still function within the sanctioned socio-cultural codes of female experiences. The female narrator 'inevitabilmente si definisce in relazione all'uomo,' Meda points out, 'che non può essere pienamente se stessa senza la controparte che la completa e integra' (60) ['inevitably identifies herself in relation to the man [and] cannot fully be herself without the counterpart who completes and complements her']. Aleramo's approach to this entrenched literary model may be radical, but her female characters (both lover and wife) remain tied to a generalized romantic discourse. The narrator in *Trasfigurazione* may not participate in the closure of the romantic plot, but she still must act within this narrative's code. Aleramo, then, refashions the epistolary genre, but does not completely free her female characters from their prescribed place within the realm of romantic literature. She does, however, allow these characters more textual freedom than do Sacrati, the Marchesa Colombi, and Serao, who also confront the role of the female protagonist within the love plot.

All four authors examined in this chapter explored how generic mod-

els, which often reflect contemporary socio-cultural conventions, succeeded in confining female characters within the romantic narrative.
These writers addressed through their acute social criticism the circumscribed roles and opportunities proscribed to women. Whether their
female protagonists suffered from a lack of financial independence, as
we saw in *Lettere di Giulia Willet* and *Ella non rispose*, or the demands of
their female roles, as in *Prima morire*, these heroines ultimately paid the
price for social transgressions.

If we look at how these authors addressed the epistolary text, we
can see some striking revisions in the traditions of the genre. Sacrati's
emphasis on the non-romantic content of the letters in her novel and
the cues offered by the extra-textual notes lead to a reading that must
acknowledge the position of women in a severely restricted society.
Her heroine becomes virtually effaced by the end of the text through
the skilful placement and length of the letters. The Marchesa Colombi's
use of a double epistolary correspondence in *Prima morire* allows for a
critique of the predominant literary schools, creating in the process a
female figure (Mercede) who is the antithesis of the romantic heroine.
In her hands, the epistolary novel serves to address, as well, the creation – through a male character – of a female archetype, a construction
taken up by Serao in *Ella non rispose*.

The very nature of epistolary texts – their unreliability as factual
documents – is emphasized by both Serao in 'Falso in scrittura' and
Aleramo in *Trasfigurazione*. While the former text uses the conventional editorial notes to comment on the genre's elusiveness, Aleramo's
novella deliberately reimagines real events. And finally, this last text
offers a glimpse, at the very least, of a striking reworking of the romantic plot, for the author focuses not on the bond between lovers, but on
that between two women. The epistolary novel, grounded in sentimental narratives, will see further and more dramatic revisions in the twentieth century. But these four authors did succeed in questioning both
the stylistic and thematic traditions of the letter novel. Their challenge,
unexceptional as it may seem today, was encoded within a narrative
model traditionally linked to the female pen, a model often derided as
pedestrian and traditional. What better forum to examine – and encode
– unorthodox ideas?

2 Literary Responses

The epistolary genre has long been considered an ideal forum for matters private, intimate, and subjective. The romantic narrative of the nineteenth century, as we have seen in chapter 1, falls within this realm, for in literary tradition nothing is more personal than the correspondence between lovers. But epistolary texts of the twentieth century often explored other narrative avenues, and the love plot frequently became a framework from which to examine concerns of both a literary and a social nature. In the next chapters, I examine how these modern works analyse the changing socio-cultural landscape of post-Second World War Italy, but here I discuss the connection between the epistolary genre and its articulation of literary movements. We saw a glimpse of this approach in the Marchesa Colombi's *Prima morire*, which lightly sketched through its double narrative the opposing tenets of Romanticism and Realism. In the following works, the engagement with literary narratives becomes both clearer and more deliberate as these authors broadened the traditional boundaries of the epistolary novel.

Throughout their history, epistolary texts have engaged in a dialogue with earlier works and with other literary genres and currents. The very nature of the genre depends on a response, both from within the text – the recipients of the letters – and from outside the text – the readers who must interpret the correspondence contained within. Almost from the birth of the genre, authors have used it to parody, imitate, analyse, but, most importantly, respond to other works using this narrative framework. Henry Fielding's 1741 spoof of Samuel Richardson's *Pamela, or Virtue Rewarded*, entitled *Shamela*, for example, gently pokes fun at the strict morality and hypocrisy underlying the original text. In 1950 Upton Sinclair took on the same novel in his *Another Pamela, or*

Virtue Still Rewarded. He plays on issues intertextual: His heroine can more fully understand her own situation by reading the original Pamela's letters. *The Three Marias: New Portuguese Letters*, published in 1972 by Maria Barreno, Maria Teresa Horta, and Maria Velho da Costa, offers a provocative feminist interpretation of the seminal 1669 epistolary novel *The Letters of a Portuguese Nun*.[1] This work comments on the very nature of the epistolary by including poems, tales, and philosophical meditations in the letters. Fay Weldon's wonderfully witty *Letters to Alice on First Reading Jane Austen* (1984) is a series of sixteen missives addressed to the author's imaginary niece. Weldon uses the letter format to juxtapose an investigation of Austen's texts (including her epistolary works) and more contemporary literature with a discussion of familial matters, creating a document that reads as part literary criticism, part personal narrative.[2] All these works address in some way the literary moment that gave rise to the original epistolary text.

Perhaps the most noted example in Italy of this interplay between epistolary texts is that posed by Guido Piovene's 1941 novel *Lettere di una novizia*, which 'rewrites' Giovanni Verga's *Storia di una capinera*, published in 1871. While both works feature a heroine unhappily sequestered in a convent, Piovene's reinterpretation focuses more on the narrative practice of writing and reading letters.[3] The very nature of epistolary texts, then, can act as a forum to examine intra- and extra-textual concerns. In this chapter I address how letter novels work through several issues fundamental to the historical nature of the epistolary: How do these works revise the traditional epistolary text while also examining the tenets of a particular moment in Italian literary history? And, second, how can this particular genre – one traditionally associated with prosaic sentimental fiction – serve as a vehicle to articulate artistic concerns? Certainly the letter novel offers an ideal forum from which to examine such debates, according to Ronald Rosbottom. While primarily considering eighteenth-century French epistolary fiction, his comments resonate for this particular study, for he calls the letter novel 'a testing ground for many serious questions concerning the craft of writing fiction,' adding that it 'demanded the best efforts of the writers toward solving the problems of narrative point of view, temporal construction, thematic consistency, and character portrayal' (300). The structural concerns of the epistolary text, then, can be parlayed into a wider discussion of narrative creation and literary genre.

In this chapter, I also focus on how the three authors under study used an examination of this literary genre as a springboard to discuss the socio-cultural role of women. Sibilla Aleramo's 1927 *Amo dunque sono* (*I Love Therefore I Am*), while not explicitly interacting with a particular literary movement, does explore the relationship between the woman writer and her artistic production, while also examining the creation of a literary work, thereby producing a meta-epistolary novel. The novel *Astra e il sottomarino: Vita trasognata* (*Astra and the Submariner: Daydreamed Life*), published in 1935 by Benedetta Cappa Marinetti, offers a reappraisal of Futurist tenets, viewed from a gendered perspective. And finally, Gianna Manzini's 1945 *Lettera all'editore* (*Game Plan for a Novel*) grapples with the parameters of post-war neorealism while revealing a personal poetics ideally suited to the epistolary genre.

Aleramo's *Amo dunque sono*, although structured around a romantic narrative, explicitly explores the creation of a literary text, and, as such, fits well within a discussion of the epistolary and its ability to comment on fictive structures. With Aleramo, it is easy to focus on the often provocative content of her works, rather than their form or structure, and many critics have neglected to consider or even ignored her intriguing use of the epistolary genre. It is significant that she took up an examination of literary origins in a letter novel. By doing so, she challenged several of the tenets of this genre, a process she first undertook with *Trasfigurazione (Lettera non spedita)* in 1914, and it is for this reason that I frame this exploration within the context of epistolary fiction.

As already discussed in the preceding chapter, Aleramo refused to adhere to literary trends or expectations, an approach that often hindered her critical and popular success. As Sharon Wood writes: '[R]ather than develop genuinely new forms for women's writing and consciousness, she is led to appropriate for her own gender a *fin-de-siècle* aestheticism quite at odds with the radical style and technique of [*Una donna*]' (*Italian Women's Writing*, 87). But rather than addressing Aleramo's literary works from outside the canon, as it were, searching for revolutionary new forms, I believe we can find substantial evidence that she challenged literary models while employing traditional genres. Aleramo believed, as Keala Jewell notes, that 'woman's profound spiritual differences from man must imply new expressive forms. Choosing to write with spontaneity and sincerity, [she] viewed her stance as an act of rebellion with the quality of a mission for a tradition of women's writing' (148). Jewell was not specifically addressing Aleramo's epistolary texts, but the insight resonates nonetheless in a discussion of the letter novel. Although as we have seen, works by Sacrati, the Marchesa Colombi, Serao, and Aleramo document that these texts are just as painstakingly constructed and weighted with multivalent readings, 'spontaneity' and 'sincerity' are considered the hallmarks of epistolary fiction. By using the cover of letter fiction to examine issues ranging from the position of the female artist in Italian society to the creation of a literary text, Aleramo expands the traditional orbit of epistolary fiction.

Amo dunque sono is composed of forty-three letters written one summer from a middle-aged woman named Sibilla to her young lover, Luciano.[4] The romantic aspects of the narrative are featured prominently, with most letters emphasizing the couple's spiritual union and physical passion. In a succinct portrayal of both the lovers and their relationship, the protagonist characterizes them as: 'La donna non più giovane e l'uomo ancor fanciullo, l'artista nota e il mago ignoto, la leonessa e l'aquilotto, e la loro crudeltà, il loro spasimo, il loro sogno nel centro dell'universo' (93) ['The middle-aged woman and the man who is still a boy, the noted artist and the unknown magician, the lioness and the eaglet, their cruelty, their longings, their dream in the centre of the universe']. The female character portrays herself, then, as the older, wiser, and more famous partner in this relationship, attributes she will continue to emphasize throughout the letters. The motive behind the correspondence is a simple one: the two have decided to separate for a month or so in order to 'purify' themselves before eventually consummating their love. Aleramo invokes several staples of epistolary fiction with this framework, for the tropes of idle waiting and separation often pervade letter texts.

Typically, it is the female character who is sequestered away in a convent or isolated country house, pining for her lover as she exists in a state of suspension, idle but for the business of letter writing. But Aleramo deliberately reworks this conceit in *Amo dunque sono*, for Sibilla is not the solitary and secluded member of the couple, but rather the one who packs her bags and departs for a new adventure (Guerricchio, 49). Aleramo creates a new type of epistolary heroine, one who is active, involved, and, despite worrying financial problems, independent. Notwithstanding an intense longing for her absent lover, for example, Sibilla does manage to accomplish quite a lot during the six weeks the two are separated. She travels from Rome to Milan to Salsomaggiore, then to Levanto and back to Rome, receives callers (including former lovers), meets with an American magazine editor, and frequents restaurants and the theatre with friends. She may miss Luciano, but Sibilla is clearly not going to sit at home and wait quietly for him. Although she calls herself 'quasi una fidanzata di guerra' ['almost a war fiancée'], she also gives herself some practical advice for surviving the separation: 'Resistere, reagire. Quanta durezza, sempre' (47) ['Resist, react. Such hardness, always']. This technique considerably tweaks the traditional theme of idle waiting, and separation, especially as it presents the female protagonist as more engaged and productive than earlier, more passive heroines.

Moreover, in another interesting deviation from this theme, the lovers' separation turns on the promised sexual congress at the end of the narrative. Sibilla's highly eroticized letters suggest the text will not conclude with a chaste kiss before the curtain drops down, as was the custom in most positive eighteenth- and nineteenth-century narratives. Rather, the protagonist is presented as a fully sensual woman, made confident (and apparently quite skilled) by previous romantic experiences. 'Un desiderio insostenibile mi circola nelle vene' ['An unsustainable desire circulates in my veins'], she writes on 3 August, although in this particular instance her ardour is inspired as much by the sight of her own naked breast after her bath as by the memory of her lover's touch (98). Even Luciano's absence does not prevent Sibilla from indulging in sexual pleasure, for she tells him candidly: 'Casta da mesi e mesi, nell'attesa dell'ora che stringerai come in una morsa le mie membra fra le tue, ho potuto stamane, senza timore, abbandonarmi qualche istante al piacer di me stessa, e poi rialzarmi, con senso di refrigerio profondo' (99) ['Chaste for months and months, waiting for the hour when you will clasp your body to mine, this morning I could, without fear, abandon myself to several moments of pleasuring myself, and then get up, with a sense of profound relief'].[5] This may be one of the few descriptions of female masturbation recorded up to this moment in Italian literature, and the episode certainly underlines the character's sensuality as well as her self-sufficiency. In this letter text, then, the author explicitly challenges the conventional image of literary heroines, which in previous centuries rarely included such productive or explicit portrayals of female sexuality. Aleramo extends the sense of intimacy implicit in the genre to a discussion of physical love for one's self, a technique all the more breathtaking as the protagonist reveals this aspect of herself to her male lover, no less. Here, the letter text serves Aleramo well, for she trades on its promise of familiarity to present a truly remarkable heroine, one comfortable with sharing the details of her sexual experiences.

But once again Aleramo confounds expectations, for while the letters seem to promise a passionate tryst between the two lovers at the novel's end, their decorous reunion is instead quite anticlimactic. 'Ogni selvaggio istinto, ogni violenza di desiderio' ['Each savage instinct, each violent desire'] is extinguished in Sibilla at the sight of her young lover; they do not kiss or embrace, but say simply 'Ti voglio bene' ['I love you'] and recognize in each other 'il volto nimbato della felicità' (125) ['a face haloed by happiness']. What are we to make of this decidedly sedate encounter? This ending is puzzling, given the rather forthright eroticism exhibited throughout the novel. I do not believe Aleramo is suddenly retreating to the safety of literary conventions, for as we have seen in *Trasfigurazione* (and certainly in *Una donna*), she was never afraid to script alternative endings for her female protagonists. Instead, in *Amo dunque sono*, she underlines the seriousness and, indeed, the sacredness of the relationship between this mismatched pair, validating Sibilla's patience and trust during the long separation from her lover. This ending, with its emphasis on the profundity of the lovers' relationship rather than their anticipated sexual union, allows Aleramo to create a more fully realized portrayal of a female character, one capable of embracing and integrating her physical and spiritual attributes.

Aleramo heightens the overt sensuality of the female character by intertwining it with Sibilla's artistry. Often her letters conflate the sensual with the act of writing, as when she tells Luciano: 'Brividi nella carne. Il desiderio di te mi agguanta fino quasi a farmi svenire. Sono a letto. Tengo il blocco di carta sulle ginocchia e la matita in mano, ma tra una frase e l'altra passano secoli' (27) ['Shivers in my body. Desire for you seizes me until I am ready to faint. I'm in bed. I have a writing pad on my knees and a pencil in hand, but between one sentence and another centuries pass']. The body as font of creativity is not a particularly original metaphor, but one Aleramo played with throughout her literary production. As Carole Gallucci writes: 'Whereas in *Una donna* the body was initially a source of repression, here it is highly, indeed almost exclusively, eroticized, clearly a source of power and remaining, as in *Una donna*, a locus of writing' (374). Gallucci sees Aleramo's reworking of this metaphor as profoundly radical, pointing out:

> For [Aleramo], the power of the letter, to inscribe and to encode, emerged from the power of the female body, to gestate and generate. Indeed, the body and the letter, corporality and inscription, were inextricably bound; paradoxically, both the body repressed and the body celebrated held out

the possibility of the word, of writing down the self. Aleramo's narrative strategy to write about the female self and the female body challenges genre and gender norms of the interwar years and proposes such a revolution. (364)[6]

This point is a fascinating one, revealing as it does the author's provocative articulation of the gendered poetics behind the creation of a literary text. The letter novel, with its intimate voice and presumably private correspondence, serves as the ideal medium for an examination of the connection between sensuality and artistry.

Aleramo's analysis of how literary texts are constructed acts as a subtext to the romantic narrative in *Amo dunque sono*, and it is in this context that the author contributes to a 'challenging subversiveness' of the letter novel (Morosoff, 88). As we have seen, Aleramo often introduces entrenched elements of the epistolary genre – such as the traditional isolation of the female character – only to subvert them. In a further example, she provides precise time elements for each letter, engaging in a classic epistolary practice, but only to turn it on its head. Each letter is dated, and many are further subdivided into specific moments in the day, such as 'mattina,' 'pomeriggio,' or 'sera' ('morning,' 'afternoon,' 'evening'). The practice lends itself to the particular frame of epistolary fiction, which is almost always in the present tense, describing events occurring often literally before the eyes of the reader. We can experience, then, with Sibilla the discomfort of her menstrual cycles, the boredom of a train ride, or even an afternoon devoted to colouring her graying hair, episodes all described in her letters. But the narrator also provides temporal cues as an invitation to reflect on events long past, such as her relationships with other lovers, as well as broader issues, like the definitions of love, happiness, and art. In effect, Aleramo contrasts the precision inherent in a form structured around specific temporal elements with the wide-ranging discussions contained within each letter. The daily and often prosaic events she describes are merely a springboard for a journey of self-exploration that allows the narrator to work out larger socio-cultural anxieties about age, relationships, financial concerns, and artistry.

This self-conscious approach to her letters allows Sibilla to more explicitly comment on artistic creation and production, using herself, as is only appropriate, as an exemplar. (Indeed, the title of this novel could just as easily have been *Scrivo dunque sono [I Write Therefore I Am]*.) Within this frame, she comments more broadly and overtly on the role of the woman artist in Italy. Throughout the novel, the narrator offers constant reminders to her young lover, himself an artist, of her fame as a writer. She relates how one fan has sent gardenias, another wants autographed copies of her books, a local photographer asks her to pose, and strangers recognize her when she ventures out for a walk. And although she devotes much of her time to her correspondence with Luciano, Sibilla does not neglect her many literary tasks, from correcting the galleys for a complete volume of her poetry to meeting with an editor from New York about including some of her short stories in his magazine. She reflects, as well, on her various literary endeavours and their public and critical reception, triumphantly reviewing the highlights and bemoaning the failures.

The epistolary narrative allows the protagonist to confide in particular the hardships faced by a female author. For while Sibilla can point to successes – she notes on 5 August that *Una donna* will be translated into Hungarian – the difficulty of her life is continually underscored. Her books may be a 'povera sfida al tempo' (59) ['poor challenge to time'] but they have brought fame, not fortune. Throughout the text Sibilla laments her lack of funds and relates the often extreme measures she takes to support herself, whether by selling the autographs of famous friends to pay for her trip to Salsomaggiore, letting an old acquaintance buy her new clothing, or fasting for two days when she is completely out of money.[7] She must rely on a pitiful advance from her publisher and financial help from her brother in order to survive. She may be well-known in literary circles, but she certainly has not been rewarded in any monetary way for her contribution to Italian literature. Indeed, *Amo dunque sono* can be read as a warning against engaging in an artistic life, as the prospects for financial independence are grim at best. By framing this discussion within the context of a letter novel, is Aleramo saying at some level that women authors are best served by relying on narrative forms traditionally attributed to female writers; that the epistolary novel, with its personal and intimate correspondence allegedly appealing to an ever-expanding female reading public, will reap the most rewards?

Certainly, even while Sibilla bemoans the lack of monetary rewards for her literary production, she is intent on creating another text, for each letter that she writes to Luciano becomes part of a larger literary project. And although she tells her friends she is writing a novel, clearly the letters to Luciano will form the basis of her new book. Sibilla examines in some detail the actual construction of the text, writing in one of the earliest letters, 'Non rileggo queste lettere, le chiudo ogni sera, cias-cuna in una busta numerata – saranno trenta, quaranta, allorché potrò consegnartele?' (16) ['I don't reread these letters, I close them up every evening, each in a numbered envelope – there must be thirty, forty, when can I deliver them to you?']. The tangible elements of letter writing – from the paper and ink necessary for each epistle, to the appearance of the lover's handwriting on the page – are fundamental elements of the letter text, creating, as it were, a metonymic bond between writer and recipient. As an artist, Sibilla is intently aware of the physical properties of a text. Indeed, she describes in a letter of 26 July how she received the original manuscript of her previous book, and how its 'tormented' appearance reflected the agonies caused in writing it.[8] The narrator of *Amo dunque sono*, then, makes clear the physical effort behind every attempt at artistic creation. By using the epistolary genre, she can more specifically trace the actual construction of the novel, as it slowly grows from a handful of letters to a thick sheaf of papers worthy of being called a manuscript.

The act of letter writing becomes by extension the first step in the cre-ative process of novel writing. In *Amo dunque sono* Aleramo moves con-siderably beyond the realm of romantic fiction, setting her discussion of artistry against the framework of the sentimental narrative. We are cued into this intertextuality when Sibilla conflates her amorous rela-tionship with her artistic agenda. The narrator undertook the project on Luciano's advice, for before leaving on his spiritual retreat he encour-aged her to 'ingannare l'attesa' ['while away the time'] by writing to him (107). She describes his request in one of her earliest letters, say-ing, 'M'hai imposto tu di scriverti e suggellare così ogni giorno molte pagine che, dicesti, potranno poi essere il libro *nostro*' (16) ['You have ordered me to write to you and to seal up many pages every day, so, you said, they could then be *our* book']. Certainly Sibilla's past liaisons have provided ample fodder for her literary production, as she remarks in her letter of 2 August, 'Qual poesia nascerà ora dal mio amore per te, dal nostro amore. Queste lettere non sono che un presentimento, un preludio. Non scrivo altro, da tanti giorni!' (96) ['What poetry will be born now of my love for you, of our love. These letters are but a pre-sentiment, a prelude. I haven't written anything else for many days!']. While the letters are framed around the relationship with Luciano, they have also served as a 'tool of self-revelation' (Morosoff, 70). As she con-structs, letter by letter, each chapter in her narrative, Sibilla discovers truths about herself and her art. The novel functions then as a form of memoir, for while it is rooted in an exaltation of Sibilla's love for Luciano, the narrator also uses the letters as a vehicle to evaluate both her romantic past and her literary works.

Even more significantly, the letters stand in for the narrator – the female artist – herself. Indeed, when Sibilla worries that the epistles have not been faithful in capturing her true self, she writes that she is comforted by a voice saying that from her letters and her books '"la tua entità si manifesta, in modi silenziosi, in modi indicibili ... ivi appari miracolosamente a chi t'ama ... l'arte suprema, la magia vera, e tu lo sai, è l'amore'" (107) ['"your true self manifests itself, in silent ways, in ineffable ways ... there it appears miraculously to those who love you ... the supreme art, the real magic, as you know, is love'"]. Sibilla conflates love with art, co-opting in the process the epistolary form by textualizing her passion in the form of letters to Luciano. The letter is more than the intermediary between lovers; it acts as the physical, spiritual, and sensual representation of the narrator. But because the protagonist is cast as a writer, Aleramo's revision of the epistolary text functions as a personalized epistle not only to Love, in the relationship with Luciano, but also to Art, in the discussion of the narrator's previous works, and through the current text unfolding before us. This is a significant evolution from the 1914 *Trasfigurazione*, as Aleramo works to create 'una scrittura che tenta di immettersi nel percorso segnato dall'istituzione letteraria' ['a writing that tries to infuse itself into the path marked by the literary institution'] (Zancan, 26). *Amo dunque sono*, then, moves beyond the romantic realm of that earlier work, fashioning a text that comments on its very construction. Aleramo's use of the epistolary genre allows her to create parallel texts, one detailing the amorous liaison that acts as catalyst to the letter-writing project, and a second underlying narrative that describes the protagonist's relationship to art and literature.

Just as the Marchesa Colombi and Matilde Serao questioned the major literary movements of their time with their fictional production, Benedetta Cappa Marinetti offered a gendered response to Futurist ideology in her 1935 epistolary novel *Astra e il sottomarino: Vita trasognata*. The work of Benedetta (her pen name) investigated the tensions engendered between female authorship and its creative production and an artistic movement that unashamedly trumpeted its misogynistic convictions. The discussion is complicated, or at least made more interesting, because Benedetta's husband, Filippo Tommaso Marinetti, was the primary founder of Futurism, and she was an early and ardent adherent of its principles.

Futurism, Italy's articulation of the avant-garde movements sweeping across Europe in the early decades of the twentieth century, advocated a complete and violent break with the stagnant and archaic social and artistic conventions of the post-unification period. Its proponents championed in their manifesto 'la bellezza della velocità' ['the beauty of speed'] and claimed 'il coraggio, l'audicia, la ribellione' ['courage, audacity, rebellion'] as essential elements of their agenda. Futurists were inspired above all by the growth of modern technology, exemplified in particular by the invention of the automobile, the airplane, and the railroad. The movement's glorification of war, its disdain for the social advancement of women, and its gradual drift into a more politicized arena have led to a simplistic interpretation of Futurism as merely the artistic manifestation of Fascist ideology. Certainly both Futurism and Fascism shared many elements and supporters, but when they are conflated into a single, monolithic cultural-political entity, the artistic contributions made by Futurists become either eliminated from critical consideration or condemned as mere Fascist propaganda.[9]

The same fate has befallen female Futurists, and, indeed, they have suffered an even greater degree of neglect, a result, I believe, of their gender and their alleged allegiance to Fascism.[10] Anna Nozzoli, for example, dismisses their artistic output as merely an 'esperienza minore' ['minor experience'] in the development of a female literary genealogy in the twentieth century (*Tabù e coscienza*, 41). Although she recognizes the artistic achievements of several female Futurists, including Benedetta, Enif Robert, and Rosa Rosa, she believes that most of them ended by blindly supporting the movement's ideal of male supremacy.

While more work needs to be done to unearth the contributions of Futurist women and to evaluate these texts within the context of the movement and, on a larger scale, within the national canon, recent efforts have revealed a treasure trove of female-authored works. Cinzia Sartini Blum offers a nuanced, balanced, and perhaps more illuminating reading of their presence than Nozzoli. She points out that although feminist and cultural critics have recently 'rediscovered' these women, they are still evaluated primarily against the production of the standards established by their male cohorts:

Their role has been perceived as a mimetic, entirely subordinated reflection of the artistic experience of Futurist men. Against this lack, I argue that Futurism is a significant episode in women's activity on the Italian cultural scene at the beginning of the twentieth-Century; it is the sole instance of Italian women's conspicuous participation in the historical avant-garde. Far from being entirely reducible to a mere imitation, the writing of Futurist women articulates a different and conflict-laden representation of the feminine. ... (*The Other Modernism*, 110–11)

Claudia Salaris's anthology offers excerpts of manifestos, articles, poems, novels, visual works, and letters from more than forty Futurist women, many of whom used the periodicals *L'Italia futurista* and *Roma Futurista* as forums for their work. More recently, Mirella Bentivoglio and Franca Zoccoli's effort to revise Futurist artistic history – appropriately titled *The Women Artists of Italian Futurism – Almost Lost to History* – examines the literary and visual production of many heretofore unknown women.[11]

These investigations make clear that despite the anti-women stance espoused in many Futurist manifestos, perhaps especially those of F.T. Marinetti, many female artists were eager to participate in this refreshingly unconventional movement. Just like their male associates, these women welcomed the opportunity to overturn antiquated artistic archetypes and narrative patterns. As Lucia Re points out,

No longer trapped in the role of exclusive objects and icons of male desire and representation ... or in the traditional nineteenth-century position of domestic angels (which the Futurists also abhorred), whose only interest in art could be an amateur one, women suddenly saw themselves instead as potential subjects and producers of art. ('Impure Abstraction,' 32)

Unlike earlier literary innovators, such as Aleramo and Serao, the female Futurists could claim they were working in and creating an utterly new artistic tradition, and therefore could ignore or repudiate the traditional depictions of female characters and experiences, depictions that previous women authors rarely succeeded in disregarding completely.

Several of these women used the same rhetorical framework popular with the Futurist movement – the manifesto – to challenge the more overtly misogynistic statements made by their male associates. Valentine de Saint Point, a Frenchwoman with personal and artistic ties to Italy, wrote *Manifesto della Donna futurista* in 1912 as a direct rebuttal of Marinetti's 1909 *Fondazione e Manifesto del Futurismo*, in which he elaborated the movement's ideology, including gender politics.[12] While Futurist women often co-opted the structure of the movement's poetics, they more importantly 'used and transformed the language of the avant-garde, the logos of male dominance, into a world that could accept the feminine voice' (Orban, 73).

Benedetta Marinetti (1897–1977) embodies the tensions and contradictions of the female Futurist: an acclaimed artist, she was also Marinetti's wife and mother of their three daughters.[13] As Re notes, 'Benedetta's juggling of family, work and politics in the 1930s gave, as she herself wittily remarked, a new meaning to the term "Futurist simultaneity"' ('Impure Abstraction,' 199). Perhaps to carve out her own identity, Benedetta dropped both birth and married names when signing her artistic works. Like many other Futurists, Benedetta was interdisciplinary, producing visual art in the form of paintings, ceramics, drawings, and set designs, as well as literary works, including three novels, collections of poetry, and essays. She is perhaps better known for her artwork, exhibited throughout Europe in the 1920s and 1930s, than for her literary production.[14]

Throughout her involvement in the Futurist movement, Benedetta 'appropriated Futurist rhetoric and imagery to forge a unique voice for herself, despite the difficulties inherent in doing so in a male-dominated movement' (Panzera, 6). Her interest in a women-centred perspective is evident in several of her works, including one of her *parolibere*, a Futurist interpretation of free verse that often included visual images along with text. In 1919, the artist signed one such effort, entitled 'Spicologia [*sic*] di un uomo'['Psychology of a man'], in a manner guaranteed to raise some eyebrows: 'Benedetta fra le donne, parolibera futurista' ['Blessed among women, Futurist free verse']. The phrase evokes the Virgin Mary, and suggests a spiritual component to the artist's poetics, an element that becomes more fully revealed in her three novels. This signature, while creating an artistic link other female Futurists, serves as well to underscore her privileged position among them. Benedetta develops more fully her gendered poetics in later literary texts. In her first two novels, *Le forze umane* (*Human Forces*) and *Viaggio di Gararà* (*Gararà's Voyage*), the central theme is 'female creativity and desire' (Re, 'Fascist Theories of "Woman,"' 90). Clearly, Benedetta's artistic agenda included an investigation of issues regarding women that the Futurist movement in general either ignored or belittled.

Benedetta's revision of the epistolary novel illustrates her concern for these issues while offering an innovative rendition of the letter text.

Astra e il sottomarino relates the tragic tale of the title characters – a young teacher and the submarine captain she meets on a train. Like Aleramo's protagonist in *Amo dunque sono*, the heroine in Benedetta's work is freed of the traditional epistolary isolation. While Astra passes most of her time in Rome, she also travels to Paris and Levanto. Emilio, the submariner, on the other hand, spends much of the novel in his vessel, conducting experiments. Interestingly, Astra's villa is just off the coast, allowing her lover to see her home when his submarine emerges from its watery dwelling. Astra's relative freedom becomes underlined when set against her lover's enforced confinement in his submarine.

In *Astra e il sottomarino*, Benedetta underscores the importance of letters while examining one of the tropes of epistolary fiction, that of the introductory note by an anonymous editor. Benedetta opens the text with a letter to her husband. While this move implicitly signals the narrative framework that follows, it also allows her to play with the tradition. This extra-textual note reminds us of Orintia Romagnuoli Sacrati's brief invocation to the Prince of Saxe Gotha preceding *Lettere di Giulia Willet*. Sacrati was seeking protection for her heroine, a move that suggested the hardships faced by literary (and real) women in early nineteenth-century Italy. A century later, Benedetta has no such worries. When she writes to her husband, '[T]i offro ASTRA' (172) ['I offer you ASTRA'], she is not asking for his approval or his protection. Rather, she praises the ability of her protagonist to bring art – and by extension, life – into the world. She writes that Astra will carry 'una irradiazione di poesia' ['an irradiation of poetry'] throughout the world, and adds: 'Poesia: tu non credi che in essa per illuminare il mondo, io credo che senza ansia spirituale e senza amore … il mondo si disgrega e si sparpaglia nel nulla' (172) ['Poetry: you believe only in it to illuminate the world, I believe that without spiritual anxiety and without love … the world will disintegrate and scatter into nothingness']. Benedetta's opening letter, then, celebrates both epistolary heroine and structure, and lays the framework for a gendered reading of her letter novel.

Benedetta uses this opening letter to claim allegiance to the Futurist movement, while also challenging the attempt by many male Futurists to co-opt the powers of procreation, claiming it instead as a right inherent to women.[15] She writes to Marinetti, 'Sono certa che questa è opera futurista e ne sono fiera' (172) ['I am certain that this is a Futurist work and I am proud of it'].[16] She points out that while the story revolves around a romantic relationship, 'ho cercato di dare il mistero del destino condizionato dalla Realtà e precisato e preveduto dal Sogno' (172)

['I have tried to show the mystery of destiny conditioned by Reality and detailed and foreseen by the Dream'], employing language fundamental to Futurist tenets. Benedetta goes on to say that while the novel has been finished for three years, she has been involved in weightier matters, namely the birth and upbringing of their third daughter. After mentioning fondly their other daughters, she writes that now Astra, her female protagonist, can join her daughters in life. The author conflates the birth of her own offspring with that of her heroine, casting herself as the generator of life and art. This introductory epistle, then, serves to assure Marinetti (and her readers) that she is indeed a card-carrying Futurist, but also underlines the female sex's capacity for biological procreation. With this prominently placed explanatory epistle, we are directed to examine in particular the portrayal of the female character. Benedetta's emphasis on childbirth appears to be a wholly conscious attempt to remove this experience from the grasp of male Futurists and reposition it in its traditional place within the female sphere.

In a second instance underlining the importance of the epistle in *Astra e il sottomarino*, a letter literally saves the heroine's life. In this episode, Astra has taken a boat out one morning, and, feeling rebellious and out of sorts, tries to row against the current. The boat capsizes, but a letter from Emilio, which she had tucked into her shirt, suddenly acts as a life vest: 'La lettera si allarga si gonfia indurisce sorregge il petto di Astra, salvagente d'amore costruito dall'amore di Emilio. Sono le sue parole scritte che realmente la riportano alla superficie. Salva!' (206) ['The letter grows bigger inflates hardens holds up Astra's chest, life jacket of love constructed from Emilio's love. They are his written words that really carry her to the river bank. Saved!']. In this dramatic example of epistolary authority, love – transcribed and made tangible through the letter – rescues Astra from her doubts and fears about her relationship with Emilio. By endowing the epistle with special powers, Benedetta by extension insists on the capacity of letter texts to transform the narrative of one's life.

The content of these letters, however, reveals how Benedetta reimagines the traditional epistolary novel, for these epistles are rarely filled with descriptions of the quotidian experiences of the lovers, or even of passionate reminiscences of their time together. Rather, the letters are vivid descriptions of their dreams, surreal inventions made all the more impressive by Benedetta's painterly approach to prose. In creating a text that is grounded in dreams and fantasy, the author positions herself within the general avant-garde atmosphere of Europe in the

1920s and 1930s. As Simona Cigliana points out in her introduction to *Astra e il sottomarino*, the novel 'si iscriveva ... nella più vasta corrente "magica" europea, quella che va dal surrealismo al realismo magico bontempelliano, cui ... il romanzo di Benedetta si avvicinava per il tagliente nitore delle immagini e dell'atmosfera' (37) ['is inscribed ... in the widest current of European "magic," which goes from surrealism to magical realism Bontempelliano, which ... Benedetta's novel approaches through its cutting elegance of images and atmosphere']. These dreams, transcribed in the letters, serve as the foundation of the novel, although the epistles are also intermixed with descriptive scenes of the lovers and their activities. Benedetta moves significantly beyond the more conventional narrative framework of romantic fiction, which has always favoured realism, for she displaces the lovers' hopes and fears into the realm of fantasy and into an explicitly Futurist sensibility.

Benedetta's debt to Futurist poetics becomes a minor subtext of the novel, signalling her adherence to the movement's literary innovations. In one letter, for example, Emilio describes the atmosphere of a particularly vivid dream as 'il cielo futurista esploso dai nervi di Boccioni e Marinetti' (182) ['the Futurist sky exploded by the nerves of Boccioni and Marinetti']. Here Benedetta pays tribute to the movement's founders, as she recognizes the role Marinetti and painter Umberto Boccioni played in fashioning Futurist poetics. The author also employs literary devices that directly evoke the artistic influence of Futurism. In one of Astra's dreams, she describes a group of *ombre*, the shades of people in limbo. One of them, called only the Signora, writes a type of *parolibera* in an attempt to prove the existence of these mysterious characters:

'Scomparsa

è

apparsa

oretsiM.' (184)

'Disappeared

she

appeared

yretsyM.'

The dream itself may not be as important in this instance as the form in which Benedetta transcribes it, for with these references to Futurism and its practices, Benedetta links her text specifically to the movement's artistic techniques.

But while she incorporates many of Futurism's literary practices, does she also champion its broader agenda? Critics have pointed out that even while revealing a willingness to examine female-centred themes in her work, Benedetta espoused an ideology that adhered to the 'equazione mussoliniana tra uomo-guerra e donna-maternità' (Nozzoli *Tabù e coscienza*, 64) ['Mussolini-like equation between man-war and woman-maternity']. While her artistic works never served as Fascist propaganda, as was the case with other Futurist authors, Benedetta apparently did support the regime's demographic campaign, in which Italian women were urged to abandon their professional activities and dedicate themselves to the role of mother in the name of the homeland.[17] Read in less political terms, the ideology underlying Benedetta's fictional production appears to recognize female fecundity as a metaphor for creativity in general. Nozzoli writes: '[L]a poetica di Benedetta si concentra infatti sin dagli esordi intorno al motivo centrale della Donna Creatrice, della femminilità come polo vitale da cui traggono origine uomini, idee, passioni' (*Tabù e coscienza*, 60) ['Benedetta's poetics are concentrated in fact from the very beginning around the central motif of the Woman Creator, of femininity as the vital pole from which are generated beginnings, men, ideas, passions']. Is she mirroring Aleramo, who as we saw in *Amo dunque sono* found in the female body a powerful metaphor for artistic production? If so, does that mean Benedetta's works are based in reductive and narrow attitudes concerning female capabilities? And how, then, does Benedetta's political-artistic poetics play out more specifically in *Astra e il sottomarino*?

The answer is not an easy one, in part because the conclusion to the text is cryptic at best. In fact, critics have been puzzling over the novel's final message since its publication, with many reading in it a tragic, dystopic conclusion to the tale of two lovers who believed they were fated to be together for eternity. Others, recognizing the impossibility of settling on a definitive interpretation, see instead a glimmer of optimism that ultimately points to a proto-feminist vision of female behaviour. Certainly, the conclusion allows the author to portray the female character along non-traditional lines, for Astra emerges as a strong and independent heroine.

On the surface, however, the novel ends in disaster: Emilio's submarine mysteriously sinks and all aboard are lost at sea. The final passage in the novel, a strange and puzzling dream in which reality ultimately obliterates fantasy, lends itself to a grim conclusion. But if we look at Astra's behaviour throughout the novel, another reading of the text becomes possible, one allowing for a more fruitful construction of its final events. Despite the love Astra professes for Emilio, she refuses to play his subservient, patient, and faithful partner. She will not keep her lonely watch from the seacoast and she will not confine herself to her room, which he suggests she do when her nerves are getting the best of her. As she writes, 'La mia carne sa tradire ma non attendere' (212) ['My body knows how to betray but not to wait']. As Blum points out in her insightful critique of the novel, perhaps the dissolution of the lovers' relationship can be viewed as a productive step in the heroine's development. Astra ultimately frees herself from the exclusive and solitary relationship she shared with Emilio, Blum writes. 'She survives because she turns her love into a desire to embrace life, implicitly rejecting Emilio's injunction to insulate herself from it' ('Benedetta's Emphatic Journey,' 29). That premise leads to a more general explication of Benedetta's vision of female behaviour, for 'Astra's desire ... runs counter to the Fascist regime's promotion of self-sacrifice, submissiveness, and domesticity as essential female values' (29).[18]

Benedetta's decision to articulate this gendered poetics resonates in particular within the framework of the epistolary text, which, as we saw in both this and the preceding chapter, offers a forum for commenting on contemporary social and literary conditions and expectations. Here, the author observed the conventions of this traditional genre, while infusing the novel with a sensibility influenced by her own particular articulation of Futurism. If we approach the novel thematically, the romantic narrative of Astra and Emilio, disclosed primarily through their dream-soaked letters, indirectly addresses the plight of women confronting a historical moment that sought to contain them into rigid socio-cultural roles. Through the device of the correspondence in *Astra e il sottomarino*, the author sets up a dialogue between a representative of a more conservative ideology – Emilio – and the woman he is meant to convert. While he is initially successful – his letter does, after all, act as a figurative life vest for the drowning Astra – the heroine ultimately appears to reject this ideology.

The question of the text's epistolarity becomes crucial in Benedetta's novel. It facilitates the evolution of the relationship between the two characters, allowing them to gradually represent polar opposites on the spectrum of gendered perspectives. The forum also, however, allows Benedetta to address issues of narrative structure and techniques, concerns fundamental to the Futurist movement. In *Astra e il sottomarino*, Benedetta appears to ultimately reject the letter text and its traditional reliance on the romantic narrative. In fact, the last several entries in the novel consist of an extract from Astra's diary, a newspaper report of the submarine's tragic fate, and the final dream. The letter serves no further purpose, for the epistolary text in Benedetta's rendition acts as a forum not merely for the construction of a romantic exchange, but also for the analysis of a poetics influenced as much by the author's gender as her participation in the Futurist movement.

Gianna Manzini's contribution to a re-evaluation of the letter text is profound; in her novel *Lettera all'editore*, the author explores the concept of memory and the fragmentary nature of time. She re-envisions these staples of epistolary fiction, recasting them in light of both a literary and a personal evolution. While she does not concern herself specifically with female-centred experiences, as did Aleramo and Benedetta, Manzini does use the vehicle of a letter text to address contemporary literary issues and movements.

Manzini (1896–1974) reveals in her works a life-long commitment to literary experimentation. A member of the Florentine school of artists that produced the periodical *Solaria*, she was initially influenced by that group's desire to create through thematic and stylistic innovations new interpretations of the novel and of literature in general. *Prosa d'arte*, as that style became known, often focused on the lyrical, fragmentary narrative evident in Manzini's first novel *Tempo innamorato* (1928) (*Enamoured Time*). Her contribution to a reimagining of traditional literary tenets was recognized from that first text and on throughout her career, which saw the publication of six novels, along with numerous short stories and critical essays. But with the 1945 *Lettera all'editore*, Manzini's contribution to a general endeavour to create alternative narratives was firmly established. In Emilio Cecchi's famous essay, he wrote that her novel revealed a rare 'complicatezza' ('complicatedness') not typically seen in European literature (7). It is especially intriguing, for the purposes of this study, that Manzini's most innovative work was an epistolary text, for we can trace through our discussion of this novel how her revision of the letter text engages concepts of canon formation and literary genre.

Like that of many Italian authors of the inter-war period, Manzini's interest in revitalizing the national literature was in part a reaction to a general artistic crisis triggered by the Fascist government's heavy-handed and often repressive approach to creative (read 'subversive') endeavours. In 1945 she was named editor of *Prosa*, an international periodical that invited vigorous debates on literary concerns. Indeed, Enzo Panareo writes that with *Lettera all'editore*, Manzini 'consegna alla storia della letteratura italiana del Novecento il documento non soltanto della sua crisi, ma di una crisi generale che in quegli anni fortunosi coinvolve tutta la letteratura italiana' (28) ['consigns to the history of twentieth-century Italian literature the document not only of its crisis, but of a general crisis that in those eventful years involved all of Italian literature']. Manzini's articulation of the 'querelle novecentesca sul romanzo' ['twentieth-century debate on the novel'] is woven throughout the novel, and, indeed, acts as catalyst to its very conception and construction (Fava Guzzetta, *Gianna Manzini*, 146).

However, perhaps because Manzini's novel does not resemble the traditional letter text, *Lettera all'editore* is not typically considered an epistolary novel. Although it opens with an epistle from the narrator to her editor, and four other such letters are interspersed throughout the novel, these letters constitute only a fraction of the novel. This fact, however, does not preclude the work from being defined as epistolary, for, as Elizabeth Campbell points out, 'if the plot is determined, advanced, and resolved by letters' the text itself can be considered a letter novel (333). While many would argue that in Manzini's case the focus is on the text proper, rather than the letters scattered throughout the narrative, *Lettera all'editore* owes much to the epistolary genre. The very title, after all, points to a suggested structure from which to read the text and prompts the reader to always locate the text within this framework.[19] Second, the letters contained within it are crucial for an understanding of the poetics underlying the author's narrative strategy. Reading the novel through the lens of epistolary fiction serves as a productive vehicle for analysing Manzini's revision of generic parameters as well as her vision of artistic creation.

Because of the fragmentary and reflexive narration, and a decidedly non-linear trajectory, the novel does not lend itself to a brief or simple synopsis.[20] Instead, *Lettera all'editore* consists of a particularly lyrical concoction of unconnected episodes, autobiographic meditations, and literary reflections. The text ostensibly revolves around a group of characters connected through familial or amorous ties. In a move evocative of Luigi Pirandello's drama *Sei personaggi in cerca d'un autore* (*Six Characters in Search of an Author*), the very origins and evolution of this *romanzo da fare* rest on the shoulders of these characters, for it is they who compel the narrator to write their stories and therefore validate their lives.[21] Manzini writes of how one day, while awaiting the daily post, a young boy leads her to the characters that she will bring to life.[22] The narrator is already familiar with these figures, for, as she writes, 'Ingiustamente li avevo abbandonati' (21) ['I had abandoned them unfairly'(9)] apparently for other projects.[23] But while she deliberates throughout the text about various editorial choices, she concedes the architecture of the narrative to the adolescent Aldo, who is secretly writing a book about several of the other characters. She attributes the novel's structure to Aldo, saying, '[I]o non facevo che dare volti, gesti, immagini, momenti, gridi, legata dal filo della mia emozione mentr'egli s'impadroniva degli avvenimenti, e sul foglietti del suo diario ne ricavaca la favola o il racconto' (22) ['I only make the expressions, gestures, images, moments, cries strung on the thread of my emotions, while he takes charge of the events and fashions the fable or story on the pages of his diary' (11)]. The novel becomes, then, a meditation on the construction of a text, as Manzini creates two figures – the narrator and Aldo – who have consciously and deliberately embarked on such a project.

The plot runs along family ties, which are convoluted and often only sketchily drawn. Briefly, Aldo is the illegitimate son of Luca, who raises him alongside his son, Sandro, although Aldo does not learn of his true parentage until after Luca's death. Amalia, Luca's wife, has a profound and intense bond with their son Sandro, and does her best to ignore the fact that Aldo is in love with Laura, Sandro's wife. Laura, increasingly unhappy in her marriage, cannot understand why her husband rejects both her and her child, and eventually commits suicide. Elide, Laura's sister, marries Memmo, who was initially in love with Laura. This summary does little justice to the intricate, often perplexing narrative contained in *Lettera all'editore*, for the family chronicles are never explained in full, but instead only alluded to, often in flashbacks.[24]

While this family history deals to some degree with the amorous ties between various members, Manzini does not privilege the romantic narrative as do other authors in this study, but examines as well the dynamics engendered by familial bonds. She is also the only writer in this book who does not systematically undertake an exploration of female roles and experiences, or at least, not in *Lettera all'editore*. Indeed, M. Assunta Parsani and Neria De Giovanni, in their study of female authors who wrote in the inter- and post-war years, believe that for Manzini 'la ricerca poetica e strutturale' ['the search for poetics and structure'] is the dominant theme in her works, rather than the motif of a woman in search of herself, as is the case in texts by Alba de Céspedes, for example (95).[25] Manzini does not ignore gender concerns, however. In her opening letter, she takes up the issue, briefly tracing an evolution within herself in regard to how she views her own sex. 'In realtà essere donna mi piaceva ormai assai meno' ['Actually, to be a woman pleased me much less now'] than when she first took up this text, she writes, adding succinctly: 'Tirannica sorte' (10) ['Tyrannical fate' (3)]. While not focusing in particular on any one of her female characters, Manzini does trace a type of female genealogy in *Lettera all'editore*. The narrator, in an elliptical recollection of years long past, writes: '"Mia madre, io, la mia bambina ...: un gruppo, una forza"' (31) ['"My mother, I, my little girl: a group, a power"' (17)]. This female line becomes more pronounced toward the end of the text, when the narrator writes that she has gradually conflated the character of Elide with that of her own mother. Certainly a portrayal of motherhood – the narrator's, Elide's, and Laura's – runs through the text, although, again, the novel concentrates on an examination of family bonds instead of discussing in any great depth gendered roles or experiences.

Alongside the story of family or romantic entanglements runs a parallel narrative, that of the narrator discussing the unfolding book with her editor. In examining the epistolarity of the text, we must turn to the letters themselves, the five epistles the narrator intersperses throughout the novel and in which she describes an evolution that is both literary and personal. But first, we must ask, who exactly is this unnamed editor to whom the narrator directs her letters? And does the editor act as the 'coscienza tecnica' ['technical conscience'] of the narrator, as Cecchi would have it (8), or is her correspondence with this figure 'il suo modo di recuperare una presenza ... all'opera e dei problemi costruttivi alla tematica del romanzo' ['her way of recuperating a presence ... to the work and to the constructive problems of the novel's thematics'], as Fava Guzzetta writes (*Gianna Manzini*, 41)? Certainly the bond between the narrator and her 'amico editore' deepens throughout the text, ending in what Manzini calls 'un piccolo angolo di'intimità' (248) ['a small corner of intimacy' (180)]. The editor acts as the catalyst for the text itself, for in her first letter the narrator responds to his request for a new novel. This technique appears similar to the brief introductions often found in traditional epistolary texts, and which we have examined in the works of Serao, in particular. This device typically serves to introduce characters, explicate their situation, and finally to legitimatize the publication of the correspondence that follows. In Manzini's case, however, the situation is quite different, in part because the text proper is not composed of letters, but also because her letters are interspersed throughout the novel, rather than just introducing it. Because the letters are few, and relatively brief, some critics have neglected them in favour of exploring the family narrative within the text itself.

But the positioning of the letters throughout the text serves as a way for Manzini to comment on both the epistolary genre, and, more generally, on an important cultural-literary debate of the 1930s and 1940s. Letter placement is certainly an important strategy in this genre; indeed, Sacrati in her *Lettere di Giulia Willet* signalled the erosion of identity in the female protagonist by excluding her letters from the final section of the novel. Benedetta ends *Astra e il sottomarino* not with letters, but with other forms of narrative, indicating perhaps the author's mistrust of the relationship engendered by the correspondence between the novel's protagonists. In *Lettera all'editore*, the letters offer short breaks between chapters devoted to the description of familial affairs. Within this privileged space, the narrator is able to comment on the construction of the text itself, while also referring to the events and relationships that form the narrative arc. The letters' significance is emphasized by their physical appearance, for they are set in italics, a device that underlines their function as 'riflessione di ciò che è stato scritto ed anticipazione di ciò che verrà' ['reflection of what had been written and anticipation of what will come'] (Parsani and De Giovanni, 109). Clearly we are meant to read these letters as integral to the narrative, but also as separate texts that characterize, to some degree, the structure of the text.

These epistles serve to define the narrative trajectory of *Lettera all'editore* while also allowing the narrator a space in which to articulate her position on contemporary literary debates. One such debate, fostered by the burgeoning neorealist movement, centred on authorial design and the aesthetic produced by that intention. Unlike many artists working in the 1930s and 1940s, Manzini declined to participate in the documentary approach of neorealism, devising instead a more interpretative methodology in creating narrative. She writes in one of the letters in her novel: 'Un'amalgama singolare si stabilisce fra ciò che vedo e ciò che immagino, dando origine a una realtà fresca d'invenzione, come appena svelata (164) ['A particular amalgam is established between what I see and what I imagine, giving rise to a fresh inventive reality, as though barely unveiled' (116)]. Her realty, then, was quite different from that of the neorealist authors. '[A]t the peak of neorealistic debates, when every Italian writer examined whether literature and art ought faithfully to represent social reality,' writes Giovanna Miceli-

Jeffries, 'Manzini expressed her belief that writers must interpret reality in a way that, once written, becomes more transparent, penetrating, and alive than when mistaken for historical events' ('Gianna Manzini's Poetics,' 94). Indeed, Manzini writes in one letter that she must 'raccontare senza uniformità, appoggiandomi ai temi che più mi son cari, o sorvolandoli proprio perché troppo mi premono, tutte queste avventure' (39) ['narrate without linear sequence, turning to themes that are dearer to me, or leaving them out just because those adventures matter so much' (25)]. Her works often explicitly engage in questioning and reinterpreting conventional stylistic elements, revealing an 'unrelenting exploration of the different, expanded functions of the novel itself' (Miceli-Jeffries, 'Gianna Manzini's Poetics,' 91). Certainly Manzini's reinterpretation of the epistolary genre, with the hybrid format found in Lettera all'editore, points to the author's desire to reimagine traditional narrative structures.

Manzini also rejected another fundamental aspect of neorealism, the ostensibly impersonal approach favoured by many practitioners of the literary movement. She elected instead to include autobiographical elements in her works. Indeed, she writes in the opening epistle that Lettera all'editore is 'una doppia avventura, personale e intellettuale' 11) ['a two-fold adventure – personal and intellectual' (4)]), admitting in a later dispatch that 'il vero romanzo per me consiste nei punti di concomitanza dell'intreccio con alcuni episodi della mia vita' (162) ['for me the real novel consists in the plot's correspondence with certain episodes in my life' (115)]. The inclusion of personal history calls to mind Aleramo's literary production, but in Manzini the incorporation of life events is not a means to reassess or even to reimagine those events, but rather an opportunity to re-immerse herself in the past. Manzini is more interested in an analysis of the sentiments evoked by recalling a particular episode in the past than in the event itself (Parsani and De Giovanni, 108). The creation of a literary text, then, becomes synonymous with the act of remembering. Manzini goes even further, for as her novel evolves in ways she had not anticipated, she is forced to re-evaluate her own lived experiences, creating what Anna Nozzoli calls 'autobiografismo critico' ['critical autobiography'] ('I "ritratti" di Gianna Manzini,' 131). Manzini's poetics invites a double discourse that focuses on both narrative and reflection. Thus, the letter novel bridges the gap and creates the connection between the 'intreccio' ('plot') of the narrative and the 'episodi' ('episodes') of the writer's life.

Because of the emphasis on past experiences and their repercussions on present-day events and feelings, Manzini's novel eschews a linear or unified structure. This practice is prevalent in epistolary fiction, which often incorporates an amalgamation of past, present, and future tenses. In Manzini's case, the rejection of a historical temporality is explicit. Such a concept of time, which the narrator refers to in one of her letters as 'c'era una volta' ('once upon a time'), is the element that 'scortava i racconti, conteneva le storie, legava i fatti, conduceva a termine le avventure, faceva crescere le bambine e le mutava in donne' (38) ['accompanied narrations, contained stories, connected facts, brought adventures to an end, made little girls grow up and charmed them into women' (24)]. But, she adds, 'Il ritmo del "c'era una volta" ... non mi riguarda più: son giunta a fargli violenza coi battiti del cuore' (39) ['The rhythm of "once upon a time" ... no longer interests me. I have come to do it violence with heartbeats' (24–5)]). The use of diverse temporal elements serves as a forum to explore the narrator's autobiographic interventions, for she often uses these past experiences as a means to explicate the present. Indeed, the narrator skips back and forth between the various moments with a defiant rejection of more traditional, linear texts.

This atemporal approach acts as a significant revision of the traditional epistolary text, for surely these fragmented and episodic segments – a direct result of Manzini's rejection of linearity – read like the epistles forming a letter novel. The seemingly disconnected and unrelated episodes of *Lettera all'editore* are instead revelatory pieces of narrative, reflection, and memory that, when stitched together, make up the text proper. This technique mirrors a more traditionally structured epistolary novel, in which the letters are linked together in a long, continuous chain to form the narrative itself.[26] By using this approach, this hallmark of epistolary fiction, Manzini creates a text that reimagines the contemporary novel. She invents a narrative composed of discrete parts, stringing them along like beads on a thread and teasing the meaning out of both their separate components and their collective assembly.

Tellingly, the act of creating an epistolary text whose ties to the objective and the linear are tenuous at best generates a maturation within the narrator herself. In her final letter to the editor, she admits to a personal evolution wrought by the demands of addressing the 'delicato e permaloso labirinto della memoria' (247) ['delicate and moody labyrinth of recollection' (180)]. She adds: 'È anche l'idea del romanzo che si è modificato in me: e sono io stessa, in ogni senso, cambiata' (245) ['The idea of the novel was modified as it went along; and I myself am changed in every sense of the word' (178)]. Throughout *Lettera all'editore*, the narrator has been commenting on the unfolding of the text in her letters; gradually, she recognizes a parallel progression within herself. Manzini speaks to the power of literature in general and the epistolary in particular as an avenue to self-awareness and growth. Engaged artistry does not simply result in a discrete work of art, but provokes as well a re-examination of the artist's sense of self, which in turn becomes implicitly enfolded into the act of creation. *Lettera all'editore* moves significantly beyond the subjective poetics of Aleramo's *Amo dunque sono*. In that text, Aleramo used the letter novel to examine and comment on the creation of a literary work without further recognizing a parallel personal evolution. Aleramo's focus on literary creation and production in her epistolary text refers back to her own work rather than opens up into a discussion of concurrent artistic movements or styles. For Manzini, however, the epistolary text, with its poetics of self-reflection and intimacy, allows her to address contemporary literary debates while acknowledging the personal metamorphosis accompanying her investigation. Her development becomes contextualized within a larger cultural discussion.

Manzini's project is similar to Benedetta's in her novel *Astra e il sottomarino*. Both works speak to the authority of narrative – in the form of a letter text – to transform lives. In Benedetta's case, her heroine is 'saved' by a letter from her lover, although ultimately their correspondence reveals the impossibility of a sustained relationship. Manzini's narrator, too, reveals a personal evolution, told against the backdrop of an analysis of contemporary literary sensibilities. The epistolary novel serves as a vehicle to investigate questions regarding artistic creation and patterns of literary production. Examining these issues through the perspective of a letter text allows for innovative articulations of contemporary literary models.

These authors also implicitly challenge issues of canon formation, for surely re-envisioning a traditional narrative pattern calls into question the very foundation of national literatures. By casting their narratives against the backdrop of literary debates, Benedetta and Manzini in particular argue for a re-evaluation of contemporary literary standards and practices. That they chose to examine this issue within the framework and context of the epistolary novel – a format, we must remember, that was often considered particular to female authors – serves as an important validation of the letter text.

3 Making Connections

The literary debates and experimentations seen in the previous chapter gradually give way to less insular texts, as authors engage more openly with the political and socio-cultural transformations of post-war Italy. These writers challenge the conventional structure and thematics of the epistolary genre through a purposeful juxtaposition of the private and the public. They use the letter novel to vividly position singular, domestic narratives against the drama of a changing society. While these works employ many of the conventions of traditional epistolary texts, these authors find in the letter format a structure and a forum to address and criticize the troubles of the modern world.

Alba de Céspedes and Natalia Ginzburg posit in their reimagining of this narrative structure a productive means of addressing social ills, seeing it as a site to nurture those connections made tenuous by the demands of a modern society. De Céspedes, for example, envisions the letter text as a forum to speak to the loss of the ideals of the Resistance. In a trenchant commentary on post-war mores, she removes responsibility for the creation of a social ethic from the dominant class, which she perceives as fundamentally hypocritical and corrupt, and instead delivers it into the hands of writers – the creators, in fact, of the epistolary. Along the way, the letter text becomes a therapeutic site for self-discovery and a means of fostering authenticity. In her two letter novels, Ginzburg creates a space for profound and committed personal interaction, counteracting the generalized social alienation she sees in post-war Italy. She finds in the epistolary structure a way of addressing the universal inability to communicate, although her approach to this problem is often ironic. In their novels, de Céspedes and Ginzburg offer an intriguing portrayal of the ethos and the evolution of post-Second

World War Italy, uncovering and addressing social problems through the use of the epistolary structure.

While both these authors tease out the correspondence between narrative structure and thematic content to address their concerns about contemporary Italy, Alba de Céspedes's 1963 novel *Il rimorso* (*Remorse*) is the most direct in deploying the epistolary as a means of exploring – and often criticizing – social and cultural mores. Perhaps more important, however, for this study, is how the epistolary acts as a redemptive space, an arena for literally rewriting the trauma and disappointments of the post-war era. Although the novel focuses on just a few months in 1961, its narrative reaches back to the civil and political struggles of the 1940s. Like many authors writing in this period, de Céspedes (1911–1997) was strongly influenced by her experiences during the Second World War, particularly her work in the Resistance movement. She broadcast anti-fascist programs on Radio Bari, and founded the literary journal *Mercurio* in 1944, which served as a forum for the cultural ideals of the partisan movement.[1] De Céspedes's commitment to a life lived with integrity, within a society that recognizes gender equality, can be read in her most important novels. The choice of genre closely reflects the author's thematic intent; whether it is the choral structure of *Nessuno torna indietro* (*There's No Turning Back*) (1938), which revolves around a group of girls coming of age in a boarding school, or the intimate diaristic structure of *Il quaderno proibito* (*The Notebook*) (1952), which reveals the gradual self-awakening of an unhappy Roman housewife.[2]

Il rimorso is perhaps de Céspedes's most striking illustration of the role of genre in illuminating and giving texture to narrative. In this text, letters and diary entries provide a means of addressing the stultifying, bourgeois ethos of 1961 Italy, as perceived by de Céspedes. Through the letters and diary, the two protagonists are able to challenge that ethos and create through their own agency more meaningful lives; indeed, their writing, begun as a personal act of resistance, eventually promises a more universal rebellion. Not all critics agree that *Il rimorso* is a 'true' epistolary novel, but see it rather as one in which the actions and motivations of the characters are stimulated by an exchange of letters. De Céspedes even alerts the readers that her novel may not fulfil conventional expectations of a letter text. In an author's note before the text proper, she writes that the characters of *Il rimorso* are fictional even if we do not know if these letters were ever sent, although clearly most were (10). Elena Gagliardi, in her excellent study of the work, asserts that the novel 'si finge un "dialogo" epistolare in cui non solo le lettere sono false, ma non costituiscono neppure una vera corrispondenza, un vero colloquio, perché il dibattito è puramente interiore: davvero la parola non riesce piú a comunicare' (20) ['pretends to have an epistolary "dialogue" in which not only are the letters false, but they do not even constitute a real correspondence, a real conversation, because the debate is entirely interior: words no longer succeed in communicating']. Certainly these letters function as interior monologues, as Gagliardi would have it, but they are much more than that. The actual exchange of letters and the reading of epistles are important as well, for it is in these moments that connections among the characters become illuminated, both to them and to the readers. Those connections – and the severing of them – are crucial to the finale scripted for each protagonist. Equally significant is the different persona each character adopts in his or her correspondences; an epistolary novel is ideally suited to register the various voices assumed by the letter writers. In the case of *Il rimorso*, these personae become especially important in a text that is so explicitly concerned with such themes as insincerity and conformity.

These themes are the backbone of the long novel, which focuses on four main characters. They are Guglielmo and his wife, Francesca; Isabella, Francesca's friend and Guglielmo's former lover; and Gerardo, a journalist who works for Guglielmo's newspaper. Francesca's sixteen letters make up much of the epistolary narrative; Isabella writes fourteen, seven each to Francesca and Guglielmo. De Céspedes underscores the value of the epistolary act by granting the majority of the letters to the character who makes the most constructive use of them. In fact, the novel turns on two plot points: will Francesca leave Guglielmo, and will Gerardo leave Guglielmo's newspaper?

Through the letters and journal entries that make up *Il rimorso*, de Céspedes traces the moral failures she finds inherent in this moment of Italian history. These failures are represented by Guglielmo, a former leader of the Resistance movement who has become an editor of an influential Roman newspaper and rising star in the conservative political party, and Isabella, a seemingly devoted wife and mother. Both, in their correspondence with each other, reveal the hypocrisy and deceit that lies beneath a façade of respectability and piety.[3] On the other end of the spectrum are Francesca, who uses her letters to Isabella as a means to acquire self-awareness, and Gerardo, whose diary entries gradually activate his long-dormant sense of personal and social responsibility. Over the course of the various epistolary exchanges and diary entries, the characters must come to terms with both an individual and communal loss of the principles and passions generated by the collective struggle against the Fascists and Germans. Guglielmo and Isabella are ultimately unable, or unwilling, to recover the ideals of the past, with the former giving up his Resistance ideals in order to continue a stultified and artificial life while Isabella, faced with the hypocrisy made evident by her letters, ends hers. Their stories serve as morality tales, an illustration of the debasement of social values found in contemporary Italy.

Isabella, childhood friend of Francesca, ostensibly content housewife and mother, represents most clearly the flourishing social hypocrisy, where a pretence of virtue is more valued than virtue itself. Her story reflects the 'angoscia diffusa, generale' (226) ['widespread, general anguish' (149)] that defines her world. Isabella participates in two sets of correspondence, one with Francesca and a complementary exchange with Guglielmo; the double correspondence represents her duplicitous nature.[4] Isabella's false piety is made apparent in these separate exchanges; with Guglielmo, who is all too familiar with her transgressions, she drops, at least in part, her mask of respectability. With Francesca, however, Isabella clings to her carefully constructed persona of modern-day saint. When Francesca writes that she has become involved in an affair, Isabella responds not with a sympathetic offer of help or understanding, but with scandalized and almost hysterical reproof. An allegedly devout Catholic, Isabella admonishes Francesca to confess her sins and to return to Guglielmo's side immediately. Isabella, whose own life is a façade, cannot understand why Francesca refuses to play the part of a docile and loving wife. 'Inoltre ti manca l'umiltà della menzogna: una dote preziosa, indispensabile alle donne' (152), she writes accusingly ['You don't possess the humility of lies: a precious gift, indispensable to women' (100)].

Isabella's insistence on upholding social mores by feigning obedience points to this particular moment in Italian history, the late 1950s, just before women actively demanded – and achieved – significant progress in their quest for social, cultural, and political recognition and parity. Indeed, this novel serves as a bridge to those of the following era, in which the authors, writing from the battlefields of the women's movement, more explicitly investigated – and promulgated – a feminist agenda. Isabella (and Francesca) exist between two worlds, the first underpinned by the gendered strictures of Fascism and the Catholic Church, and the latter shaken by the impassioned social insurrections of the late 1960s and 1970s. Isabella, along with many women of her generation, deferred to the expectations of her world, unable or unwilling to challenge the traditional patriarchal forces that created those expectations.[5] Rather than working toward forging a more authentic self, as Francesca does, Isabella hides behind a veil of piety, comfortable in a milieu that rewards compliance and complacency.

If Isabella's complicity with the conventionality of her worlds is made apparent in her letters to Francesca, her duplicity is revealed in her exchanges with Guglielmo. Although Francesca clearly expects her correspondence with her friend to be private, Isabella uses the situation to begin a correspondence with Francesca's husband, pleading concern about Francesca's emotional stability, and suggesting that she be institutionalized.[6] But when Isabella writes to Guglielmo, she dances around the reason for Francesca's disquiet, hinting at his wife's amorous activities rather than simply telling him the truth in her first letter. Her epistles are in turn flirtatious (she is clearly in love with him), reproachful (of Guglielmo's indifference to his wife and to her), and sanctimonious, a mirror of her extreme hypocrisy. This hypocrisy takes the form of sexual betrayals, for we learn toward the end of their correspondence that Guglielmo and Isabella had at one time indulged in an affair, begun while Francesca was in the hospital giving birth to her son. Isabella has also seduced Gianluca, Francesca's first suitor, and even admits in her final letter to a casual affair with a stranger that she picked up on a train. Her sensual appetite, which she blames on her 'need for love,' embodies an inherent disloyalty to her loved ones and reflects a more general betrayal of social and personal relationships (353).

Isabella's sexual sins, revealed so potently in her letters to Guglielmo, may be shocking and distasteful, but more alarming is her unwillingness to accept responsibility for them. Instead, she claims, in a breathtaking demonstration of self-delusion, 'Le mie intenzioni sono sempre innocenti: che cosa, in seguito, le snatura?' (518) ['My intentions are always innocent: what is it that, afterward, deforms them?' (353)].[7] By the end of her epistolary exchange with Guglielmo, however, Isabella appears to show some signs of self-awareness, for she is forced by his letters to confront their affair, her marriage, and her relationship with Francesca. Is her suicide then an act of redemption, an indication that she is willing to atone for a lifetime of disloyalties? Isabella may have received some insight into her actions, for certainly Guglielmo's letters coldly point out her many failures. But her letters make clear that while pretending to be guided by her religious faith, Isabella is driven more by a slavish devotion to social appearances. The role of the epistolary narrative is crucial to the conclusion to Isabella's narrative, for even after her death the fiction of her reputation as a devoted wife will remain intact. Her husband discovers the letters from Francesca, but because her friend knew nothing of Isabella's transgressions, these epistles highlight instead her piety. Letters, then, can influence a narrative even from beyond the grave. In Isabella's case they perpetuate the image she has so carefully constructed of herself and presented to the world.

But by ending Isabella's narrative in death, de Céspedes punishes her lack of responsibility, her refusal to participate in an honourable and positive life. Guglielmo, Isabella's partner in deception and disillusionment, has had even more opportunity to create such a life, and, as one who fought against the forces of repression, even a duty to do so.[8] As a hero of the Resistance and a promising journalist, Guglielmo embodied the ideals of this era: courage, truth, passion, and sincerity. But in the years since the war, he has become subsumed by the ideology of the prevailing conservative political and social forces, abandoning his earlier ideals for a life of wealth, privilege, and prestige. Like Isabella's, Guglielmo's betrayals are both personal and collective, and they are made worse by being hidden behind a mask of propriety. Guglielmo, however, is ultimately more complex (and more sympathetic) than Isabella, for he is fully aware of his faults, even if he continues to accept rather than change them. As M. Assunta Parsani and Neria De Giovanni point out, 'Guglielmo rappresenta la classe borghese che ha preso coscienza dei propri limiti, senza per altro avere la capacità di evolversi' (51) ['Guglielmo represents the bourgeois class which has realized its own limits, but does not have the capacity of evolving']. His relationship with Francesca reveals the extent of his gradual adoption of a cynical conformity. When they first met, just after the war, they were bound together by 'il fervore di una comune fede politica, la medesima ansia di una vita impegnata ed autentica' (Crocenzi, 33) ['the zeal of a common political faith, the same anxiety of an engaged and authentic life']. Fifteen years later, their marriage is a sham; they share no interests, no beliefs, and no goals, and have long since abandoned any sexual or sentimental intimacies.[9]

But although Guglielmo willingly advocates conservative social norms, his awareness of that conformity saves him from the end scripted for Isabella. As the only protagonist connected to all three other main characters, he plays a pivotal and ultimately positive role in their lives, redeeming at least in part the overall sterility of his life. Again, this occurs through his letters, as Guglielmo forces Isabella to face the truth behind her pretence of propriety. He goads Gerardo into quitting his position as foreign correspondent at the newspaper, freeing him to become the novelist he aspires to be. And finally, recognizing his wife's struggle against the bourgeois conventionality he has so eagerly embraced and attempted to instil in her, he puts up no legal or emotional obstacles when she finally does leave him.[10]

But what is Guglielmo's role in the epistolarity of *Il rimorso*? Although he decries letter writing as a useless exercise, over the course of his correspondence with Isabella he becomes more and more dependent on her epistles, growing anxious and irritable when her letters fail to arrive regularly.[11] He refuses to talk to Isabella about Francesca's situation by telephone, saying he prefers letter writing: 'Così mi pare di scrivere un diario' (297) ['In this way it is as if I were writing a diary' (196)]. The letters allow him a space in which he can write freely and intimately, an opportunity no longer afforded by his weekly newspaper editorials, which must conform to the party line and which he often delegates to his underlings, so as to concentrate more fully on his epistles to Isabella. Guglielmo uses his letters as an opportunity to examine how his life has so completely deviated from the ideals of the immediate post-war period. His letters are the voice of his generation, one that has sold out to 'un mondo dove gli ideali sono sbaragliati dagli interessi' (420) ['a world where ideals have been replaced by material interests' (282)]. But while Guglielmo recognizes the gravity of his personal and communal betrayal, he is too firmly entrenched in – and too fully rewarded by – powerful social and political forces to change his life. He may claim that '[i]l fascino della corrispondenza epistolare, a parer mio, consiste nella sua inutilitá' (414) ['The fascination of correspondence, to my mind, lies in its uselessness' (278)], but clearly his life serves as a biography of a failed generation.

While de Céspedes uses the vehicle of letter writing to examine and illustrate the moral failures of the conservative class controlling contemporary Italy, Francesca's and Gerardo's letters serve a redemptive role, leading to a rejection of their characters' stultifying milieu and the beginnings of a more authentic existence. Francesca's letters to Isabella are an exercise in self-analysis, for through them she revisits her life, tracing the loss of the ideals of her youth. Although she hoped to build a productive and equitable partnership with Guglielmo, their marriage has become a fraud. Francesca has buried her youthful aspirations and passions, succumbing inexorably to the stifling weight of a life governed by the expectations of others. She describes her situation in physical terms, indicating how thoroughly social conformity has permeated her very being: '[M]i rendevo conto che le ore vuote, le giornate inutili, le voci moleste, ci si attaccano addosso come una gomma che non possiamo staccare senza portar via anche la pelle' (440) ['I realized that the empty hours, the useless days, the humble voices become attached to us like an incrustation that we can't pull off without tearing away our skin, too, painfully' (297)]. Francesca is keenly aware of the risk she takes by remaining in this environment; she watched helplessly as her only real friend, Andreina Serra, a former partisan, became ensnared by a life of wealth and superficiality and ended up numbing her pain with an addiction to sleeping pills. 'Dove sono le passioni di un tempo?' ['Where are the passions of the past?'] Francesca asks herself at a dinner party, surrounded by blank and hypocritical faces. 'Coloro che mi circondano non hanno più alcuna passione. Nessuno sarebbe più capace di salvarsi. E neanche di perdersi' (255) ['The people who surround me have no passion any more. Nobody would be capable now of ruining himself. Of ruining himself or saving himself' (169)].

But does running off with a lover constitute leading an authentic life? Is that a frivolous, self-indulgent act, one that would only underscore the superficiality of her world, with its adulterous marriages, or a daring act of self-authentication? And doesn't Matteo, her jealous, possessive boyfriend, pose as dangerous a threat to Francesca's sense of self as her cold and neglectful husband? The affair itself is ultimately of little importance; more significant is the process of self-assessment it triggers in Francesca. In the end, Francesca decides not to continue her relationship with Matteo, whom she met in an impossibly idyllic setting: on the isolated Isola Rossa while recuperating (*sans* husband) from an operation. In this anonymous setting, she was released from the pressures of being a rich man's wife, and found with Matteo the freedom of expression sadly lacking with her husband. Indeed, the motivation for Francesca's self-revelatory letters to Isabella is the inability of this couple to communicate. These letters stand as an intermediary between Francesca and Guglielmo, a correspondence moderated by Isabella, who writes to both of them. Only toward the end of the text, after Francesca has made her decision to leave Guglielmo, is she able to write directly to her husband, pointing out that she is no longer the woman who once passively played the role of his wife.

Francesca's letters, of course, have inspired this change, since the physical writing of those epistles precipitates her decision to leave her husband. As she writes to Isabella early in their correspondence: 'In fondo sono già partita. Sono partita nell'impostare la prima di queste lettere' (100) ['I have already left. I left when I mailed the first of these letters' (64)]. The letters have forced her to undertake the 'rivolta profonda' ['profound rebellion'] necessary to escape the world of conformity and hypocrisy (Crocenzi, 34). The epistolary practice, then, is an integral component of Francesca's evolution, guiding the process of self-awareness and compelling her to act on the consequences of that awakening.[12]

But although Francesca is finally able to redefine her narrative, her destiny at the end of the text is still intertwined with that of a man: Gerardo, whom she meets for the first time at the newspaper office where she has gone to say a final goodbye to Guglielmo. It is with Gerardo that Francesca will begin her new life, a life founded on honesty and mutual respect. Perhaps de Céspedes, writing before the woman's movement reached its apogee a decade after this novel was published, was unable to envision a life devoid of male companionship for her heroine. But although Francesca's decision to begin a life with someone she has known for mere hours may seem abrupt, the two characters are bound by so much – including a life centred on writing – that their partnership is inevitable. Indeed, their writing has prepared them for this encounter, for through Francesca's letters and Gerardo's diary, both have found the fortitude – and the necessity – to break with their hypocritical and superficial lives.

Like Francesca, Gerardo turns to his writing for self-awareness, although in his case, it is a correspondence with his own self. Before turning to his narrative, we must address his mode of writing, the diary. Why doesn't he participate in the epistolary exchanges of the other characters? And how is the use of a journal different from that of a letter? The first question is easily answered: Gerardo's exclusion from the epistolarity of the text emphasizes his own ongoing endeavour to extract himself physically and psychically from the superficiality of his world. His diary entries illustrate his profound and mostly solitary struggle as he attempts to find the courage to leave his job and begin a potentially penurious life as a novelist. By limiting his participation in the narrative to his journal, de Céspedes recognizes Gerardo's detachment from those around him, while also allowing his voice to be present in the text and underscoring his talents as an author through the entries themselves.

The choice of the diary as a vehicle for Gerardo's path to self-awareness is an appropriate one for an epistolary novel. The two types of
narratives are often conflated by both authors and critics, for both are
first-person expressions of self. Indeed, the demarcation between novels written in diary and letter format can be fluid: witness *Va' dove ti
porta il cuore* (*Follow Your Heart*), Susanna Tamaro's novel examined
in the following chapter, which I label an epistolary text and others
believe represents a diary novel. Both diary and letter novels, while
often focusing on private matters, can also be used for broader analyses
of socio-cultural conditions. [13] De Céspedes herself recognized the far-
reaching abilities of the diary text in revealing both the personal and
the political; in her novel *Il quaderno proibito*, for example, the protagonist's use of a journal to examine her role as wife and mother allows
for a telling indictment of post-war Italy. In *Il rimorso*, Gerardo's diary
entries also become a forum for wide-ranging discussions on the *zeitgeist* of contemporary Italy.[14] But more important for his particular narrative, the journal inspires Gerardo to action, just as Francesca's letters
finally impel her to take decisive steps in her project for self-actualiza-
tion. As H. Porter Abbott writes in his examination of diary fiction, 'any
writing in the first person ... [is] action that exerts an influence on the
writer.' He adds, 'The unique advantage of fiction in the diary mode
is its capacity to expose this ordinarily unnoticed reflexive action by
giving the writing itself a role in the plot' (9). Gerardo's twenty-four
journal entries – exercises in self-reflection – track his evolution from a
listless young journalist, untethered to any particular set of principles,
to a gifted novelist finally recognizing the importance – both to himself
and to his work – of leading an exemplary life.

But before he can arrive at that point, he must, like Francesca, work
through his own personal history, carrying on in his journal a dialogue
with himself and his past. Abbott points out that fictional diarists are
often writers, as the genre lends itself to 'a kind of laboratory in which
the real author examines the behavior of his or her medium in the course
of day-to-day living' (50). Gerardo's lengthy journal entries mediate his
life as he gradually begins to turn it into a fictional account. The result
is a sense of serenity and accomplishment missing from his journalistic
endeavours. 'Maravigliosa [*sic*] mattinata trascorsa lavorando, leggen-
do,' he writes in one entry. 'Profondo senso di benessere' (398) ['Wonderful morning: writing, reading. Deep sense of well-being' (267)].

This sense of tranquillity, inspired by his writing, cannot be sustained,
however, when confronted with the conformity and artifice around

him. Both Gerardo and Francesca must leave the security engendered by Guglielmo (as his employer and her husband), and extricate themselves from meaningless affairs.[15] With this accomplished, they are free to devote themselves to their writing, a redemptive act that both inspires and reinforces their new-found sense of authenticity. In one of his last diary entries, Gerardo draws a telling picture of Francesca at work, a sight that aroused for the first time a feeling of genuine tenderness:

Voglio annnotarlo. È stato nel vedere le mani di Francesca sui foglietti che adopera per scrivere. ... Mani non particolarmente belle, ma aggraziate che, scrivendo, palesano insieme l'abilità di un operaio e l'applicazione di una scolara. ... Nello scrivere, le mani di Franscesca si deformano leggermente, decadono, direi: in una condizione, una classe diversa. Sembrano rallacciarsi, come anelli di una lunga catena, ad altre mani che hanno lavorato. (553–4)

I want to make a note of it. It was when I saw Francesca's hands on the little narrow sheets of paper she uses for writing ... They are not particularly beautiful hands, but graceful, and writing, they display the ability of a craftsman and also the application of a student. ... As she writes, her hands become slightly misshapen, I seem to see them joining, like links in a chain, a long line of other people who have worked. (377)

This description describes what connects the two to each other – their writing – as well as connecting Francesca, and by inference Gerardo, to a long lineage of authors. That creation of a partnership – both professional and personal – between Francesca and Gerardo is underscored by the physicality of their space, for their tiny apartment in Milan is dominated by a table '[t]anto grande che ciascuno di noi sembra avere un tavolo per sé: una fila di libri al centro come un muro divisorio' (553) ['So big that each of us seems to have a table to himself: a row of books down the center like a dividing wall' (377)]. As Piera Carroli points out, writing both unites the couple and frees them from their former lives. 'La scrittura è indispensabile per mantenere il contatto con la parte più profonda di se stessi, quella più autentica che alcuni personaggi vogliono celare e altri, Gerardo e Francesca, cercano di far emergere, frammento per frammento' (103) ['Writing is indispensable for maintaining contact with the most profound part of oneself, the most authentic part which some characters want to conceal and others, Gerardo and Francesca, try to bring forth, bit by bit'].

But what form will their writing take, now that Francesca has ceased her correspondence with Isabella, and Gerardo has finished the last notebook of his diary? Francesca will begin writing stories again, an activity she dropped after marrying Guglielmo.[16] Gerardo will publish his diary as a novel, for in writing it the line between his own narrative and a fictional one has become blurred. 'Nel romanzo mi costruisco' (166) ['In the novel I am constructing myself' (110)], he writes in one journal entry, revealing how the act of writing itself promotes the process of self-awareness and growth. Like Sibilla Aleramo's narrator in *Amo dunque sono*, examined in chapter 2, the letters, or in Gerardo's case, the diary entries, become the novel itself. In both these texts, the act of writing diary entries or letters fosters creativity and self-awareness. Gerardo will create a life – his life – through his writing, revealing the integral relationship between art and literature, but also, importantly in this novel criticizing the insincerity of post-war Italy, between art and authenticity.

With the conclusion of *Il rimorso*, de Céspedes pins her hopes for a more ethical future on a pair of writers, entrusting to them the task of creating a society free of conformity and hypocrisy. The old guard, represented by Guglielmo and his partisan cohort, failed to sustain the values of the Resistance movement in the new Italy, succumbing instead to the facile and ignoble temptations of a bourgeois conventionality. Rather, it is up to Francesca and Gerardo and their generation to recreate a society based on truth and decency. This project is rooted in their writing, for it is through self-expression – letters and diaries – that they learned to reject the false and embrace the true. The epistolary text, then, bridges the movement from passive acquiescence to active commitment, allowing the characters of *Il rimorso* to address the social failures of their world and pen narratives and lead lives correcting those failures. The task will not be easy, as Gerardo notes in the final words of the novel, as both he and Francesca confess their fear. De Céspedes may allow them a partnership of support and respect, but she recognizes that the work of transforming Italian society will be arduous and prolonged. The first step, however, has already been taken. When Gerardo expresses doubts to his sister that he can strike out on his own and publish a novel, asking, '"E se tutto questo, romanzo incluso, non servisse a niente?"' she replies: '"Ti avrà servito a vivere. Non basta?"' (485) ['"And what if all this – including the novel – were of no use? … It will have helped you to live. Isn't that enough?"' (329)]. De Céspedes leaves the reader with the hope that if life is transfigured through writing, perhaps society can be transformed by those whose writing recognizes the importance of fostering authenticity and accountability.

In Natalia Ginzburg's two epistolary novels, the letter as narrative structure functions as a canvas for both critique and rejection of social and familial alienation. While the search for connection – through the mechanism of written correspondence – traditionally drives the epistolary impulse, in *Caro Michele* (1973) the central characters are for the most part unable to relate to each other or to society at large on any meaningful level. Contrary to expectations, the epistolary novel becomes the ironic site for a stunning lack of connection. *La città e la casa* (1984), however, speaks instead to the possibility of true communication contained within the letter structure. In this work, several characters use their letter exchanges to more deeply understand others, although the promise of intimacy proves to be transitory in nature, as they cannot sustain this new-found connection beyond the epistolary relationship. Through the narrative structures of these novels, Ginzburg points to the difficulty in developing and maintaining those fundamental relationships that would offer the most solace in a world she felt marked by social isolation. She saw the family institution as particularly threatened by an increasingly busy and modern society. Ginzburg positions the letter novel in a way that seeks to address – on a narrative and personal level – her generalized anxiety about the state of the world.[17]

Ginzburg wrote comfortably in a number of genres, including the novel (*Tutti i nostri ieri* [*All Our Yesterdays*] and *Lessico famigliare* [*Family Sayings*]), the short story ('La madre' ['The Mother']), the drama (*Ti ho sposato per allegria* [*I Married You for Happiness*]), and the essay ('Il mio mestiere' ['My Trade']), to cite several of her most acclaimed works. She did, however, express a preference for the first-person narrative, even avoiding the use of an omnipresent narrator by writing dramas and epistolary novels.[18] Her letter novels generally did not receive the critical attention of her earlier, more autobiographical works. Whether that is a function of the genre, which many considered old-fashioned and unwieldy, or a preference for the author's riveting life story is unclear.[19]

Caro Michele, however, is a compelling exploration of a post-war world in chaos, of a society losing its grip on the pre-war values based in family, work, and a commitment to addressing and alleviating civic problems. The social criticism inherent in Ginzburg's finest texts is woven here into the minutiae of the letter exchange, for the trivia of the characters' lives only emphasize their helplessness in the face of a

changing ethos. Letters, like diaries, often act as chronicles of the picay-
une details of a life, creating whole lives through an accumulation of
detail. The epistolary format serves Ginzburg well in this respect, for
she was a master of the particular and in her letter novels the epistles
are replete with quotidian details.[20] Alba Amoia speaks of Ginzburg's
texts in general when she writes:

> Against a backdrop of emptiness and loneliness, Ginzburg records every-
> day family conversations and events, gradually building up tension over
> insignificant facts until they converge in an explosive climax. She gives so
> much attention to the minutiae of daily life to demonstrate that they can
> upset the social equilibrium, throw a household into disorder, and deter-
> mine the behavior and fate of her characters. (64)

Certainly the letters in *Caro Michele* are grounded in this detail, in this
record of the fleeting pleasures and less-fleeting drudgeries of daily life.
Ginzburg's gift is to distil from these details fully fleshed-out portraits
of her characters. Even more intriguing is what lies beneath the occasionally tedious presentation of these seemingly banal lives, for under
the accumulation of detail is buried a primordial scream, a cry for help,
for connection, or simply for attention, to which the letter structure
lends itself easily.

The catalyst for the novel's correspondence – reflected in its title – is
the eponymous character's sudden departure from Rome to England in
1970. The twenty-two-year-old Michele, an aspiring but unsuccessful
artist, has taken up half-heartedly with an unspecified militant group,
and is fleeing his political enemies. A conventional plot is practically
non-existent. Rather, the text revolves around those writing to Michele,
including his mother, Adriana, needy, lonely, and obtuse about life in
general and relationships in particular; Angelica, Michele's sister, who
is struggling with a failing marriage and their father's death; Mara,
Michele's scatter-brained but good-hearted ex-girlfriend, whose infant
son is of uncertain parentage; and Osvaldo, Michele's ex-lover, whose
genuine compassion and insight set him apart from the others. The
thirty-seven letters making up the novel reveal the family's history,
its gradual disintegration, and its sense of resignation – represented in
part by Michele's violent and solitary death at the hands of reactionary
thugs – about the future.[21]

This atmosphere of despair and decline permeates the text, illustrated
by the scores of failed relationships and a generalized listlessness and

lack of genuine commitment to any political, professional or social entity by the younger generation (Michele, his sister, and Mara). Ginzburg's own pessimism about contemporary society, which she considered to have lost its moral moorings, is readily apparent. [22] Her works reveal what she sees as a climate of personal detachment, a condition mirrored and perpetuated by the epistolary format. On a structural level, the narrative is an apt metaphor for a world in which connections are lost or never made. In *Caro Michele*, for example, many of the letters cross each other in the mail, avoid responding to queries or requests, or miss their recipients completely. Some of the characters are without phones or move frequently, further thwarting attempts at communication.

Letters could – and should – bind these characters together, providing a space to reflect upon and further cement a common familial or romantic history. After all, the epistolary structure is predicated on the forging of a connection between letter writer and recipient. Even if those letters are never sent or received, the simple act of writing the epistles typically strengthens the bond and increases the understanding between writer and recipient from the writer's point of view. How intriguing and significant, then, that Ginzburg chooses instead to subvert this tenet of epistolary fiction, for the letters in *Caro Michele* emphasize the estrangement each character feels toward the others and toward their world in general. As Anne-Marie O'Healy writes, 'The novel dynamically represents an attempt at communication, accompanied by the unspoken recognition that the task is impossible' (*A Woman Writer*, 193).

If the letters do not signify or foster human connection, what then do they represent? Certainly they provide 'a pretext for introspection,' O'Healy believes (*A Woman Writer*, 193). Indeed, several of the characters, most notably Adriana, use the letter less as a means of communication than as a vehicle for acquiring a greater sense of self, a technique we saw in *Il rimorso*, with Francesca's therapeutic letter writing. Adriana's earlier letters reveal a clingy woman, left lonely and bewildered by the recent rejection of her long-time lover, the death of her ex-husband, and her son's flight to London. By the end of the novel, the epistles have guided Adriana toward a semblance of dignity, although she has done so only by retrieving memories of happier times with Michele.

That reliance on the past and its recuperative value is explicitly tied to the narrative structure of *Caro Michele*. The fragmentary nature of the text, with its jumble of narrators and their criss-crossing letters, reflects, again, a generalized inability to forge personal and familial connections. What saves the characters, and the novel, from complete hopelessness is the comfort provided by the past. As O'Healy writes, 'In an orphaned world where the present is meaningless and the future does not exist, many of [Ginzburg's] recent characters turn their gaze to the past. Memory is an important theme in these works; in the end it is the only value that is salvaged' (*A Woman Writer*, 33).

In *Caro Michele*, the letter format allows both Adriana and Osvaldo to find refuge in the past. Adriana, in her last letter, recalls a song that Michele sang one day: Her happiness in that particular moment is relived in the writing of the epistle. Osvaldo, who has travelled to Michele's home in Leeds to learn what he can of his death, writes to Angelica about the comfort he finds in remembered experiences. The importance of memories, he points out, only becomes apparent as one ages, adding that he, Adriana, and Angelica succeed in 'coltivare le memorie' (155) ['try[ing] to remember'] (161) in part because 'nella nostra vita non c'è nulla che valga i luoghi e gli attimi incontrati lungo il percorso' (155) ['there is nothing in our lives at present that can compare with the moments and places we experienced in the course of our lives'] (161).[23] Those remembered moments are precious even before they become memories, Osvaldo continues. 'Mentre io li vivevo o li guardavo, quegli attimi o quei luoghi, essi avevano uno straordinario splendore, ma perché io sapevo che mi sarei curvato a ricordarli' (155–6) ['While I was living these experiences, they had an extraordinary intensity because I knew that later I would turn to recall them' (161)]. Significantly, this reflection comes in the last letter of the novel, a fitting conclusion to both an epistolary tale and a portrayal of loss and resignation. Osvaldo lives his life twice, once in the actual living, and then again in the remembrance. So, too, unfolds the letter text; first in the narration of lived experience contained in each epistle, a 'curving back' of memory, and then in the reading of this narrative.

By focusing on the value of memory, Ginzburg explicitly links the narrative structure of *Caro Michele* to its overarching theme. Epistolary fiction generally lives in the present: Letters may describe past events or anticipate future ones, but mood and reality are firmly grounded in the here and now. It is today that matters; the immediate always takes precedence over the past. Just as Ginzburg subverts the letter text to show how alienated the characters are from one another, despite the ready means of communication, here she revises the genre's reliance on the present to point to the importance of the past. The present and the future, for this particular family, offer no hope or redemption. 'It is only in cultivating the bittersweet sensations of memory that their lives take on a momentary, vibrant reality,' writes Rita Signorelli Pappas of the characters (90). The epistolarity of *Caro Michele* offers a corporeal embodiment of this act of remembrance, for the letters are tangible representations of the record of the past.

This theme of remembrance, anchored in the epistolary structure itself, is best exemplified through the relationship between Michele and Osvaldo. This relationship has not been examined critically or in depth. However, if we approach their bond through the lens of epistolarity, it becomes clear that Ginzburg considered this relationship fundamental to the theme of (dis)connection. The importance of their relationship is not immediately apparent in a cursory examination of the novel's correspondence. First of all, the two men write each other only once. Indeed, Osvaldo writes only two letters in the entire novel. But the significance of an epistolary correspondence often works in reverse proportion to its frequency; because Osvaldo is allowed only two letters, they resonate in particular in this collection of written communications. Letter placement also reveals important information about the relationship between letter writer and recipient. The single exchange between Michele and Osvaldo occurs at the mid-point of the novel's correspondence, a place that marks its significance in the text's narrative arc. Osvaldo's is the final epistle, written to Angelica from Michele's home in Leeds.[24] Significantly, this second letter acts as a final commentary on the work as a whole. The communication between the two men may be brief and limited, but Ginzburg underscores its importance by its physical placement in the novel, even using it to close all the correspondence in the book.

The connection between the two men is further emphasized by the deliberate arrangement of key letters, a technique afforded, clearly, by the epistolary structure. On 15 February 1971, Michele writes three letters: to Angelica, Mara, and Osvaldo. In the first two, he immediately announces his intention to marry Eileen, an American woman he has met recently. To Angelica he requests that she obtain and send him the documents he will need to marry abroad. To Mara he asks that she continue to write to him, as her letters, full of entertaining descriptions of her capricious adventures, amuse him. He also sends her some used baby clothes from his fiancée, for she has two children. Perhaps Michele feels a momentary sense of guilt or responsibility for one of them, who may be his as well. The letters to Angelica and Mara are brief, practical, and like all of his other letters up to this point, lacking in any warmth or emotion.

The letter to Osvaldo, however, completely changes tone, revealing the depth of Michele's feelings toward him. This revelation is all the more pointed by the letter's proximity to the two others written the same day. This letter is also the last of the three; as if Michele needed to practise breaking the momentous news with others before finding the words to tell his former lover. While with Angelica and Mara he announced his engagement without any preamble, with Osvaldo he engages in some preliminary small talk, thanking him for keeping Adriana company, and excusing himself for not communicating more frequently. Finally he drops his bombshell: 'Ti comunico una cosa che forse ti stupirà. Ho deciso di sposarmi' (90) ['I am writing to tell you something that may amaze you. I have decided to get married' (92)]. If the two men have had an amorous relationship, as becomes clear when the letter continues, then certainly Osvaldo would be surprised by this news, although Michele has had girlfriends in the past. He takes pains to assure Osvaldo that he is attracted to this woman because of her intelligence, rather than any sexual or physical charms she might possess. Indeed, he writes, 'Non è bella. Anzi in certi momenti è quasi bruttissima. Molto molto magra. Coperta di lentiggini' (90) ['She is not pretty; in fact sometimes she is very homely. Extremely thin. Covered with freckles' (92)]. She has large eyes like Ada, Osvaldo's former wife; 'Però è più brutta di Ada' (90) ['However she is homelier than Ada' (92)]. His allusion to Ada reminds Osvaldo of his own former marriage, which serves to stem any criticism from Osvaldo about this new (heterosexual) relationship. We find out later, however, that Michele only marries Eileen to help her with a drinking problem. Their marriage lasts eight days.

Although Osvaldo remarks in his final letter that Michele lived only in the present, the 15 February epistle concludes with a poignant evocation of their past relationship, and reveals how much this affair still lives in Michele's heart. He directs Osvaldo to a bureau drawer in his basement apartment in Rome, where he has left a blue-and-white striped cashmere scarf, a gift from his father. In one of the very few passages in the novel in which Michele exposes his feelings, he writes: 'Vorrei che tu andassi a cercarla e la portassi. Sarei contento di sapere che hai al collo quella sciarpa, quando cammini per il lungotevere, uscendo dal tuo botteghino. Non ho dimenticato le nostre lunghe passeggiate sul lungotevere, avanti e indietro, col sole che tramontava' (91) ['I wish you would get it and wear it. I would like to think of you with that scarf around your neck when you leave your shop and walk along the Tiber. I have not forgotten our long walks back and forth along the Tiber at sunset' (93)]. Michele still pines for their moments together, and wants to bind Osvaldo to him – almost literally – with this gift.

Osvaldo writes back by return mail, lamenting that the treasured scarf is no longer to be found. He has, however, purchased one himself, and wears it, pretending it was once Michele's. 'Mi rendo conto che è un surrogato,' he adds. 'Ma d'altronde noi tutti viviamo di surrogati' (92) ['I realize it is a substitute, but all our lives are made up of substitutes' (94)]. One could read this in a literal sense, for surely Michele and Osvaldo, in their relationships with Eileen and Ada, have cast these women in the role of surrogate loved ones. Just as the simple object of the scarf represents the past the men shared, so does this brief exchange of letters contain the expression of their love. Osvaldo alludes to this when he describes his own, mundane activities, finishing with 'cammino per il lungotevere, sto con le mani in tasca appoggiato al ponte e guardo il sole tramontare' (92) ['I walk along the Tiber, and with my hands in my pockets stand leaning over the bridge watching the sun set' (94).) He is left standing where Michele abandoned him, gazing off into the sunset they once enjoyed together, his scarf wrapped carefully around his neck.

Just as the scarf stands in for their communal past, so does the letter symbolize any human contact between the two men. These two letters are achingly heartfelt, revealing perhaps the only authentic connection between the various characters. It was a missed connection, however, a fact Osvaldo recognizes in his last letter, for the two men were too dissimilar for a permanent relationship. But, again, the epistolary correspondence means that they can relive, to some degree, their relationship. Through the letter, Michele and Osvaldo can evoke those evening walks. Certainly Osvaldo is capable of this act of remembrance, and he writes that he hopes that in Michele's last moments he had 'in un lampo conosciuto e percorso tutte le strade della memoria' (156) ['suddenly discovered the past and looked back' (161)]. Here Osvaldo gets the last word – the last letter – and it is his wisdom and grief that mark the end of the novel. The letter, then, serves as the only means of contact, although ultimately this intimacy is transitory.

Is it important that this relationship is a homosexual one? Certainly this is the one true romantic attachment in the text, infused with genuine feeling and regard. Perhaps because Osvaldo is endowed with a maturity and self-awareness not evident in the other characters, he in particular was able to extend and express a real connection with his lover. But with this attachment Ginzburg is further emphasizing how even true and heartfelt ties are doomed by the modern social ill of alienation. Perhaps their relationship fails because homosexual affairs were generally not sanctioned in Italy at this time. The two men received no social or familial support, as those around them were constrained both by the prohibited nature of the affair and a general sense of detachment from others. The significance of Michele and Osvaldo's homosexual relationship is not satisfactorily addressed in the text, but it ultimately becomes part of the web of missed or failed connections underpinning the novel. Ginzburg's *Caro Michele* turns the epistolary format on its head; the exchange of letters in the novel underscores the lack of connection among the characters, rather than forging relationships. It speaks, then, to the author's sense that the rapidly modernizing post-war world affords little opportunity for profound and positive relationships. By emphasizing the past – through the examination in particular of Osvaldo and Michele's affair – Ginzburg also rewrites the letter novel, for she emphasizes in their letters the depth of a particular relationship but also an inability to sustain it.

The epistolary structure of *La città e la casa* (1984) further illuminates the theme of failed relationships found in *Caro Michele*, although a significant evolution is evident, for in this later novel the exchange of letters offers genuine if short-lived moments of understanding and intimacy. Here, Ginzburg examines more than the breakdown of individual families; she is concerned as well with a general lack of civic or personal responsibility. In this work, the author reveals more powerfully the struggle for connection among the various characters, although many of the letter writers fail to correctly interpret the motivations, aspirations, or personal histories of the others, underlining a generalized inability to express themselves with directness and clarity. Indeed, the epistolary structure itself points to the letter's role in both creating bonds and revealing the failure of those bonds to sustain themselves outside of the narrative pattern. [25]

The letter text has the potential to transform relationships, offering a redemptive opportunity in a society that has lost its power to shape lives. Two letter exchanges in particular reveal how the epistolary process can ameliorate troubled relationships. A brief description of the characters involved in these exchanges will help contextualize the epistolarity of this text and its function as a transformative medium. I focus in particular on Giuseppe, a middle-aged journalist who leaves his home in Rome to live with his more successful brother in Princeton, New Jersey; his gay son Alberico, a rising film director-screenwriter who suffered a lack of paternal involvement in his formative years; and Lucrezia, Giuseppe's married ex-lover. Through the first letter exchange, between Giuseppe and Lucrezia, the characters attempt to recuperate the emotional closeness they once shared as lovers. Their letters take up roughly one-third of the ninety-plus letters in the narrative and are generally the longest of the epistles, and a final exchange between the two concludes the novel, a significant epistolary positioning. Giuseppe listens as Lucrezia writes about her latest lover, her decision to leave her patient and loving husband and to sell their beloved home, the birth and unexpected death of her infant son, and her struggles as a single parent raising her children (one of which she believes is Giuseppe's). For her part, Lucrezia listens to Giuseppe describe his shock at his brother's marriage, the same brother's untimely death, his decision to marry the widow, Anne Marie, his passion for his new wife's daughter, and the death of his new wife. Over the course of the novel, Giuseppe and Lucrezia share parallel experiences on either side of the Atlantic Ocean, both discovering forbidden desire while undergoing similar losses and heartaches.

But what is striking and instrumental about their correspondence is the way they make use of it to evaluate both their shared history and their current concerns. The letters, as in their traditional generic capacity, become the arena for greater self-awareness, which in turn acts to bring improved understanding between the two. At the beginning of their correspondence in particular, the missives suffer from an overriding sense of misunderstanding. Giuseppe refuses to admit that he fathered her son, Graziano; Luciana insults him by calling their long-over affair 'bloodless.' Ultimately, however, the two cannot move past the connection they have made on paper. This is made apparent by the circularity of their correspondence, a technique that reveals the epistolary genre's role in creating and underlining thematic developments. Here, the reader is cued to interpret this relationship by the closure of two key letters. In the first, written by Lucrezia just before Giuseppe leaves for the United States, she takes the opportunity to say goodbye by letter, rather than in person, as she had originally planned. She goes on to enumerate what she will remember of him:

> I tuoi pochi e lunghi capelli. I tuoi occhiali. Le tue maglie col collo rivoltato, blu d'inverno, bianche d'estate. Le tue gambe magre e lunghe, da cicogna. Il tuo naso lungo e grande, da cicogna. Le tue mani grandi e magre, sempre fredde anche quando fa caldo. Così ti ricordo. (40–1)

> Your long, thinning hair. Your glasses. Your jumpers with their roll collars, blue in the winter, white in the summer. Your long, bony legs, like a stork's. Your big, long nose, like a stork's. Your big, bony hands that are always cold even when the weather's hot. That's how I remember you. (37–8)[26]

In the final letter of the novel, in the novel's final passage, Lucrezia writes the same words practically verbatim. This second time, however, the words are not just the platitudes of a casual ex-lover and friend, but a heartfelt recognition of how close they have become over their two-and-a-half-year correspondence. Through their letters Lucrezia has finally been able to understand Giuseppe thoroughly. She writes: 'Non è vero che non so più come sei. So benissimo come sei. Ti ricordo come se ti avessi davanti' (236) ['It isn't true that I no longer know what you are like. I know very well what you are like. I remember you as if I had you here in front of me' (219)]. But although in this text Ginzburg points to the letter as a vehicle for greater comprehension, for Lucrezia and Giuseppe, that understanding will come to naught. As Giuseppe points out in his final letter, he may want 'immensamente' (immensely) to see Lucrezia, but they have experienced too much in the past years to reconnect in any place except on the written page. 'Siamo stati troppo tempo lontani e sono successe, a te e a me, troppe cose' (233) ['We have been apart for too long, and too many things have happened, to you and to me' (216)].

This failure to move beyond the epistolary connection reveals a more general inability to connect on a wider scale, within the family for instance, or within the community at large. The letter exchange may foster temporary intimacy, but it does not promise a more permanent connection. For Ginzburg, the transformative promise of the epistolary is defeated by the overwhelming lack of connection on a more universal level. This becomes tragically apparent in the correspondence between

Giuseppe and his son Alberico. Over the course of his sojourn abroad, Giuseppe forms with Alberico one of the closest relationships in the novel, cut short, however, by the young man's brutal death. The two men write infrequently, but as we saw with *Caro Michele*, the frequency of a letter exchange does not always reflect its importance. In *La città e la casa*, Giuseppe writes only six of his twenty-nine letters to his son. But six of the seven letters Alberico writes in the novel are to his father, underscoring the importance of this correspondence in his life. The two had virtually no relationship at the onset of the novel; Giuseppe admits in a letter to his brother that he won't even miss his son when he moves to the United States, because he never sees him. Indeed, Giuseppe has never been involved in Alberico's life, for when he and his wife divorced the young boy lived with his mother and had little contact with his father. Giuseppe's own immaturity and Alberico's bohemian lifestyle have also hampered any true understanding between the two men. Certainly when the two now see each other this lack of personal connection casts a pall on their meetings. Giuseppe writes of this strain in an early letter to Lucrezia: 'Quando siamo insieme, facciamo un'estrema fatica a dirci le cose più semplici' (9) ['When we are together we find it extremely difficult to say the simplest things to each other' (11)].

Alberico makes the first overture in their correspondence, writing a letter of condolence to Giuseppe when he learns about the unexpected death of Ferruccio, his uncle and Giuseppe's brother, in Princeton. He writes as well about his own situation; he has set up house with Nadia, a friend, and Salvatore, his lover. The uneasy relations between father and son are evident when Alberico admits that he decided against attending his uncle's funeral in the United States because he did not want to cause 'confusione' (82). But what is more striking is the affection that comes through in the note; Alberico addresses the epistle to his 'Gentile padre' ['Respected father'] and closes by writing 'Ti abbraccio' (82) ['With love from' (76)]. Giuseppe is struck by this tone, writing back immediately to say how grateful he was for the letter, one of the few he has received from his son, and one that he will keep carefully in his wallet, 'sul mio cuore, come un bene raro e prezioso' (83) ['next to my heart, like something rare and precious' (77)]. He closes his letter in a similar way, indicating an unsuspected depth of emotion for the son he freely admits he neglected. These tender last words are all the more striking as only a handful of the nearly one hundred epistles in the novel end with anything other than the name of the letter writer. The correspondence with Alberico will allow Giuseppe to atone for that neglect, and forge a new kind of relationship, more fraternal than parental, with his adult son.

Their relationship unfolds along parallel lines, for both undergo similar experiences that help further cement their blossoming attachment. Both father and son, for example, are involved in creative endeavours: Giuseppe writes a novel during his stay in the United States and Alberico finishes one film and begins writing another. The letters themselves can be read as an offshoot of this creativity, as both men clearly feel more comfortable with the written word than with verbal communication. Another shared experience is played out within the family arena, for both become surrogate father figures. Alberico gives his surname to the unwed Nadia's child, an act that presumes an increased sense of maturity and responsibility. For his part, Giuseppe becomes involved in the life of Chantal (Anne Marie's daughter) and her new baby girl, especially after the young mother temporarily abandons the child. Clearly, each has moved from searching for 'protettori' (protectors) to becoming one himself. Alberico wants to give his new daughter the 'protezione paterna' (paternal protection) that had been missing from his early life, and Giuseppe hopes to correct some of the mistakes he made with the young Alberico by becoming a more conscientious and involved father. As both men are forced to mature through their role as paternal protector, their own relationship deepens and becomes more meaningful.[27]

We are cued to this transformation through the epistolarity of their exchange, for Alberico addresses his final letter to his 'Amato padre' (222) ['My dear father' (207)], and Giuseppe returns the sentiment by calling him his 'Amatissimo figlio' (224) ['My dearest son' (208)]. But the relationship is truncated by Alberico's untimely death during a street mêlée involving his friend Salvatore.[28] The tragedy is foreshadowed by the loss of the children in their lives: after Nadia is killed in a similar brawl, her parents remove their young grandchild from the reluctant Alberico, who would have liked to raise her himself. And Chantal reclaims her daughter, leaving Giuseppe alone and bereft. Neither man is allowed to develop fully his new role as father figure, the ground on which they reached a clearer understanding and appreciation of each other. But although their budding relationship ends in tragedy, they are at least granted the opportunity to develop such a bond. The epistolary exchange makes this evolution possible, by allowing the two men to communicate their shared experiences through the written word.[29] In his last letter, Alberico writes that they are better suited to such an arrangement, for although he is happy to host his father should he return to Rome, he points out: 'Per un breve periodo, potremo convivere, non troppo a lungo, perché non piacerebbe né a te né a me' (222) ['We could live together for a short time, not for too long because you wouldn't enjoy it and neither would I' (207)]. Just as Lucrezia and Giuseppe were able to work out their misunderstandings through their correspondence, so Giuseppe and Alberico use this medium to rewrite their own family narrative, enriched by their new experiences as fathers.

In *La città e la casa* Ginzburg privileges the epistolary exchange over all other types of communication, allowing the narrative structure to create the space for a detailed and focused look at the evolution of relationships. Just as in *Caro Michele*, the letters provide the only productive means for this examination, for both works are steeped in an overwhelming sense of loss and defeat. At the ends of these novels, Michele and Alberico are killed in senseless street violence, Adriana and Lucrezia must come to terms with the dissolution of their respective relationships, and Osvaldo and Giuseppe are left facing a solitary life. But the epistolary correspondences offer a source of healing, of finding a means of connection in the isolated society depicted by Ginzburg. Indeed, the letters, especially in *La città e la casa*, resist the author's inherent pessimism, for the epistolary exchanges offer authentic, albeit brief moments of connection across family or social lines. Ginzburg certainly makes use of the epistolary format to comment on the alienation she saw in 1970s Italy, for only through this structure are her characters afforded both comfort and connection.

Alba de Céspedes and Natalia Ginzburg move the epistolary novel beyond its traditional task of presenting personal and intimate narratives. Although both authors base their texts in correspondence among lovers, family members, and husbands and wives, the conventional protagonists of this genre, they also succeed in transforming their narratives into a more public forum, addressing larger societal issues. The authors use the framework of the letter exchange to speak to – and perhaps even challenge – the social climate of post-war Italy. In *Il rimorso*, de Céspedes rejects the conservatism and hypocrisy of the ruling class, arguing instead for an active and sincere commitment on both a personal and universal level. Tellingly, those most able to foster this sense of *impegno* are writers, who must move from writing their own personal narratives to creating an engaged and authentic ethos. Ginzburg is more pessimistic about the likelihood of vanquishing the overriding sense of alienation she sees in contemporary Italy. But her letter novels do allow for a glimpse – if transitory – of redemption and connection through their intimate revelations.

4 Addressing Women

The epistolary novel of the 1970s and 1980s continued the evolution noted in the preceding chapter, opening up its narrative to address social, cultural, and political concerns. The works studied in this chapter, however, are concentrated explicitly on the complex and even problematic arguments crucial to the feminist movement. By using the letter novel to explore these issues, such as abortion, motherhood, and women and work, the authors energized both the conventional literary model and the topics being examined. These new texts remain tied to the women's epistolary tradition, however, for while the thematic content no longer focused on the traditional romantic entanglements discussed in chapter 1, many of them do address amorous or sexual relationships. But the examination of female experiences, societal expectations, and cultural practices that was often relegated to the background or subtext of earlier letter novels becomes in these modern works the core of the narrative. By structuring their texts around a discussion of topics pertinent to women's lives, these writers created a cultural and literary context for a discussion of the political goals of the feminist movement. The epistolary text brings the private (letters) directly into the public sphere – into public readership. In other words, the personal may be political, as one feminist slogan would have it, but the political is also literary.

The political can also be historical, as becomes clear in Isabella Bossi Fedrigotti's 1980 novel *Amore mio uccidi Garibaldi* (*Kill Garibaldi My Love*), which employs the epistolary novel as a means to reinsert women within the historical record. Bossi Fedrigotti's text re-envisions female experiences during a particularly crucial moment in Italian history: the Risorgimento. Two other authors have instead called attention to the literary, social, cultural, and political changes of the more recent past. Oriana Fallaci's 1975 novel *Lettera a un bambino mai nato* (*Letter to a Child Never Born*) served as a touchstone for the clamorous and divisive Italian debate over legalized abortion. Dacia Maraini's *Lettere a Marina* (1981) (*Letters to Marina*) eloquently presented alternative visions of female sexuality and the bonds among women. Along with those feminist-era works are two texts that fall into the so-called 'post-feminist' period, when the heady and tumultuous fervour engendered by the legal and social successes of the 1970s evolved into a more temperate approach to cultural change. *Dolce per sé* (*The Violin*), a 1997 novel by Maraini, revives many of the earlier concerns of the feminist movement, analysing through the letters of her unmarried heroine such topics as work and women as well as contemporary expectations of the female role. On the other hand, Susanna Tamaro's 1994 bestseller *Va' dove ti porta il cuore* (*Follow Your Heart*) appears to render the relationship between mothers and daughters – a key cultural reference point for many feminists – in terms that are decidedly anathema to the movement's philosophy.

Fallaci's and Maraini's approach to the epistolary text belied its critical reputation as a genre mired in the highly circumscribed literary and social expectations of previous centuries. Instead, the two authors co-opted it as a provocative means of addressing feminist issues. Barbara Zaczek says of their efforts: 'They reclaim the female epistolary tradition as part of their literary heritage, and restore it to the modern reader through the process of revision and rewriting' (*Censored Sentiments*, 19). Their works illustrate what Elizabeth Campbell sees as a defining element of feminist epistolary fiction: a focus on women 'concerned most of all with seeking their individual identity' (334). In her examination of works from such disparate national literatures as those of Argentina, Australia, Brazil, India, Senegal, and the United States, Campbell recognizes a common thread, one that can be tied easily to the Italian texts under study. All these works, she writes, 'use the letter as a subversive and freeing agent and also as a mirror in which [the authors] not only seek themselves and/or another but attempt to change their lives to reflect the mirror image' (332). A discussion of these novels elucidates how the use of this particular literary genre transformed political or social debates.

The novels belong to a tradition of women's writing that helped create and shape a feminist consciousness, as Anna Nozzoli points out. 'È chiaro, infatti,' she writes, 'che il romanzo o il racconto di impianto femminista non soltanto rispecchia una realtà emergente nell'attuale contesto socio-politico, ma a sua volta esercita una determinata funzione presso il pubblico dei lettori, divenendo strumento di diffusione su larga scala della nuova coscienza femminile' (*Tabù e coscienza*, 148) ['It is clear, in fact, that the feminist novel or short story not only mirrors an emerging reality in the current socio-political context, but exercises in its turn a particular function with its reading public, becoming an instrument to disseminate on a large scale the new female conscience'].[1] In the process, these authors produced an astonishingly extensive and innovative body of literature. Adalgisa Giorgio writes that since the 1970s, '[w]omen have made an enormous contribution to the regeneration of the novel in Italy by making its form, content and language more pliable and thus able to represent and interpret the concerns of men and women in a fast changing world' (236). Perhaps more important is the critical attention paid to these authors. Unlike earlier moments in Italian history, when female writers were often neglected or even disparaged, these contemporary authors have been more fully integrated into the study of the national literature, 'thus ensuring [their] inclusion in the Italian literary canon' (236).

While it would be misleading to suggest that all books written by women in the 1970s and 1980s advocated a feminist agenda, many did, and those works shared a number of pertinent themes.[2] Along with headline-making issues such as abortion and divorce, these novels focused on the patriarchal family structure, female sexuality, the maternal role, women at home and in the workplace, and sexual violence. Many of these texts were highly experimental, creating hybrid genres, although as a rule these works had in common certain narrative structures. Giorgio notes that first-person narratives were often used 'as a means of self-reflection and self-knowledge,' a technique evocative of the consciousness-raising practices of feminism, a topic discussed in more depth below (220). 'Their fragmented, a-temporal structures convey the protagonists' fragmented perception of self and reality,' she continues. The use of the present tense and an informal linguistic register 'suggest the topicality and urgency of what is narrated' (220). Nozzoli, too, believes the fragmentary and diaristic style of many of these texts was a deliberate narrative strategy that served to underline the development of their female protagonists. She writes:

È chiaro, infatti, che la scelta della disorganicità contro l'organicità, del frammento o del diario contro il romanzo tradizionalmente inteso, non debba attribuirsi a propositi estetizzanti o a intenti sperimentali, quanto piuttosto alla volontà di calarsi tout court in una dimensione frantumata, alla necessità di partire da zero per ricostrurire i modi e le forme di una nuova espressività. (*Tabù e coscienza*, 166)

It is clear, in fact, that the choice of unorganic unity against organic unity, of the fragment or of the diary against the traditionally understood novel, must not be attributed to aesthetic purposes or experimental intentions, but rather to the willingness to descend completely into a shattered dimension, to the necessity to begin from zero to rebuild the methods and the forms of a new expressiveness.

While Giorgio and Nozzoli do not specifically address the use of the epistolary text in feminist literature, clearly these narrative techniques fall squarely within the realm of letter fiction. It is through the narrative space created by the intersection of epistolary fiction and feminist ideology that I propose to examine the novels under study in this chapter.

We'll begin with the past. Isabella Bossi Fedrigotti's novel *Amore mio uccidi Garibaldi* tweaks epistolary tradition: the fictional correspondence in her novel intertwines the private with the political, forcing a re-evaluation of a critical moment in Italian history. The author uses the correspondence between a noblewoman and her husband to subvert gender roles, destabilize the historical record, and situate the female subject within the male-centred chronicle of the fight for national unification.

Because of the epistolarity of the text, coupled with the emphasis on women's history, *Amore mio uccidi Garibaldi* occupies a singular space within the conventional category of historical fiction. The historical novel has long been a staple of Italian literary production: since Alessandro Manzoni introduced the genre in 1827 with *I promessi sposi* (*The Betrothed*), such texts have flourished over the ages despite the vagaries of narrative trends.[3] Women writers came later to this genre, but their works have generally been as acclaimed as those of their male counterparts.[4] While historical novels often feature famous, lesser-known or fictional protagonists, women-authored historical fiction typically gives voice to the marginalized, those whose lives have been erased from the historical record. Anna Banti's *Artemisia* (*Artemisia*), Renata Viganò's *L'Agnese va a morire* (*Agnes Goes Off to Die*), Elsa Morante's *La storia* (*History: A Novel*), and Maraini's *La lunga vita di Marianna Ucrìa* (*The Silent Duchess*), among others, have been fundamental in question-

ing and countering traditional accounts by locating their female protagonists in such historically significant, male-centred spaces as the
Renaissance art studio, the partisan camp, the Second World War, and
the aristocracy in eighteenth-century Sicily. The narrative approach of
these women-authored historical texts is as innovative as their subject
matter, for often these writers introduce non-conventional documents
relating to the domestic arena directly into the works. These materi-
als, including diaries, household accounts, and, especially significant
to this study, letters, enable the authors to reconstruct the lives of both
historical figures and fictional characters using intimately revealing
first-person primary sources. Unlike *Amore mio uccidi Garibaldi*, however, none of these texts uses letters exclusively to explore how the private – in the form of the epistles – becomes intertwined with the public
– in the form of the historical record. Rather, these works examine how
female experiences can illuminate heretofore-accepted knowledge of
historical events and movements.[5]

Because Bossi Fedrigotti's novel is planted so concretely and vividly
in a particular historic moment, it is appropriate to consider the literary significance of this subject. *Amore mio uccidi Garibaldi* represents a
body of artistic endeavours that explore how unification history resonates in particular with our understanding of contemporary Italy.
Norma Bouchard, in her important collection of essays that examine
novels and films revolving around the Risorgimento, considers Italy's
'foundational story' crucial to understanding identity formation in
post-Fascist Italy (18). But while seminal works depicting this moment,
such as the film *Senso* (*Sense*) (1954) and the novel and eponymous film
(1958 and 1963) *Il gattopardo* (*The Leopard*), have received considerable
critical attention, Bouchard points out that only recently have historians and cultural, literary, and feminist scholars taken up contemporary
texts that offer alternative narratives. By alternative, she refers to those
works that do not point to a single and cohesive trajectory from unification to modern state, but rather seek to explore a more multifaceted
approach in understanding Italy's evolution as a nation-state.[6]

This evolution was played out against a particularly gendered vision
of nation building. Indeed, the female figure was often conflated with
the idea – or ideal – of Italy. As Alberto Mario Banti points out, in the
socio-cultural discourse defining the new nation, 'la patria è madre'
['the homeland is mother'] was the most prominent trope (55). The
image of a 'Mother Italy' helped give birth to the rigid gender roles considered appropriate and necessary for a country struggling to obtain

independence and forge a national identity. '[G]li uomini hanno dei ruoli che esprimono la loro profondo mascolinità ..., le donne ne hanno altri che testimoniano della loro femminilità' ['Men have roles that express their profound masculinity ..., women's roles are witness to their femininity'] writes Banti (61). For the women, that meant an often simplistic bio-cultural directive: 'conservarsi pure, essere buone figlie, buone spose, buone madri' (61) ['keep chaste, be good daughters, good wives, good mothers'].

The creation of gendered spheres of activity was reinforced by such pseudo-scientists as Cesare Lombroso, who claimed to prove through his phrenological studies that women were intellectually inferior to men and therefore should be relegated to the domestic arena. But the 'cult of domesticity' was countered by the birth of a proto-feminist movement in Italy and the rise of a growing class of women novelists, journalists, social reformers, and teachers. (A more extreme rejection of gendered roles was proffered by Anita Garibaldi, who fought valiantly alongside her husband.)

Bossi Fedrigotti's novel exemplifies the larger project of reimagining both the Risorgimento and the gendered roles and experiences of this particular historical era, with an emphasis on the female. The letter novel works as the ideal vehicle for a narrative positing an alternative and even subversive vision of accepted history. Because of the epistolary genre's historical relationship with female authors, its capacity for challenging social codes has been generally unaddressed by the (male) critical establishment. As we will see shortly, the letter novels of Maraini and Fallaci, with their frank discussions of female sexuality, male-female relationships, and abortion, reveal how the epistolary novel can question traditional expectations of female roles and posit new modes of existence. A narrative that emphasizes a female perspective on historical happenings lends itself in particular to the epistolary genre, for the structure allows a personal, behind-the-scenes rendition of the official version of events and movements. Certainly *Amore mio uccidi Garibaldi*, by allowing the female protagonist to articulate her own story through her own use of letters, proposes a counter-narrative to the authorized history of the Risorgimento.

The novel itself unfolds in the Trentino area in 1866, during the Third War of Independence, when Italy allied itself with Prussia against Austria-Hungary. This brief military conflict would finally end the decades-long period of the Risorgimento, leading the way to the creation of the modern Italian nation. In the novel, the author concentrates on

a fragment of time in both the unification and the lives of the two protagonists. Count Fedrigo Bossi Fedrigotti is a somewhat impoverished
landowner; his wife, Leopoldina Lobkowitz, is born of a noble family from Bohemia. After their marriage the couple settles in Bolzano,
then an Austrian province.[7] Fedrigo eventually joins up as an officer
with the Austrian army, although he is inspired more by the stipend
it promises than any impassioned patriotism. His absence triggers the
exchange of letters, through which the couple is able to dismiss the
conventional socio-cultural roles of husband and wife and invent their
own. For these few months, as we shall see, Fedrigo is able, even on
the battlefield, to shed what he sees as the burden of masculinity while
Leopoldina defies contemporary prescriptions of female behaviour by
embracing and expressing – albeit privately – her sensuality.

The first part of the novel is made up of Leopoldina's letters to her
mother immediately after the marriage; the second half takes up Fedrigo's epistles to his wife as he moves with the Austrian army from one
encampment to another. Although the narrative action in this latter half
revolves around military successes and defeats, the novel is not a traditional chronicle of war. As the author explained in an interview, 'Certo
che gli uomini combattevano … non mi importa, non mi interessa di
scrivere dell'erorismo e della forza dell'uomo in combattimento. Chi
resta a casa a combattere sono le donne. È un altro tipo di eroismo che
m'interessa di più' (Beverly, 37) ['Certainly men were fighting … but
that's not important to me, I'm not interested in writing about heroism and men's strength in fighting. Who stays at home to fight are the
women. It is another type of heroism that interests me more']. As with
many such novels, 'the historical background, meticulously detailed
though it is, remains precisely that' (36).

More important are the reflections on both socio-cultural expectations and literary modes that arise from a recreation of this moment,
reflections made more apparent by the personal nature of the epistolary
structure of the text. In order to draw clearly the distinction between
historical context and private or domestic life, and to set the letters'
point of reference, Bossi Fedrigotti intermingles the correspondence
with straight narrative that traces the political, legal, and diplomatic
progress of Italian unification. With this structure, the novel continues
the literary legacy of Morante's *La storia*, which alternates factual, dry
reports of the war with the poignant narrative of an unmarried Roman
woman struggling to raise her son. In other words, History versus history. By setting the family chronicle physically apart from the official

record of the times, these authors emphasize the private rather than the public face of history.

The private, personal sphere has long been recognized as the female domain, and in *Amore mio uccidi Garibaldi* this domain is made visible by the narrating voice of Leopoldina. Her letters to her mother, although often discussing the impending war, reveal as well the minutiae of domestic and familial life. Although only one of Leopoldina's missives to her husband is preserved in the text, through Fedrigo's replies we continue to observe how she bears witness to a specifically female perspective of Italian unification. With her letters, women's history – hidden, neglected, even derided – moves to centre stage, an important task of female-authored historical fiction, which often, like Morante's text, strives to reinscribe women within the historical context and render their stories 'official.' In the process, these works give 'voice to the submerged and to those who haven't spoken,' as Maria Ornella Marotti writes, while 'creat[ing] a space marked by female difference and subjectivity' (Marotti and Brooke, 66). In *Amore mio uccidi Garibaldi*, Leopoldina's experiences, rooted in the domestic and familial, become as important as those of her husband, far away in the traditional male sphere of battles and business. This juxtaposition of the private and the public is reflected in the novel's title, a quotation from one of Leopoldina's letters. The full quotation reads: 'Amore mio, uccidi subito questo Garibaldi. Lo trovi, gli spari e torni da me un eroe per tutti e non solo per gli occhi di una moglie incinta' (67) ['My love, kill this Garibaldi immediately. Find him, shoot him and return as a hero for everyone and not only in the eyes of a pregnant wife']. The phrase directs the reader to the novel's mindful interweaving of the personal and the political, foregrounding and privileging the private over the novel's historical content.

Through this correspondence, and, I would argue, because of it, the couple is able to reach a greater mutual understanding, creating in the process a singular marriage that gradually extricates itself from the chains of prescribed male and female gender roles, especially for Leopoldina.[8] Her epistolary relationship with her husband translates into a freedom to express herself in ways antithetical to traditional expectations of womanly behaviour. As Lucia Re points out, women's access to reading and writing was rigorously limited during this period in Italy, as conservative social institutions worked instead to define the female role as one based on the moral education of their children. This cult of domesticity resulted in a 'strategic and profound opposition to women's learning anything that may have taken their minds beyond the walls of the family home' ('Passion and Sexual Difference,' 165). Bossi Fedrigotti's heroine, however, defies the restrictions on both female consumption and production of writing. In her letters to her mother, Leopoldina often describes what she is reading (usually novels), and notes in one particular epistle that she has already devoured the books her mother sent her. Although with her correspondence Leopoldina is not producing literature as such, she is involved in the creation of a narrative, one that reflects both a personal subject (herself) and the larger socio-political concerns of Italy and Austria. By confining her writing to a non-threatening genre considered appropriate for women, Leopoldina balances her own personal desire to narrate her history with the social forces pressuring her to replace the pen with a less subversive tool, such as the embroidery needle. As Re points out, women of this period often had to hide their literary aspirations, for fear of familial or public censure. 'Whatever writing women engage in must remain private,' she writes (164).

In *Amore mio uccidi Garibaldi*, it is with the seemingly innocuous format of the epistolary correspondence that Leopoldina reveals an unwillingness to conform to nineteenth-century ideology concerning women.[9] First, she firmly asserts her displeasure upon discovering that she is again pregnant. (She already has two children; she will go on to have a total of five.) Instead of embracing maternity, Leopoldina writes of the financial imposition this extra mouth will cause, and of how difficult it would be to raise yet another child during a time of war. She demythologizes the image of the maternal figure, a crucial element of the social and cultural propaganda of the Risorgimento.[10] In her private mode of expression – the letter – Leopoldina is able to reject what she sees as the burden of motherhood (although she does finally accept and welcome this child, along with her other offspring).

Leopoldina uses the vehicle of the letter to challenge not only the role of motherhood, but also the expectations of female behaviour attached to that role. Here, the letter becomes a significant arena for spurning social expectations as Leopoldina begins to explore her own sensuality. In a time in which women were expected to act as paradigms of wifely and maternal virtue, overt expressions of female sexuality were strictly prohibited, especially among the upper classes.[11] Certainly there is no indication in our introduction to Leopoldina that she is even capable of such behaviour. Indeed, in Fedrigo's letter to his mother announcing his engagement, his primary attraction to Leopoldina seems to be

her capacity for childbearing: 'Non è bella affatto, ma a me piace. ...
Ha ventotto anni, è sana, sanissima, ed è grande quasi come me' (18)
['She isn't pretty at all, but I like her. She is twenty-eight years old,
healthy, very healthy, and is almost as tall as me']. He goes on to ask
his mother to write to Leopoldina, and to praise in particular 'le qualità
morali' ['the moral qualities'] of his future bride (18).[12] Clearly he does
not expect his wife to harbour or to demonstrate any signs of sexual
appetite. And there is nothing to indicate that their separation and subsequent correspondence, three years after they marry, would give rise
to such feelings in Leopoldina. But through these letters, she succeeds
in rewriting herself, an act that continues the legacy of earlier women,
such as Sibilla Aleramo, whose narratives often explicitly acknowledged female needs and experiences.

One letter in particular demonstrates how the epistolary structure
fosters the act of rewriting the self. Leopoldina writes a letter of astonishing frankness on the eve of Fedrigo's departure. 'Appena finisco di
scrivere sarò da te, e per una volta tanto sarò io a cercarti, anche se non
è la regola' (66) ['As soon as I finish writing I will be at your side, and
for once I will be the one to seek out you, even if that isn't the rule'].
Her use of the word 'regola' is telling, for it indicates that Leopoldina
willingly and wilfully breaks the code of femininity. She will be the one
initiating sexual relations that night even if Fedrigo, as her husband,
customarily takes on that duty. Bossi Fedrigotti emphasizes the importance of this epistolary act in several ways. First, although Leopoldina
writes daily to her husband, the letter she tucks into his luggage is the
only one to him included in the text. Secondly, the placement of the letter, at the very midpoint of the novel, signals its importance, for it signifies a new emphasis in Leopoldina's life, one centred on redefining her
relationship with her husband through an examination of gender roles.
Fedrigo welcomes his wife's new-found sexual boldness, responding in
kind in letters that verge on the explicit. It is through their correspondence that Leopoldina and Fedrigo find a way to break through the
strict rules governing the social codes between husband and wife: this
forum allows them a freedom and an intimacy not previously available
in their marriage. Fedrigo responds eagerly to Leopoldina's challenge
of these social codes, writing that he will come back from his military
experiences a changed man: 'nelle lettere, ho scoperto diversa anche te'
(112) ['I have discovered in your letters that you have also changed'].

The epistolary nature of the text lends itself to these moments of self-
discovery. As Anne Bower writes in her discussion of twentieth-centu-

ry letter novels, this format allows women characters in particular to 'increase their power or sense of self through the opportunity to write their own truths. Their material conditions may not change greatly ... but their words shape their own lives and the lives of others' (12). We see this transformation, stimulated by the exchange of letters, in *Amore mio uccidi Garibaldi* as both Leopoldina and Fedrigo re-evaluate and recreate not only their marriage but also their roles within it. Within the context of historical fiction, this transformative act becomes especially significant for those figures typically left out of official chronicles. The epistolary novel, Bower writes, 'positions the subject – whether fictional character or literary scholar – as one who, no matter how alienated and isolated, has found a tool with which to reclaim herself or himself as active respondent to and shaper of his or her past, present, and future' (9).

The redefining of the female presence in *Amore mio uccidi Garibaldi* is signalled at both the beginning and end of the novel. The novel opens with a description of the portraits of the family's ancestors, with a particularly detailed account of those belonging to Fedrigo. The narrator then notes that the portrait of Leopoldina, which once hung semi-hidden above a piano, was later moved 'per metterla accanto allo sposo' (10) ['to put her next to her husband']. Leopoldina's place in the family – and by extension in the family history – is recognized as being as important as that of its patriarch. By situating the portrait next to that of her husband, the author also underscores the relationship between the two; they are partners, sharing the same concerns that arise from raising a family during a time of economic and political uncertainty. This partnership is mirrored by the narrative structure, for the epistolarity of the text emphasizes the continuous conversation – carried out in letters – between Leopoldina and Fedrigo, which serves as the stimulus for this couple to redefine, if only for a few months, their marriage covenant.

But are they able to sustain this new-found freedom? Certainly they intend to; indeed, in one of his last letters to his wife before he returns home, Fedrigo writes, 'Leopoldina mia, sai che ti chiederò molte più cose di una volta' (129) ['My Leopoldina, you know that I will ask much more of you than before']. Clearly he hopes to continue the partnership begun in their correspondence and initiated by his wife. But although we cannot know definitively whether Leopoldina and Fedrigo are able to maintain in person the new roles they carved out on paper – and at a distance – the epilogue implies that it was not possible. In this section, a few short pages that summarize the lives of the protagonists and their children, Bossi Fedrigotti returns to the portraits of Leopoldina and Fedrigo. Instead of emphasizing their placement next to each other, as she did in the opening section, the author now notes how these pictures are startlingly devoid of the passion and companionship that made up their letters:

> Non ci sono più lettere, e i ritratti della scala non lasciano capire come sono cambiati i loro caratteri. Mostrano il bisnonno, ormai fiero conte-principe, maturo e un po' burbero. La bisnonna, con una dignità che ha dimenticato gli abbandoni della giovane Leopoldina, lo guarda dall'altro muro. Lui non è più tenero, lei non è più romantic. (136)

> There are no more letters, and the portraits on the staircase do not reveal how their characters have changed. They show the great-grandfather, by now a proud count-prince, mature and a bit churlish. The great-grandmother, with a dignity that has forgotten the whims of the young Leopoldina, looks at him from the other wall. He is no longer tender, she is no longer romantic.

The sombre and unapproachable figures seen in the official portraits are only given life in their intimate and lively letters. The epistolary structure of the text, then, constructs a space outside of the constricting framework represented by the couple's formal portraits. This framework, Bossi Fedrigotti implies, represents those socio-cultural forces that worked to enclose men and women within carefully delineated modes of behaviour.

Bossi Fedrigotti's use of the epistolary to reveal a woman's history is emblematic of her project to challenge the official interpretation of this moment in Italy's past. The letters serve to weave singular life stories within the broader chronicle of this time of political and social upheaval, creating a history that runs parallel to that documented in official texts. Those historians and novelists who attempt to recuperate women's history often focus on a single character, casting her experiences – albeit behind the scenes – as worthy of study and recognition. As historian Gianna Pomata writes, 'The variable and multiple richness of women's identity is particularly contained in their experience of life, and one finds it more in the course of individual lives than in the vague corps of movements, classes, or institutions' (168). Certainly that is the case in *Amore mio uccidi Garibaldi*, which highlights Leopoldina's domestic and marital life. But Bossi Fedrigotti uses the female condition as a pathway to look at another marginalized history within the concerns of official Italian history. She takes a significantly different view of the period of Italian unification, choosing to focus on those fighting *against* independence rather than glorifying the arduous but ultimately victorious march toward autonomy.

By positioning her two protagonists as pro-Austria, Bossi Fedrigotti offers an atypical perspective of the Risorgimento.[13] This perspective is emphasized by the differing ideologies of Fedrigo's large and extended family, which is cast as a microcosm for Italian society in general. His brothers, who face dramatically different financial situations as a result of their family's diminishing wealth, straddle both sides of the military and political conflict. While several fight valiantly to preserve Austrian dominion, others are drawn to the promise of a new world, one offering prosperity, liberty, and autonomy. But while most unification histories trace the triumphal path to nation-state, Bossi Fedrigotti focuses on the pro-Austrian characters to challenge the roll call of official history, which typically highlights the powerful and the victorious.[14] In her text, for example, General Giuseppe Garibaldi, the leader of a group of volunteer soldiers who helped liberate southern Italy and who fought in northern Italy in 1866, is not the heroic saviour of the country, but rather a 'brigante' ('brigand'), as Fedrigo writes to his wife (84).

But the author further complicates the issue by painting the Red Shirts – Garibaldi's solders – in sympathetic terms. She endows Fedrigo with the ability to see the humanity in his adversaries, creating a nuanced portrayal of those most directly affected by the military contest. Fedrigo's letters describe a regiment continually left in the dark by its superiors, who play whist and lounge about while the enlisted men are forced to go on twelve-hour marches in the bitter cold. In several letters Fedrigo writes movingly of the respect and compassion he feels for prisoners taken by his regiment; although they represent the enemy, he sees only a group of battered and bewildered young men fighting far from their homes. The author refuses to grant victor status to either side; the mostly uneducated and poor enlisted men are instead victims of a larger movement outside of their control. The vision of history presented in this text is not just that of women, struggling to accept wartime deprivations on the home front, but also that of the simple soldier, lacking a voice in the game of war.[15]

Bossi Fedrigotti's text examines those excluded from the traditional renderings of official History by producing personal life stories that parallel those already secured within the pages of history books. Women, as seen in Leopoldina's letters, are granted their own history, rooted in the domestic. But because the story of this woman is told in correspondence – in both senses of the word – with that of her husband, both characters can question the official articulation of history. They do this by challenging gendered expectations of behaviour, Leopoldina at home (and perhaps especially in the bedroom) and Fedrigo on the battlefield. Both these characters demonstrate willingness – freely expressed in the privacy of their letters – to reimagine the role of wife and husband. As Bossi Fedrigotti points out in her epilogue, only through the exchange of letters is this couple able to rewrite the narratives expected of them. The epistolary structure in *Amore mio uccidi Garibaldi* ultimately endows both the text and its characters with the capacity to reshape both personal and official history.[16] Letters, then, can write/right history.

Fallaci's *Lettera a un bambino mai nato* is not generally considered a traditional epistolary text. Despite the promise of its title, traditional structural epistolarity is simply not present. For example, chapters do not begin or conclude with salutations from the letter writer to the recipient, nor are there extra-textual editorial notes explaining the origins of the correspondence. There are a number of more subtle epistolary conventions contained in the text, but these have been overlooked by critics, who perhaps have been more interested in the novel's controversial content. However, I believe that reading this novel through the lens of epistolary fiction – as we are cued to do by its very title – offers a rich interpretation of the text's structure and meaning, situating it within the context of women's literature of 1970s Italy.

Although Fallaci's international reputation as an important if polemical writer stems in part from *Lettera a un bambino mai nato*, she remains perhaps most famous for her investigative journalism. Her incisive and often combative interviews with world leaders, collected in *Intervista con la storia* (*Interview with History*) (1974), best captures her rendition of New Journalism and puts her solidly in the camp of Tom Wolfe, Gay Talese, Truman Capote, and Norman Mailer. Fallaci's investigative writings encompass a vast range of subject matter, from the American space program (*Se il sole muore*, 1965 [*If the Sun Dies*], and *Quel giorno sulla luna*, 1970 [*That Day on the Moon*]), to the Vietnam War (*Niente e così sia*, 1969) (*Nothing and So Be It*), to the Greek revolutionary and her former lover Alexos Panagoulis (*Un uomo*, 1979) (*A Man*), to the volatile political and religious situation in the Arab world (*Insciallah*, 1990)

(*Inshallah*). In her final works Fallaci (1929–2006) reflected on the events of 11 September 2001, terrorism, and Islamic fundamentalism in *La rabbia e l'orgoglio* (2001) (*The Rage and the Pride*) and *La forza della ragione* (2004) (*The Force of Reason*). Her works reflect a commitment to social and political justice, a commitment she believed evolved from her early involvement with the Resistance movement in her native Florence.[17]

In all of her works, Fallaci becomes a part of the text, 'not merely an observer or an investigator, but a catalyst, and something more than that, interacting energetically with the people she meets' (Gatt-Rutter, 10). Because of this personal involvement in her works, the author is often confused – or conflated – with her female protagonists. Like Sibilla Aleramo, Fallaci admitted her writings were rooted in her own life experiences, but believed all authors pillage their personal histories for inspiration.[18] Unfortunately, some critics have not been able to see past the similarities between Fallaci's experiences and those of the unnamed protagonist of *Lettera a un bambino mai nato*. Santo Aricò, for example, writes that the novel 'dramatizes an intensely personal situation from Fallaci's life and becomes a subtle form of journalistic, memorializing literature' (160).[19]

Lettera a un bambino mai nato, published during the height of the abortion debate in Italy, was hailed by both sides of the movement, who saw in the multi-valenced novel support for their own ideology and political agenda. Aricò notes that the text's fluidity allows its readers to make up their own minds as to whether the female protagonist supports or opposes legalized abortion (163). This skilfulness in presenting a variety of viewpoints certainly played a part in the book's success.

Fallaci's literary tactics also point to her capacity for creating a text with a plurality of meanings, allowing the reader to participate in the novel's resolution. This is, of course, a hallmark of epistolary fiction, for the genre's very structure calls for an active partnership with its readers. Janet Altman believes epistolary readers contribute to the enfolding of the text through the lens of their own life stories. 'We read any given letter from at least three points of view – that of the intended or actual recipient as well as that of the writer and our own' (111). In Fallaci's case, her epistolary text becomes the means for both a personal and a civic discussion, as readers bring to the text their own experiences. This novel, then, acts as a literary illustration of the feminist goal to personalize the political, and it does so through its epistolary format, by calling on its readers to read and respond to the letters contained within it.

What I find interesting about the text is how Fallaci reinterprets the traditional letter novel to interrogate the genre while at the same time demystifying social and cultural conventions. She uses the protagonist's situation as a springboard to reflect on such diverse issues as motherhood, male and female roles, social institutions such as the family and marriage, the privileged position of science and medicine, and, of course, abortion. The protagonist, a single, professional woman who must decide whether to continue or cut short an unexpected pregnancy, creates a free-form dialogue with her unborn child through a series of thirty-two letters.[20] She finally decides to have the child, but she continues to interrogate her own – and society's – expectations of the maternal role. Eventually, however, the heroine loses the fetus, for which she is held accountable through an imaginary trial. This trial becomes a forum featuring the novel's multiple viewpoints. At the end of the text, the protagonist must confront the verdict of her unborn male child and her own evolving philosophy regarding the value and significance of life and love.

By limiting the narrative trajectory to a span of a few months, the novel captures a brief fragment of the protagonist's life, a single '"letter" to the unborn child rather than a lengthy narrative' (Marrone, 108). The text stands, then, as a snapshot of a specific cultural and political moment, just as a brief and fragmented correspondence – whether factual or fictional – often illuminates a particular juncture in time through its emphasis on events unfolding in the present. By limiting the time frame of the narrative, Fallaci can focus more closely on some of the fundamental concerns of the feminist movement, such as motherhood, women and work, and the social expectations brought about by a person's gender. Examining the epistolary elements of the text reveals how the text takes up such issues through the conventions of such a genre.

Much attention has already been paid to the author's presentation of the abortion issue, from the fact that the protagonist feels passionately about her right to terminate her pregnancy – even without the necessary legal or social support – to her assumption that life does begin at conception (or shortly thereafter), as she writes in the first letter, 'Stanotte ho saputo che c'eri: una goccia di vita scappata dal nulla. ... Esistevi' (7) ['Last night I knew you existed: a drop of life escaped from nothingness ... You existed' (9)].[21] The arguments for or against abortion are presented with sensitivity and in full, for Fallaci encapsulates through the interventions of various characters in the novel – especially in the imaginary trial – the variety of opinions generated by such a contentious topic. But *Lettera a un bambino mai nato* is more than a pro- or anti-choice manifesto, and because the abortion issue has been studied in depth, I choose to focus on other, often overlooked aspects of the text that surface through the novel's epistolary form.

Fallaci's nuanced examination of motherhood, for example, bears analysis, especially in light of the novel's epistolarity. Here, the author's decision to use a decidedly non-objective, first-person narrator – typical of letter novels – allows for a reconstruction of the maternal figure. While initially unwilling to accept the burden of single parenthood, the novel's protagonist eventually decides to continue with her pregnancy. 'Mi prendo la responsabilità della scelta' (10), she announces in her second letter ['I take the responsibility of the choice' (12)]. It is with these words that Fallaci creates a vision of motherhood based on acceptance and responsibility, positing a 'regenerative notion of maternity,' as Robin Pickering-Iazzi calls it (325). The narrator sees as part of the maternal pact an obligation to expose her yet unborn child to the harsher realities of life. Through a series of fairy tales, parables, and lessons drawn from historic and religious sources, she tries to instil in her child an idea of the world's deep-seated inequalities, along with a desire and ability to instigate a change for the better. Social change depends in part on an interrogation of the institution of motherhood, especially as it had been structured and circumscribed in conservative Catholic Italy. Fallaci clearly envisions and supports non-traditional family arrangements, depicting them as an arena for the progressive ideologies that lead to political and legal advances. The very structure of the text, then, with its emphasis on a loving but autonomous mother, creates an innovative portrait of the maternal figure.[22]

This narrative experimentation is based in part on the exchange between the protagonist and her unborn child, for Fallaci revises the conventional correspondence of letter texts, creating a free-form conversation between the heroine and the child. While the child does not directly address the mother until the end of the text, when he is given a voice in the proceedings of the imaginary trial, I believe that this character still participates in the dialogue begun by the mother. They communicate, in short, through a series of photographs. These pictures, taken from a newspaper article tracking the physical development of a human being, become touchstones for the protagonist, a means of conceptualizing the fetus growing within her. In fact, the photograph of a three-week-old embryo serves as the turning point in the mother's decision regarding her pregnancy. 'Ma ho deciso per te: nascerai,' she writes. 'L'ho deciso dopo averti visto in fotografia' (9) ['(But I've decid-

ed for you: you will be born. I did so after seeing you in a photograph'
(11)]. While staring at the picture, she finds the comfort and strength
necessary for the hardships she envisions as a single mother, saying 'la
paura m'è passata: con la stessa rapidità con cui m'era venuta' (9) ['my
fear went away as quickly as it had come' (11)]. Clearly, this is not a traditional epistolary exchange, but one that creates instead the physical
and emotional presence of the fetus, while also allowing the protagonist an opportunity to address directly her preoccupations, fears, and
aspirations for her child.

This correspondence, signalled by the fetal photographs, triggers reflections on the gendered expectations of society. The narrator
embraces an inclusive vision of humanity that has little to do with one
specific sex. Women may face entrenched obstacles ranging from the
legal to the social to the linguistic, but being female is also, she promises, an 'avventura che richiede un tale coraggio, una sfida che non
annoia mai' (13) ['an adventure that takes such courage, a challenge
that's never boring' (15)]. And while men are spared 'many humilia-
tions, much servitude and abuse,' they also suffer under other, equally
debilitating, cultural expectations (18). Finally, she tells her child, 'io
sto cercando di spiegarti che essere un uomo non significa avere una
coda davanti: significa essere una persona. ... È una parola stupenda,
la parola persona, perché non pone limiti a un uomo o a una donna,
non traccia frontiere tra chi ha la coda e chi non ce l'ha' (14) ['Child, I'm
trying to tell you that to be a man doesn't mean to have a tail in front:
it means to be a person. ... *Person* is a marvelous word, because it sets
no limits to a man or a woman, it draws no frontier between those who
have that tail and those who don't' (17)]. Part of the narrator's agenda
in restructuring society is to produce a child who sees him/herself as
a person able to create a sense of identity that ignores traditional roles.

Perhaps the best example of such a person is the one the narrator
offers of herself, for throughout the text she consistently challenges stereotypical images of the feminine, maternal figure. She says early on that
her ex-lover – and the father of the child – no longer has a place in her
life, nor a vote in her decision to continue with the pregnancy.[23] When
she does decide to keep and raise the child, she plans to do so alone,
without the traditional familial arrangement. The family, she writes, 'è
una menzogna costruita da chi organizzò questo mondo per control-
lare meglio la gente, sfruttarne meglio l'obbedienza alle regole' (36) ['is
a lie constructed the better to control people, the better to exploit their
obedience to rules and legends, by people who organized this world'

(42)]. As a single mother, the narrator immediately encounters the disdain of society at large, from the scornful and rough treatment from her male doctor, to the shocked disbelief of her pharmacist and tailor, to the unspoken but explicit hope of her boss that she will abort. Rather than feeling pressured into conforming to their expectations, she constructs a new vision of family, one that embraces the bond between mother and child: 'Dormiamo insieme, abbracciati. Io e te, io e te ... Nel nostro letto non entrerà mai nessun altro' (51) ['We'll sleep together, our arms around each other. You and me, me and you ... no one else will ever get into our bed' (59)]. The mother's alternate version of the family unit reveals her determination to transform social institutions, especially those that rely on traditional female roles. Motherhood, the narrator posits, deserves recognition as a legitimate and potentially productive aspect of female life experiences, despite its lack of acceptance in 1970s Italy, when it was almost exclusively deemed an oppressive institution.

The role of a professional woman is also reconstructed by Fallaci, who revises a fundamental component of traditional epistolary fiction to address this issue. As I discussed in the Introduction and in earlier chapters, heroines of such conventional texts often found themselves locked up in convents or sequestered at country estates, the letter the only means of communication with their lovers or loved ones. Modern epistolary fiction by women often makes use of the same conceit, and Elizabeth Campbell even calls isolation 'essential to the epistolary urge' (338). But Fallaci employs this technique only to revise it completely, revealing again how the text's narrative structure serves to emphasize and reinforce its feminist ideology. In *Lettera a un bambino mai nato*, one of the narrator's principal concerns is her professional life, which is depicted as both the site and the inspiration of her strength. While the protagonist's actual profession is never specified, she apparently works in a creative field, one that calls for both dedication and ambition. When offered the chance to go on an extended business trip abroad, the narrator is thrilled at the opportunity. However, she suffers complications with the pregnancy, and is told to stay 'still and flat' in bed (35). The narrator is completely isolated, dependent on a friend for meals and company, and removed from the intellectual and professional environment that serves as a source of energy.

But rather than observe the traditional tenet of epistolary isolation, Fallaci significantly reworks this technique. First, rather than isolate the narrator as a means to help her 'look inward,' as Campbell would have it (338), Fallaci uses this situation as a springboard for discussing the

nature of the world, an outward-looking proposal. While the protagonist is lying flat in her bed, she concocts a series of fairy tales meant to
reveal injustices stemming from the imbalances between the genders or
among social and economic classes. Although some critics seem more
interested in tracing the autobiographical elements of these parables,
others have noted the transgressive nature of these tales. Zaczek writes:
'In bringing the real life examples under the guise of fairy tales, Fallaci
reverses the role played by such stories in conduct books. One might
call them anti-examples, since the traditionally accepted values undergo a careful scrutiny and ideals are measured against reality' (*Censored
Sentiments*, 172). By interjecting fairy tales into the text, the author also
reveals an innovative approach to genre. Just as she rewrites the epistolary text in order to address contemporary issues regarding women's
roles and choices, so Fallaci reimagines the fairy tale as a site for challenging social hierarchies, rather than endorsing them. By examining
the world's inequities, Fallaci also opens up the text, moving it from a
personal and intimate exchange between mother and child to a more
sweeping analysis of social issues. For the author, isolation and inactiv-
ity do not restrict or limit the protagonist to a blinkered self-examina-
tion. Rather, the circumstances serve as an opportunity to communicate
universal truths. The epistolary structure emphasizes this approach, for
it becomes a means to share those realities with both the child and the
reader at large.

Fallaci breaks the convention of the isolated heroine in a second,
more dramatic way, for she eventually liberates the woman from confinement to her bed, her apartment, and, by extension, the domestic
sphere. The author does this by allowing the woman another choice,
this time between continuing her regimen of bed rest or travelling on
assignment for her job. Although she accepts responsibility for the
fetus, the protagonist refuses to make any more accommodations for
it, especially those compromising her professional life. In a particularly
poignant and honest passage, she recognizes that she is better fit for a
career than for motherhood:

> Il mestiere di mamma non mi si addice. Io ho altri doveri verso la vita. Ho
> un lavoro che mi piace e intendo farlo. Ho un futuro che mi aspetta e non
> intendo abbandonarlo … Io non ti ammazzo, sia chiaro: semplicemente,
> mi rifiuto di aiutarti ad esercitar fino in fondo la tua tirannia. … (62)

> The job of a mother doesn't suit me. I have other duties in life. I have a job

that I like and I intend to go on with it. I have a future awaiting me and I
don't intend to abandon it ... I'm not going to kill you, understand: I simply refuse to help you exercise your tyranny to the end. ... (71)

Although her male doctor calls her a 'murderess' (72) for undertaking
the arduous voyage, a female doctor agrees with her decision, saying it would be 'against nature' to spend the remaining months of her
pregnancy in bed (64). Tellingly, the narrator's reaction to travel and
work is one of ecstasy and emancipation: 'Dacché ho ripreso la vita di
sempre, mi sembra d'essere un'altra: un gabbiano che vola' (65) ['Since
going back to my regular life, I feel like a new person: a seagull in flight'
(74)]. Even though she has travelled to a strange and exotic country, the
narrator is back in the professional milieu and thus she finally feels at
home – not closed up in her apartment, but actively engaged with the
world.

Epistolary heroines often undergo another form of trial along with
isolation, although this test is more temporal than physical or spatial.
The sense of idle waiting animates many epistolary texts, as the correspondents anticipate first letters and eventually reunions with their
loved ones. In *Lettera a un bambino mai nato*, this feeling of expectation
is driven by the evolution of the pregnancy, as the narrator periodically checks the photographs of fetal development to determine how
her own child is maturing. But Fallaci shatters that sense of anticipation
in two ways. First, she releases the protagonist from bed rest and from
epistolary isolation, allowing her to resume an active life that explicitly
revolves around her own needs, rather than those of her pregnancy.
While the child's development remains important, she is no longer
anchored passively to her bed awaiting its birth. Second and more significantly, the pregnancy does not, in fact, come to term, aborting as
it were the anticipated encounter between mother and child, between
letter writer and recipient. Despite the woman's best intentions, the
fetus is pronounced unviable while she is on her journey; in fact, she
discovers at the end of the novel that it actually died only a few weeks
after conception. This early loss nullifies the child's presence for some
critics. Indeed, John Gatt-Rutter sees the child as a 'textual figment (of
the narrating mother) within a textual figment (of the published book)'
(63). He goes on to add that 'the child is "created" by the voice of the
mother; he is a child of her text and cannot subsist independently of
her text any more than the biological child can subsist independently
of her womb' (83).

I would argue that the character of the child is not merely a conceit conjured up by Fallaci as a means to investigate such issues as choice, responsibility, and a commitment to address social ills. Rather, the child and his untimely demise signify how thoroughly he has mastered the lessons instilled by his mother. We must go back to the origins of the epistolary novel, however, to understand how Fallaci ultimately reveals the consequences of the exchange between the protagonist and her child. As discussed in the Introduction, letter fiction was tradition-ally divided into two distinct types, based either in sentimental/erotic or educational narratives. *Lettera a un bambino mai nato* contains ele-ments of the sentimental epistolary novel, for the mother's bond with her child is heartfelt and profound. But Fallaci creates an alternative vision of the love relationship, one based not on erotic attraction but rather on respect, dignity, and autonomy. In the second model, a men-tor or guide serves a critical role in instructing his or her young charge how to negotiate social expectations (Altman, 196). The text clearly fol-lows this pattern, for the mother is intent throughout the novel on edu-cating her child, through her own example and through her stories and homilies, about personal and civic obligations. At the end of the text we learn how successful this instruction has been. These lessons cul-minate in the novel's imaginary trial, in which all the characters weigh in on the guilt or innocence of the mother in the loss of the child. An entire range of viewpoints is presented, echoing those letter novels that contain epistles from a variety of correspondents, allowing a diversity of perspectives. Through this convention, Fallaci incorporates the myr-iad of positions on the issue of choice and abortion.[24] The two doctors argue about whether the mother was selfish to continue with her work; her female friend maintains that 'maternity is not a moral duty' (96); her boss claims she was more interested in keeping her job than her baby; and her parents profess unwavering support for their daughter and refuse to judge her. But finally, only the child can determine his mother's guilt or innocence.

Tellingly, he is presented as an adult, capable of making his own decisions, although clearly his mother's lessons played a crucial role in his own choice. That choice, of course, was not to live, for as he tells his mother, her despondent and one-sided presentation of the world's inequities finally convinced him against accepting life. 'Nel mio uni-verso che tu chiamavi uovo, lo scopo esisteva: era nascere' ['In my uni-verse, which you called the egg, the purpose existed: it was to be born'], he says. 'Ma nel tuo mondo lo scopo è soltanto morire: la vita è una condanna a morte. Io non vedo perché avrei dovuto uscire dal nulla per tornare al nulla' (91) ['But in your world the purpose is only to die: life is a death sentence. I don't see why I should have had to emerge from nothingness just to return to nothingness' (103)]. Despite his harsh words, he forgives his mother, and even promises to be born 'some other time' (103). The child has more than taken his mother's words and example to heart, for he embodies the attributes of choice and responsibility, traits the protagonist has striven to instil in him. Equally significant is the lesson the mother has learned from her relationship with the unborn child, a lesson learned through the reciprocity of the epistolary structure. Despite her innate pessimism, she has discovered the joys of life and its sense of promise, pointing out that 'domani è un giorno colmo di opportunità' (96) ['tomorrow is a day brimming with opportunity' (108)]. She intends to embrace life '[a]nche con le sue ingiustizie, le sue tristezze le sue infamie … E intendo viverla ad ogni costo. Io corro, bambino. E ti dico addio con fermezza' (98) ['even with all its infamies, and I mean to live it at all cost. I'm running, Child. And I bid you a firm good-bye' (110)]. Indeed, although the mother's health is itself in danger, due to complications from the miscarriage, she nevertheless recognizes and celebrates the inevitability of life. She concludes her final letter with one more lesson: 'Tu sei morto. Ora muoio anch'io. Ma non conta. Perché la vita non muore' (101) ['You're dead. Maybe I'm dying too. But it doesn't matter. Because life doesn't die' (114)].

Fallaci's decision to revise the epistolary genre results in a highly subjective analysis of feminist ideology. She personalizes the relationship between mother and child, reimagining the maternal figure through the exchange between the two figures. In doing so, she contextualizes the position of motherhood in contemporary Italy, reconstructing the female role to embrace alternative visions of life experiences. By incorporating and then reversing several traditional elements of the letter text, such as the isolation of the heroine and her sense of idle waiting, Fallaci rejuvenates the epistolary genre to better reflect the often-unconventional circumstances and choices of modern women, whose roles became less rigid than in previous generations. Fallaci highlights those choices in the novel's dedication: 'A chi non teme il dubbio / a chi si chiede i perché / senza stancarsi e a costo / di soffrire di morire / A chi si pone il dilemma / di dare la vita o negarla / questo libro è dedicata / da una donna / per tutte le donne' (5) ['To those who do not fear doubt – To those who wonder why / without growing tired and at the cost / of suffering and dying – To those who pose themselves the dilemma / of giving life or denying it – this book is dedicated / by a woman / for all women' (6)]. This dedication also speaks to the universality of the text; the nameless protagonist's story reflects 'a chapter in a potential biography of contemporary female experience' (Marrone, 116). The letter format reinforces the connection between the intimate and personal and the more universal truths Fallaci paints. The epistolary text's reciprocal structure means that the reader has been, along with the fetus, the beneficiary of the narrator's sermons on choice and responsibility. Fallaci's insistence on the importance of these attributes, on actively committing to creating a better, more just world, reflects the rhetoric of the women's movement.

Like Fallaci, Dacia Maraini often uses her literary projects as a forum to address social problems, creating fictional texts deeply infused with a feminist aesthetic. Throughout her long career, Maraini has focused on the female protagonist, grounding her investigation of the status of women within a wider examination of historical, political, and cultural conditions. As Vera Golina points out, for Maraini's heroines 'understanding and comprehending the self – their fundamental quest – requires first and foremost an understanding and evaluation of society, the world they inhabit, and of the life conditions surrounding them and the family structure' (147). Ultimately, Maraini's feminist ideology, highlighted against the quotidian experiences of her heroines, promises nothing less than a complete transformation of society.

As the country's premier feminist author and spokeswoman since the 1960s, Maraini – like Fallaci – has gained an international following, resulting in numerous literary prizes, honorary degrees, a growing body of critical work devoted to her literary production, and a recognition rarely afforded a female author from Italy.[25] Despite this recognition, Rodica Diaconescu-Blumenfeld posits that both Maraini's overtly feminist aesthetic and her status as a female author have led to a critical blindness and neglect. Nor is this atypical for women authors, she maintains, for 'not only do they write the scandal of women as desiring subjects, but further, they write difference into dimensions that the canon cannot recognize' (7). Maraini, too, acknowledges the seemingly inherent prejudice against women authors, and often makes a discussion of female writers and writings a part of her fictional projects.[26] In both *Lettere a Marina* and *Dolce per sé*, for example, Maraini examines female artistry, its critical reception, and its importance in a personal evolution grounded in a gendered sense of self. Interestingly, both of these works are epistolary novels, which allow her to investigate these issues through the forum of a traditionally 'female' literary genre. Maraini's attention to the construction of literary texts is reflected in the wide variety of venues she has chosen throughout her career, from novels to films, from essays to short stories, from poems to dramas. [27] For Maraini, generic choice is inextricably intertwined with thematic content, especially as it pertains to an examination of female roles. As Grazia Sumeli Weinberg notes, 'La scelta dei vari generi letterari ... mette in evidenza il rapporto della scrittrice con la storia, rapporto sincronico che, assumendo l'aspetto di un processo, dà causa, tramite la forma, alle costrizioni sociali che tuttora operano sulla condizione del soggetto femminile' (23) ['The choice of various literary genres ... reveals the author's relationship with the story, a synchronized relationship that assumes the aspect of a trial, gives a motive, through the form, to the social constructions that still operate on the condition of the female subject'].

This symbiotic relationship between form and content – between narrative structure and female authorship – is perhaps especially apparent in Maraini's epistolary novels, *Lettere a Marina* (1981) and *Dolce per sé* (1997), both of which focus on women writers. Both texts are closely tied to feminist ideology and practices, with the first novel more clearly a reflection of the impassioned and revolutionary rhetoric of the women's movement of 1970s Italy and the second, discussed below, a meditation on that same ideology, but at a considerable remove. *Lettere a Marina* investigates such fundamentally feminist issues as relationships between mothers and daughters and men and women, alternative sexualities, and the bonds between women. By casting her text as a portrait of various female roles and figures, Maraini restructures the epistolary narrative, opening it up to include aspects of female experiences long neglected in literature, history, and culture. As Barbara Zaczek puts it, *Lettere a Marina* 'constitutes, then, an attempt to reclaim the female epistolary tradition, to use letters as a way of preserving women's lives and their stories' (*Censored Sentiments*, 160).

The epistolary text, which revolves around the twin concepts of authorship and self-definition, allows Maraini to reimagine the female writer, investigating in the process both the genre and this literary figure. In *Lettere a Marina*, the connection between narrative format and female authorship is underscored throughout the text. The plot itself is practically non-existent; rather, the novel is composed of roughly eighty letters addressed to the title character from her ex-lover, Bianca, who has briefly taken up residence in a sleepy Southern resort town. Bianca's reason for this deliberate isolation is both personal and literary: 'Per scappare da te per finire il romanzo a cui lavoro ormai da due anni senza molta convinzione,' Bianca writes Marina in the first letter (5) ['To escape from you to finish the novel I've been working on half-heartedly for more than eighteen months' (7)].[28] But the 'real' text in *Lettere a Marina* is not the novel Bianca finally succeeds in completing, but rather the loose narrative contained in the scores of letters she writes. We saw a similar narrative strategy in Aleramo's *Amo dunque sono*, in which the narrator's letters became the literary project at hand. In Bianca's case, her personal narrative, consisting of dreams, memories, reflections on the various familial, sentimental, and sexual relationships she has had, as well as those she experiences during her sojourn, stands for the literary text itself. Indeed, at novel's end, as Bianca prepares to leave town, we discover that she has not even sent these impassioned letters. Instead, she intends to reread them while on the train, an act that both recuperates her narrative and emphasizes its intertextuality. By casting her heroine as both writer and reader, Maraini intensifies the reciprocal nature of the epistolary. Significantly, it is the letter format itself that provides Maraini with the foundation for the discussion of literary antecedents and their connection with contemporary female artists.

Before focusing on Maraini's revision of the letter text, I would like to examine the poetics underlining the narrative and at the root of the generic experimentation. Like Fallaci, Maraini has turned a fictional account of a heroine's social and cultural development into a broader exploration of feminist ideology and practices. Perhaps the most striking aspect of *Lettere a Marina* is the relationship at the heart of the correspondence, for the romantic-sexual entanglement revolves around two women, rather than a man and a woman. Maraini and others writing feminist novels of this era often explored what Nozzoli calls 'il diritto di una nuova etica sessuale' ['the right of a new sexual ethic'], often including alternative sexual identities or practices (*Tabù e coscienza*, 160). Certainly the year in which the book was published (1981) was a propitious moment in the history of lesbian literature, as feminist theoreticians and authors began to seriously grapple with the issue of female sexuality outside of heterosexual relationships.[29] Maraini confounds the issue to some degree, for her protagonist is not, strictly speaking, a lesbian, but rather bisexual. Tommasina Gabriele believes Maraini deliberately included a bisexual heroine, for through this character's sexuality, the author 'condemns both the system of compulsory heterosexuality *and* the pressure to adhere to one sexual identity at a time' (247). Gabriele rightly suggests that the novel's most significant innovation is that it 'confronts the minefield of loving across the boundaries: the woman who loves women also loves men' (247).

But Maraini does not cast the lesbian relationship in idyllic terms, for the affair between Bianca and Marina was fraught with the same tensions, difficulties, and even violence found in many of the heterosexual liaisons described in the novel.[30] Indeed, all the relationships portrayed in *Lettere a Marina* seem doomed by a cycle of infidelity, a threat of emotional and/or physical violence, and a lack of mutual understanding. Maraini, then, opens up the traditional romantic narrative, challenging both conventional *and* alternative choices for women. This act of examining traditional female experiences is fundamental to the feminist movement; what is even more provocative is questioning as well those alternative experiences – like lesbianism – that many in the women's movement automatically assumed were productive and rewarding.

Bianca's non-sexual relationships with other women become a forum for an examination of two feminist practices important to the Italian women's movement, and it is here that Maraini focuses on the intersection of the literary and the political. Again, I would argue that it is through the vehicle of the epistolary text that both these feminist practices and an overarching feminist poetics become apparent. In the practice of *affidamento*, or entrustment, for example, two women enter into a relationship in which one acts as a mentor to the other. Their relationship is predicated not on similarities of class, age, social position, level of education, or professional status, but rather on differences in these areas. Despite the apparently unequal positioning of the pair, *affidamento* creates 'a bond of reciprocity in which the diversity between the women enriches their experiences, their perspectives of themselves and the world around them' writes Virginia Picchietti (*Relational Spaces*, 31).[31]

By structuring the epistolarity of the text around a relationship between two women, and by including within those epistles lessons learned from life experiences, Maraini emphasizes the potentially edifying aspect of female bonds. Although there is no written correspondence between Bianca and Basilia, her uneducated, put-upon neighbour, I believe the epistolary format of the text calls attention to this practice of mentoring, or *affidamento*, for both women benefit from their interactions. Basilia, self-defined by her position as wife and mother, acts as maternal figure to Bianca, teaching her through a re-enactment of

traditional storytelling the narratives of female wisdom and authority. As Picchietti notes, 'Through Basilia, Bianca is able to glimpse the
ancient roots of a maternal discourse based on women's subjectivity
and power' ('Symbolic Mediation,' 114). Basilia, too, grows through
her interactions with the more independent Bianca, finally leaving the
domestic space that has enclosed her throughout the text to enjoy a
meal at a restaurant.

If Basilia 'helps Bianca replant her roots in a symbolic community of
women,' as Picchietti has it, she does so not only through a dynamic
based on trust and guidance, but also through the ideology of sisterhood ('Symbolic Mediation,' 114). The site for these bonds often grew
out of the practice of *autocoscienza*, or self-awareness, which was modelled on the American women's movement's use of consciousness-raising sessions as a means of self-exploration. In Italy, small groups of
women met to share their personal experiences and – for perhaps the
first time – acknowledge the value of such an act while also theorizing its role within the ideology of the feminist movement. As Lucia Re
points out in her reassessment of *autocoscienza*, '[T]he ability for women
to have their own spaces and opportunities for critical reflection gave
the *autocoscienza* groups the opportunity to develop a new sophisticat-
ed type of analytical and simultaneously political feminist discourse'
('Diotima's Dilemmas,' 58). This vehicle for individual self-awareness
extended, then, into a more general and politicized tool for transforming social and cultural expectations for women. Again, I argue that
this practice becomes underscored through the use of letters, for it is
through the epistolary structure that Bianca is able to fully explore the
significance – both personal and political – of bonds with other women.

In *Lettere a Marina*, Bianca's ties to the practice of *autocoscienza* are
complex and reach into areas of artistic and personal development.
They are literal and figurative, thematic and stylistic. In her letters,
she remembers fondly her own experiences with such an *autocoscienza* group, and, indeed, attributes the creation of a gendered self – and
artistic voice – to these encounters. She writes to Marina: 'È il piccolo
gruppo che mi ha ridato voglia di scrivere mi ha riportato a galla cose
che credevo morte e sepolte. E anche il bisogno di parlare con te se non
fosse per il piccolo gruppo ... non sarei qui a scriverti' (40) ['It is the
little group that gave me back the desire to write, that brought things
to light that I thought were dead and buried. And also the need to talk
with you; if it weren't for the little group ... I wouldn't be here to write
to you'].[32] She states quite clearly, then, the link between the practice

of a feminist poetics and a woman's personal (and artistic) development. The practice of *autocoscienza* – as exemplified through her letters – allows Bianca to articulate and evaluate her experiences, which become transcribed in her letters and, concurrently, her book. For Maraini, the practices engendered by the feminist movement not only serve to advance a woman's personal situation, but also allow her to generate artistic projects (such as Bianca's) that will ultimately transform the cultural and social landscape.

But Maraini portrays the act of *autocoscienza* as a dynamic that extends beyond the literal or textual, for Bianca's relationships with Basilia and other women offer the bond of sisterhood that typically arose from the *autocoscienza* experience. In her letters, Bianca describes her female family members, including her mother and sister; childhood and adult friends; unknown women who inhabit the small town where she has taken refuge; and even her literary muse, Emily Dickinson. Surely these epistles work as a kind of consciousness-raising session themselves, for through them and their portraits of various female experiences Bianca finds the support and strength necessary for both her artistic endeavours and her own personal growth. She positions herself within this continuum of female figures, locating through their shared history a sense of fellowship. As Picchietti says, 'narrating life experiences prove[s] beneficial for Maraini heroines ... It is a liberating practice of self-articulation and -definition, and creates for them a sense of female community not out of common victimization, but rather out of the perception of a shared historical past and collective action in the present' (*Relational Spaces*, 137).

This use of letters as a mechanism to promulgate the ideology of the feminist movement points to a new poetics for the epistolary text. Maraini's choice of a traditional 'female' genre to explicate and reflect on issues relating to women's artistic production and self-development has been misunderstood by some critics. Bruce Merry, for example, writes that she 'has been versatile in her use of the diary and letter format in order to extract the innermost emotions from the heart of women' (200). He conflates the epistolary with the sentimental, unable or unwilling to recognize the potential for a radical aesthetics within the letter text. Barbara Zaczek, on the other hand, sees *Lettere a Marina* as 'an attempt to reclaim the female epistolary tradition, to use letters as a way of preserving women's lives and their stories' (*Censored Sentiments*, 160). She points out that Maraini confronts and dismisses the stereotype of a 'feminine love letter as an uncontrolled flow of sentiment' (156).

Although the correspondence is rooted in the romantic-sexual liaison between two women, the letters themselves are not limited to an examination of their affair, but rather are the starting point for a discussion of female relationships in general. Pauline Dagnino sees a connection between *Lettere a Marina* and the revolutionary revision of the letter text *The Three Marias: New Portuguese Letters*, thereby tracing a genealogy of female-authored epistolary works.[33] Just as the three Marias of the Spanish work reached back to establish a connection with the original Mariana of *Letters to a Portuguese Nun*, Dagnino writes, 'Maraini's achievement in [*Lettere a Marina*] is the inscription of the woman in the text in the recreated conditions of female development' (197).

Maraini challenges both the thematic and stylistic conventions of the epistolary text, redefining its structure and objectives by viewing it through the lens of a feminist poetics. The conventional isolation of the female protagonist, for example, becomes in Maraini's hands a reflection on both literary and social expectations of female behaviour. Bianca indeed removes herself from the vicinity of her former lover – a necessary condition if letters are to ensue – but she does so willingly. Unlike earlier heroines who languished in their solitude and isolation (think of Diana in Serao's *Ella non rispose*), Bianca quickly establishes relationships that satisfy her emotional, intellectual, and even sexual needs. Even more important, by sequestering herself Bianca is able to achieve her professional and artistic goal of finishing her novel. This is a significant evolution in the literary depiction of female artists. While Aleramo's heroine in *Amo dunque sono* only briefly alludes to her current literary project in her letters to her lover, Maraini's Bianca announces her artistic intentions in the opening epistle. Even more, Bianca weaves into her two texts (the novel and the letters) a discussion of women's issues. She contributes, then, to the literary and cultural production of the feminist movement, an important step in the diffusion and eventual acceptance of its ideology. Maraini significantly revises the stereotype of a suffering and lonely epistolary lover, portraying instead a composed, active, and independent woman capable of casting her own concerns within larger social issues. She does this explicitly, to comment on and encourage the sort of engaged and committed activism necessary for political, cultural, and social change in 1970s Italy.

Maraini's vision of cultural transformation, a transformation rooted in feminist ideology, is reflected in the stylistic choices she brings to her works. By reimagining the textual conventions of the epistolary novel, a genre once considered particularly suitable for the alleged effusions of female writers, Maraini challenges canonic hierarchies. Like Maraini, some critics see the act of reclaiming those conventions as a necessary and productive strategy for modern women writers. Elizabeth Campbell, in her study of contemporary female-authored epistolary texts, writes: 'Epistolary fiction, with its fragmentation, subjectivity, abandonment of chronology, repetitiveness, associative and sometimes seemingly illogical connections, and, most of all, unconventional use of language, embodies the definition of *l'écriture féminine*' (335). She goes on to call epistolary writing both 'subjective and emotional' (336), an interpretation that seemingly perpetuates the same perceptions about female authorship that have traditionally excluded it from critical acceptance. I believe, however, that Campbell is instead calling for a reworking of those critical assessments that sanction the rational over the illogical, the precise blueprint of the modern *bildungsroman* over the looser and perhaps more playful postmodern narrative.

In *Lettere a Marina*, Maraini does indeed experiment with the 'subjective and emotional' attributes of letter texts. She often employs a stream-of-consciousness style, with no commas, colons, or semi-colons in the text, and no textual divisions to mark dialogue. The result is a succession of long, elliptical, and sensual passages lush with meaning and metaphor. By formulating the novel in this seemingly loose and unstructured manner, Maraini calls attention to the presumed anti-literary nature of letter texts for which the genre – and its female practitioners – have been castigated. But in her hands, the epistolary text's traditional attributes serve as a vehicle for a subversive revision. Throughout the work, for example, Bianca struggles to finish her novel, and her letters are replete with references to the difficulty she has in envisioning its structure. She talks about the 'piccolo cimitero di segni neri' (44) ['small cemetery of black crosses' (44)] that result from her crossed-out and marked-up pages as she labours over the book's construction. Artistic production, in this depiction, is a deliberate and often agonizing process, the very antithesis of the alleged effortless and spontaneous letter text. As *Lettere a Marina* progresses, Bianca continues to have doubts about her work, but is finally able to complete the novel, finishing it in an intoxicating two-week period. Surely the painstaking, deliberative, and arduous effort involved in literary production in *Lettere a Marina* is meant to contrast with the more free-flowing letters contained in the text. And, if so, Maraini then comments on the construction of the letter text and on literary models in general, arguing for a reassessment of those critical measures that evaluate canonic literature. She also inserts female authors into this reassessment, for in Italy most have been omitted from literary histories.

Maraini continues this project of challenging critical appraisals of genre and female authorship by rejecting an objective and authoritative perspective. She allows her narrator to act 'as the organizing and the uniting force' of the text, but not as its sole voice (Zaczek, *Censored Sentiments*, 156). Like Fallaci, Maraini opens the work to a multivoiced discourse, moderated but not overshadowed by Bianca and her life story. In the process, Maraini validates a variety of female experiences. Bianca literally treats these female figures as subjects, casting them as protagonists in their own life narratives as well as in her letters. Bianca's epistles act as the intersection between those life narratives and her novel, for she frequently moves back and forth between the real and the fictional. As she sits before her typewriter, she tries to imagine 'le unghie dei miei personaggi,' adding, 'Dalle dita dalle unghie si capisce certe volte più che dalle facce' (20) ['the fingernails of my characters. One can sometimes tell more from someone's fingers and nails than from their faces' (22)]. She moves immediately into a description of Marina's prickly 'cactus feet,' effectively folding her ex-lover into her narrative. In the process, she erases the space between novel and letter, between fiction and fact.

This erasure comes full circle in the novel's conclusion, in which Bianca again conflates texts and genres. After rereading her novel (and fearing it a failure), she writes her last letter to Marina, promising to reread all the epistles while on the train to her next destination. In this passage, Maraini emphasizes the act of rereading and of reassessment, and, by extension, of critical inquiry. Bianca may judge her novel deficient; the novel may indeed *be* deficient. But Maraini is pointing instead to the act of appraisal, an act she places squarely in the hands of a woman, a figure traditionally excluded from the critical establishment. In *Lettere a Marina*, a woman not only writes the texts – the novel and the letters – but is also allowed to evaluate them. I would argue that the letters, too, signify a completed text, as worthy of critical investigation as a novel. Indeed, the act of rereading the letters serves to demonstrate their meaning, confirming for Bianca their value as both a personal record of her love affair and as a more universal document of female experiences and shared female bonds. These letters further serve as illustrations of such feminist practices as *autocoscienza* and *affidamento*. Maraini's final revision of epistolary conventions, then, in *Lettere a Marina*, turns on the transformation of women-authored epistles into a manifesto for living, a blueprint for exploring female roles and experiences, both literary and real.

The exhilarating early days of modern feminism, which saw the publication of *Lettera a un bambino mai nato* and *Lettere a Marina* among other texts fundamental to literary feminism, gave way to a women's literature with a less overt political agenda and a more critical approach to gender issues. While the texts emerging from the legal and socio-cultural battles of the 1970s and 1980s did not necessarily espouse a homogeneous and unvarying ideology, a general feminist poetics binds many of them together. The works published later, in the years of so-called *dopofeminismo* or 'third wave' feminism, share fewer stylistic or thematic affinities.[34] This 'fragmentation of feminism,' as Sharon Wood notes, has led to a less conclusive picture of a distinct female literary tradition despite the recent popular and critical successes enjoyed by many Italian women writers (*Italian Women's Writing*, 214). She points as well to an evolution in narrative style among these later (and typically younger) writers, as they became increasingly less connected to the early feminist movement. 'Literature by women in this period moves away from the plain realism ... practiced by writers of the 1970s as an extension of political activism, to an exploration of the "female style" adumbrated by [Sibilla] Aleramo half a century before'('Feminist Writing,' 165). But while these women created works less obviously indebted to a feminist endeavour, they increasingly experimented with narrative structure and voice.

How did the female-authored epistolary novel fare during this critical moment in Italian women's literature? To better reveal how this genre can be tied to feminist concerns, I examine Susanna Tamaro's *Va' dove ti porta il cuore* (1994) and Maraini's *Dolce per sé* (1997), texts that offer strikingly different perspectives on women-centred epistolary narratives. Maraini's novel offers an illuminating example of how a traditional genre such as the letter text can be successfully revised in order to participate in and advance a feminist poetics. She continues the project begun with *Lettere a Marina*, in which the epistolary novel was the site of an extensive examination of female experiences, told through the prism of feminist practices. In *Dolce per sé*, Maraini proposes an ideology of inclusion, thereby advancing the Italian feminist project of developing a cultural genealogy for women. This politics of inclusion, which decentres traditional romantic bonds between men and women, focuses instead on non-conventional, non-sexual relationships between women, an outgrowth of the lesbian liaison witnessed in *Lettere a Marina*. In order to address the evolution of feminist concerns, Maraini meditates on the construction of the letter text itself, and especially the marriage between its structure and its politics.

Va' dove ti porta il cuore appears instead to offer an interpretation of the letter novel that is more reactionary than innovative. The work reintroduces many of the traditional epistolary tropes that had been long abandoned or challenged by other women writers, and emphasizes those conventions most detrimental to female literary production and to the expression of an authentic female self. The novel itself was accorded the critical disdain often granted to runaway bestsellers considered more popular than literary. Tamaro's other works, including the novels *La testa fra le nuvole* (1989) (*Head in the Clouds*), *Anima mundi* (1997), the children's book *Cuore di ciccia* (1992), and the short story collection *Per voce sola* (*Just for One Voice*) (1991), were well received, and the recipients of literary prizes.[35] But her venture into lighter fiction generated scorching reviews. Remo Ceserani and Pierluigi Pellini, in their essay on the development of the Italian novelistic tradition, dismiss Tamaro's works, and particularly *Va' dove ti porta il cuore*, as 'sugary,' even though many of her short stories are replete with frightful descriptions of abused and abandoned children, violence, and horror (18). Perhaps the choice of a 'woman's genre,' with its reputation of being anti-literary and overly sentimental, spurred some of these negative appraisals.[36]

Other critics have seen in the work a reflection of the more conservative Italy of the 1980s and 1990s, a time when the women's movement no longer played as visible a role in shaping cultural identity. Giancarlo Lombardi writes that the novel 'perfectly bespeaks the contradictory nature of an advanced society when conservatism and progress still rub shoulders, a society in which some women can still act as their own worst enemies' (*Rooms with a View*, 168). Fulvio Senardi finds the work hostile to the social transformations of the 1960s and later, especially in regard to feminism and sexual liberation. If *Va' dove ti porta il cuore* does indeed reflect Italy's general drift toward conservatism, I would argue that it does so in part through its adherence to conventional epistolary practices.

Tamaro's letter text features a protagonist who became increasingly more prevalent in women-authored texts of the 1980s and 1990s: a grandmother. Adalgisa Giorgio, in her investigation of contemporary women's literature, notes that mothers, daughters, sisters, and grandmothers were often incorporated in these texts as a means to explore '[b]lood genealogies and the female family lineage' (224). In *Va' dove ti porta il cuore*, this examination of a female heritage is the underlying impetus of the epistolary structure, for the novel revolves around the letters sent by Olga, an elderly widow, to her granddaughter, living in the United States. The letters, written over a period of less than two months and which remain unsent, contain long expositions of the mundane affairs of Olga's house and garden, ruminations on the dynamics within her family, and the revelation of a long-buried secret, her affair with a married man.

Tamaro's novel plays with an essential narrative trope of the letter text: the physical isolation of the protagonist. As we have seen in both *Lettera a un bambino mai nato* and *Lettere a Marina*, modern authors often radically revised this traditional trope to paint a portrait of female independence. Initially Olga seems to embody this spirit of self-sufficiency, for she continues to live alone in her large house despite her doctor's concern that a recent illness necessitates hospital care. But unlike Bianca's in *Lettere a Marina*, Olga's decision to seclude herself means cutting herself off from all human contact, except for the occasional visits of a neighbour couple. And, unlike Maraini's protagonist's, her physical isolation is paralleled by an emotional disconnect that dooms her attempts at genuine self-exploration. In fact, Olga's unsent letters merely underscore her inability to connect with others, a character flaw she herself points out when she writes to her granddaughter of 'gli anni di incomprensioni e malumori della nostra convivenza' (11) ['the years of misunderstanding and bad feeling when we lived together' (14)].[37] The wintry desolation that Olga sees in her garden, the wounded blackbird she fails to save, the poignant descriptions of a loveless life, her own physical decline and imminent death, all reflect a profound emotional sterility. While the narrator profits from her solitude to review the tragic events of her life, her seclusion serves only to underscore a complete detachment from the world around her.

Olga's isolation is linked to her history of emotional abandonment, a recurrent trope in more traditional epistolary texts. Indeed, as Katharine Jensen points out in her study of seventeenth- and eighteenth-century letter novels, this 'culturally dominant, masochistic version of femininity' was a model for the female author writing about love (2). Tamaro's work reinforces this particularly gendered ideology based on cultural perceptions of female passivity and compliance. In the novel, all of Olga's romantic and familial relationships eventually lead to a sense of desertion. The protagonist, frustrated by an emotionally distant marriage, had a heartfelt, erotically charged liaison with Ernesto, a young doctor. The affair, which produced a daughter, Ilaria, lasted only a few years until Ernesto was killed in an automobile accident. Ilaria, who would grow up wilful and rebellious, produced her own daughter – the unnamed granddaughter – by an unknown lover, and was then herself killed in a car accident, leaving Olga to raise the young girl. The granddaughter, like her mother, would grow increasingly distant from Olga, and eventually leave for an indefinite sojourn in America, breaking off all contact with the older woman. Olga's sense of abandonment and rejection dominates the letters she writes, situating her squarely within the epistolary tradition.

However, despite this detachment from everyone, and while Olga's life story appears centred on traditional male-female relationships, such as those with her husband and her lover, her real concern is firmly rooted in a history of the female members of her family. Indeed, this female genealogy is underscored by the novel's dismissal of the paternal figure. While Olga's family secrets concern a missing (for Ilaria) or absent (for the granddaughter) father, it is still the connections among female family members that remain the text's focus. These connections stay fixed within the family sphere, revealing that it is at this conjunction between narrative development and ideology that *Va' dove ti porta il cuore* fails to fully break free of the conventions long established by the genre. For while other authors, notably Maraini, question those generic strictures calling for an emphasis on male-female relationships, and present new paradigms of productive female experiences outside those relationships, Tamaro offers no subversive plot that would free Olga from what Jensen calls 'the practice of epistolary femininity' (3).

Instead, the inevitability of the grim (female) family legacy is underscored, as Olga tells her granddaughter, 'L'infelicità abitualmente segue la linea femminile. Come certe anomalie genetiche, passa di madre in figlia' (39) ['Unhappiness is generally transmitted through the female line, passing from mother to daughter the way some genetic abnormalities do' (49)]. Olga's epistles include a litany of misunderstandings, missteps, and misdemeanours among the various women in her family, tracing this chronicle of misery as far back as her own grandmother. And although Olga claims to repudiate this legacy, she appears through her letters to shackle her own granddaughter to this procession of unhappy women. In her penultimate letter, she symbolically passes on to the young woman a simple object, a cake mould that evokes a baking session shared between the two of them in happier times and that serves as a token of domesticity, the historical sphere of female family genealogy. Olga points to the importance of the cake mould when she writes, 'Questo stampo apparteneva a mia nonna cioè alla tua trisavola ed è l'unico oggetto rimasto di tutta la storia femminile della nostra famiglia' (159) ['This pan belonged to my grandmother – your great-great-grandmother – and it's the only object we have left to show for all the female side of our family history' (198)]. By bestowing this object on her granddaughter, an object resonating with the weight of female history, Olga promulgates the very family history she has denounced.[38] As Laura Rorato points out in her study of Tamaro's works, the author's characters are often 'forced to realize that unhappiness, like genetic illnesses, can be transmitted from one generation to another, becoming, with the passage of time, even more fully rooted and harder to eradicate' (65). It is significant, however, that Olga's granddaughter has chosen to leave her aging relative, and to reject so completely any contact with her. Perhaps Tamaro means to suggest that this chain of female unhappiness will be broken by future generations. After all, Olga's granddaughter has chosen to go to the United States, historically seen as a place where women's rights are more advanced. But while the possibility of the granddaughter's ultimate rejection of Olga's repressive ideology would offer a significant revision of Tamaro's underlying poetics, there is scant textual evidence for it. Because the letters that Olga writes are so intent on describing her own history, we do not have any sense of how the granddaughter will respond. The granddaughter is not afforded a voice; a narrative choice that tilts the novel toward the grandmother's perspective. The epistolarity of the text, then, reveals its ideology, for the one-sided correspondence only emphasizes the repressiveness of the family's female history.

The cultural subtext of this novel is matched by its reactionary position in the ongoing debate over the literary merits of the epistolary text. The work's fundamental theme is found in its title, an exhortation that when directed to the granddaughter encourages her to follow her heart's dictates. Colleen Ryan astutely argues that Tamaro is proposing through this pronouncement 'a human solution to solitude, emptiness, and unmediated regrets' (361). If viewed from a purely literary perspective, however, this theme reinforces the perception of the epistolary text – at least those written by women – as inherently nonliterary and grossly sentimental. This perception is as old as the genre

itself. We have seen in the Introduction how the male critical establishment coupled the epistolary mode with women's writing and then
devalued it as a literary genre. Tamaro's novel implicitly plays into this
paradigm. *Va' dove ti porta il cuore*, packaged as the last *cri de coeur* of an
unhappy and frustrated woman, acts as a treatise endorsing the traditional dichotomy between sentiment and intellect. While Laura Rorato
argues that the author attempts to rescue the heart from its position
as a hackneyed sentimental symbol, I believe that Tamaro instead falls
into that very trap. The grandmother's advice to her granddaughter,
for example, includes avoiding the 'eccessiva rigidità alla mente' (72)
['excessive rigidity of her mind' (90)] manifested by Ilaria, and obeying
instead her heart's desires . Olga ends by endorsing a life philosophy
based on the anti-intellectual, a particularly peculiar act given that she
herself was once an intelligent and curious young woman. Perhaps her
frustrated intellectual ambitions – her father refused to allow her to
attend university – are partly responsible for a focus on sentimental
values later in life. While Tamaro may have intended to comment on
the limited academic and professional options available to that generation of women, the overwhelming emphasis on a more sentimental
approach to life undermines such a critique. Indeed, the thematic focus
of the novel celebrates those very literary precepts that have traditionally marginalized the epistolary genre while classifying it as a female
mode of expression. The impulsive and the instinctual are privileged
over the deliberate and the rational, a binary dichotomy that has traditionally served as a literary appraisal of female authorship as well as a
more generalized social perception of female behaviour.

Tamaro's novel and its conformity with the more limiting tenets of the
epistolary genre become more striking in light of Maraini's innovative
treatment of the same narrative structure. With *Dolce per sé*, Maraini
furthers her project of interrogating various literary genres while sub-
stantially radicalizing them through an infusion of her own feminist
ideology. At first glance, however, there is much that links the two
texts. Like *Va' dove ti porta il cuore*, Maraini's novel focuses on an older
woman writing letters to a younger one; here, it is Vera, a middle-aged
playwright, who writes intermittently for about six years to Flavia, the
young niece of Vera's lover, a violinist. Both authors incorporate aspects
of the sentimental and the instructional narratives typical of early epistolary texts, as both Olga and Vera examine their own amorous history,
while offering to their young addressees direction on how to navigate

the rocky shoals of womanhood. Both protagonists had atypical or extramarital relationships: Olga and her lover were both married to others, while Vera, who is divorced, was involved with a man almost twenty years her junior. Both narrators take up in their letters the birth and demise of those amorous liaisons.

The differences far outnumber any similarities between the two novels, however, evident, significantly, in the authors' generic approach. Olga's sense of frustrated desires and ambitions is fuelled in part by her physical and emotional isolation. Vera, on the other hand, is liberated from the traditional seclusion of epistolary texts. As a playwright, she is an active participant in the theatrical milieu, travelling frequently around the world to supervise productions of her plays. Unlike Olga, Vera is able to be self-reflective while participating in the world around her. *Dolce per sé* is also devoid of the motif of abandonment that so haunts *Va' dove ti porta il cuore*. By portraying a confident, productive, and solitary female protagonist, Maraini frees her from the tangles of erotic plot. The character forges a narrative trajectory through her letters that focuses on self-expression and self-determination.

While both texts revolve around the relationship between an older woman and a young woman or girl, Maraini's novel more profoundly illustrates the practice of *affidamento* or entrustment that was evident in *Lettere a Marina*. Rather than structuring her work around family ties (grandmother/granddaughter, for example), she creates a non-conventional coupling, one between a fifty-year-old woman and a six-year-old girl. Maraini moves considerably beyond the primary relationship found in *Lettere a Marina*, which, while including examples of the practice of *affidamento*, still revolved around the narrator's affair with Marina. In *Dolce per sé*, Maraini shifts her focus, this time containing the love relationship within the letters themselves and structuring the novel around a relationship not based on familial or generational ties.

The protagonist understands the uniqueness of this female relationship, pointing out to Flavia in her second letter, 'che non mi sei parente, che non mi sei coetanea' (21) ['you are not related to me, we are not the same age' (16)].[39] Nor is the bond maternal, for Vera treats Flavia as a young adult without any overtones of a mother-daughter relationship. Maraini emphasizes the mentor/initiate characteristics of this relationship while at the same time practising an inclusionary politics of feminism.[40] By this I mean Maraini articulates a feminist philosophy that embraces a variety of relationships and life experiences. Rather than privileging traditional relationships, such as those between husband

and wife or parent and child, she reveals the benefits of non-conventional bonds, especially those between women.[41]

Maraini uses the powerful yet intimate format of the letter to initiate a young woman into a life structured around a feminist poetics. This sense of initiation is heightened in a letter that refers to a rite of passage for all young children: the loss of their baby teeth. The seemingly innocuous incident of Flavia losing a tooth evokes one of Maraini's early poems, entitled 'Le poesie delle donne' ('Poems by Women'). In this poem, the author describes the violent loss of a 'dente di miele' ('baby tooth'), an experience that propels the young girl into adulthood, with its attendant expectations of female behaviour. While the loss of a tooth in Dolce per sé is not as explicitly linked to an initiation into a gendered social role, Maraini is clearly engaged with this issue throughout the novel. She considerably reworks the illustration of this rite of passage from the poem to the novel. In 'Le poesie delle donne,' a male figure – the father – initiates the young girl into the adult world, tying her loose tooth to a door handle that he then kicks shut. While the poem focuses on the paternal role in the indoctrination into female behaviour, in the novel Flavia's tooth falls out without any intervention. In Dolce per sé it is the young girl who controls the moment in which she moves from childhood to adolescence. I would argue that this re-representation of the tooth incident is a deliberate strategy on Maraini's part, for it endows the female figure with a high degree of agency and self-determination. This passage, which imparts a message of female self-determination, encapsulates a fundamental aspect of the feminist poetics Maraini articulates in the novel.

The narrator's initiation into the ideology of feminism and her alternative vision of female existence is strikingly different from that of Va' dove ti porta il cuore, whose protagonist emphasizes an irrevocable sense of destiny that dooms her own granddaughter. Throughout her letters, Vera often discusses her friends, all of whom have cast off the weight of femininity and forged lives far different from societal expectations of female behaviour. By creating this roster of strong and productive women, the protagonist fights the perception of female weakness and passivity that imbues Tamaro's text. She uncovers and criticizes those social practices that limit female experiences, such as the 'arcaico codice linguistico' (28) ['archaic code of language' (24)] that once forced women to express themselves through such physical ailments as headaches and fainting spells.

The reference to 'Le poesie delle donne' also challenges perceptions of female literary production, a particularly appropriate allusion for *Dolce per sé* in light of the categorization – and denigration – of the epistolary text as a 'woman's genre.' In her poem, Maraini addresses the inability (or unwillingness) of the literary establishment to recognize the value of an artistic endeavour that does not conform to canonic strictures.[42] By referring to this poem, Maraini recuperates female authorship from the margins of canonic literature, while also interrogating the construction and politics of genre. In the novel, her project is bipartite, involving a specific thematic analysis as well as a broader examination of the production and reception of the literary text. Implicit in her work is an awareness of how these aspects of the text are shaped by the knowledge that some genres and modes of literary expression have been categorized by gender.

Maraini comments directly on this process, challenging the false and potentially restrictive link between what women artists produce and what they are allowed or expected to produce. In one of her first letters, Vera recounts the story of Flavia's mother, who renounced a promising career as a pianist in order to raise a family: 'Il marito, i parenti, la gente intorno avranno davvero riconoscenza per queste rinunce professionali? O non sarà che, dopo averla costretta a scegliere fra professione amata e maternità, la tratteranno con sufficienza dicendo: "In fondo le donne sono poco portate per l'arte"' (25) ['Husbands, relations, friends, have they had any recognition of what it meant to her to give up a career? Or is it that having forced her to choose between a career she loved and motherhood, they then respond pretentiously by saying, "In the end, women aren't all that gifted"' (20)]. In her commentary on how female artistic production is often circumscribed by gender, Maraini offers by extension a neat reproof to those critics of the epistolary text who scoffed at the letter text precisely because it was considered a marginal female genre.

While Tamaro's text reproduces the very anti-literary attributes traditionally assigned to the epistolary, Maraini finds alternative ways to address, interpret, and present its conventions. Throughout the novel Maraini challenges the authority of established, male-authored texts, creating in the process a critical essay on the canon. Vera's letters offer a veritable feast of literary references, alluding to works as diverse as Proust's *Swann's Way*, a Brechtian drama, the poetry of Michelangelo and Leopardi, Pirandello's treatise on humour, and Dostoevsky's *The Idiot*. While Maraini's treatment of these texts reveals an appreciation of the original work, she also enters into a dialogue with them that challenges their canonical authority. For example, the first letter opens with an act of remembering, and the narrator supports this narrative move by citing a passage from Leopardi's *Ricordanze*: 'Dolce per sé; ma con dolor sottentra / in pensier del presente, un van desio / del passato' (7) ['Sweetness itself; but underneath the pain / the present thought, vain longing / for the past' (unnumbered)]. The epistolary text often focuses on the past, and certainly in *Va' dove ti porta il cuore* and *Dolce per sé* the past becomes fertile terrain for an examination of family histories. Not only does Maraini evoke the bittersweet sensation of memory in her very title, itself appropriated from a canonical author, but her narrator depicts memory as a communal font of wisdom, shared among women. While Olga describes a female genealogy that is bound by ties of oppression and misery, Vera emphasizes the productive attributes of a shared female history. She writes of that 'memoria femminile che è entrata nel mio bagaglio sapienziale come un talento innato: cercare, studiare, cogliere, mettere da parte, cucinare, trasformare, accudire, cibare' (184) ['female memory that has become part of my mental baggage, like some inborn talent. To look, to study, to pick, to put on one side, to cook, to transform, to make ready, to nourish' (195)]. This passage, taken from Vera's final letter to Flavia, alerts the young girl to the recuperative and generative elements of womanhood. The citation of Leopardi's poem, with its allusion to desire for the past, becomes an opportunity to examine the role of memory in female experiences. The desire to maintain a genealogy speaks ultimately to the inclusionary politics underlying Maraini's work, in which both male and female cultural history can be fonts of inspiration and creativity.[43]

Her interest in the construction of a literary text often manifests itself in an analysis of the production of language itself. In *Dolce per sé*, this concern is translated into equipping the young Flavia with a series of modes of communication and self-expression. Again, the contrast between Tamaro's more conventional text and Maraini's is striking. In *Va' dove ti porta il cuore*, the narrator is only able to offer her granddaughter a rhetoric based on an anti-intellectual and often overly sentimental system of knowledge. Vera provides her young charge, in contrast, with a series of 'languages,' each appropriate for the interpretation and articulation of different life experiences.[44] She also shares with Flavia the language of music, as manifested through Flavia's uncle, the violinist. She remembers an intimate moment with her former lover, when he played Bach for her and she listened 'non solo con le orecchie ma con la pelle, sdraiata nuda sul letto' (109) ['not only with my ears but through my skin, while I lay stretched out naked on the bed' (113)]. The musical language spoken here, which is met by an equally non-verbal reception, transcends linguistic boundaries. Why this attention to various languages, oral or non-verbal, physical or musical? I believe that Maraini deliberately investigates various linguistic modes as part of her project to bring to the foreground alternate means of self-expression. The lesson for Flavia is clear: different methods of communication both enrich and elucidate different life experiences.[45]

While Maraini welcomes non-verbalized forms of communication into her catalogue of languages, as an author she naturally favours the written word as a form of expression. In *Dolce per sé*, the written text is also the playwright-protagonist's chosen vehicle of expression. A discussion of why Maraini privileges written texts leads nicely to an examination of how she recuperates marginalized modes of authorship, especially as they pertain to the epistolary novel. Again, we must turn back to *Va' dove ti porta il cuore* in order to fully recognize Maraini's narrative innovations. Tamaro's text concludes with a relatively closed narrative: The grandmother records in a letter her final piece of advice, and we are led to believe that, because of her precarious health and advanced age, she will then die offstage. The novel follows the more traditional pattern of epistolary texts, in which the work comes 'to a motivated state of arrest and equilibrium, producing a strong sense of closure' (Altman, 148).[46] *Dolce per sé*, however, features a more open ending. There is no sense of resolution and no indication of how the life stories of Vera and Flavia will unfold, indicating that life, learning, and relationships are ongoing and not finite. It also proposes that Vera's influence on Flavia will continue after the letters stop, creating a female genealogy. At the end of the novel, Maraini leaves the reader with an exhortation to pay close attention to the written word. 'Io sono una lettrice appassionata,' Vera tells Flavia, adding:

E mi sembra che solo attraverso la lettura riesco a 'vedere' al di là delle immagini che si vedono a giornata. Quando riusciamo ad andare oltre lo stereotipo scopriamo che le pupille della persona osservata sono gremite di storie non raccontate, che la sua pelle conserva l'odore del latte materno, che le sue mani, per quanto vizze, sono percorse dallo spirito del rinnovamento. (185)

I myself am an avid and passionate reader, and it seems to me it is only through reading that I am able to see beyond the images sold to us each and every day. When we are able to get beyond stereotypes, we can see how the eyes of the person being observed are full of untold stories, how their skin still smells of mother's milk, and how their hands, however withered, are driven by the spirit of renewal. (197)

Maraini's text is left open because the stories it contains cannot be resolved; readers must bring to them their own insights, using their own sets of languages.

This reciprocal relationship between narrator and reader is fundamental to the epistolary format. Indeed, as Janet Altman writes in her structural study of the letter text: 'The epistolary reader is empowered to intervene, to correct style, to give shape to the story, often to become an agent and narrator in his own right' (91). While most epistolary texts share this impulse, Maraini's text makes explicit the role we as readers have in its creation. In it, Maraini entrusts us, as readers, with the feminist poetics promulgated in the novel. In Vera's first letter to Flavia, the young girl becomes the symbol of epistolary communication. The narrator recalls a family vacation in which Flavia surprised her uncle by knocking at his hotel room, claiming to be the maid with a letter, and then shouting 'Sono io la lettera' when he opened the door (10) ['I'm the letter!' (4)]. Maraini inscribes the letter onto the figure of this young girl, conflating the epistolary with the burgeoning female subject. By doing so, the recipient of the letters – both within and outside of the text – becomes implicated in the act of producing a literary text infused with an inclusionary poetics.

What does this narrative strategy, this slippage between the production of a literary text and its politics, have to do with the epistolary? By underscoring how the letter text can act as a document that engages in a dialogue with its cultural content and with its readers, Maraini addresses the genre's secondary status. She challenges those critics who denigrate the genre as a vehicle good only for producing fictions of limited scope. Instead, Maraini highlights the intersection between the creation of a letter text and its underlying politics, casting the reader as an intermediary in this process. Along the way, we are meant to embody the letters as Flavia has, becoming advocates of the author's feminist poetics, that is, the inclusionary ideology that informs her work.

Bossi Fedrigotti, Fallaci, and Maraini cast the concerns of their heroines within the framework of larger social and literary issues: female history, female sexuality, changing roles of women, female authorship, and the reconstruction of the canon. I would posit that they did this deliberately, to comment on and encourage the sort of engaged and committed activism necessary for political, cultural, and social change. The epistolary text provides the ideal forum for such a strategy, for the authors are able to address the correspondence between literary narrative and socio-cultural ideology. *Amore mio uccidi Garibaldi* offers an exciting revision of history, engraving within official chronicles a woman's perspective. The letters in *Lettera a un bambino mai nato, Lettere a Marina,* and *Dolce per sé* serve as a bridge linking the poetics and the politics of the feminist movement. Fallaci and Maraini create in these novels a dialogue with their readers – with us. We are the recipients of these epistles; we are called to meditate on social expectations, to ponder the potential in all of us, but, most of all, we are called to transform the literary into reality.

Postscript

Female authors in Italy have significantly revised the letter novel since the early 1800s, steadfastly focusing throughout this evolution on the role of women in Italian society. These authors have consciously and often ingeniously tied narrative structure to thematic content, creating powerful texts that reflect – and challenge – contemporary literary and socio-cultural norms. Indeed, as demonstrated in the preceding chapters, it is difficult to address these novels without examining how their epistolarity fosters a deeper understanding of their poetics.

A brief overview of the works studied here encapsulates the connection between structure and content. As we saw in chapter 1, the more traditional letter novel, one hinging on romantic relationships, provided the foundation for a critical appraisal of female roles in nineteenth-century Italy. Orintia Romagnuoli Sacrati, in her novel *Lettere di Giulia Willet*, gradually removed the heroine from active participation in both her life and the text, subtly denouncing how restrictive social expectations can erase female identity. In *Prima morire*, by the Marchesa Colombi, the dual correspondences between the two sets of lovers represent differing literary modes – romantic and realist – and their attendant expectations of female conduct. Only one of the two heroines, Mercede, defies the social proscriptions demanded of her gender, but in the process is excluded from the epistolary exchange. Matilde Serao, in her analogous short stories 'Falso in scrittura' and 'La vita è così lunga,' takes up several of the conventions of epistolary fiction, only to reject them as she considers their effect on female protagonists. The intervention of an anonymous editor, for example, is used primarily to address the issue of the creation of female characters, rather than to advance the narrative. In the introduction to her novel *Ella non rispose*, Serao confronts head-on the slippage between women's fictional and real letters, taking up an argument begun in the earliest discussions of epistolary texts and defending the literary merits of letter novels. Like the heroine in Sacrati's *Lettere a Giulia Willet*, the protagonist in Serao's novel is also effaced from the text, literally dying once her role in the production and reading of letters is complete. In all these works, epistolary conventions regarding the romantic narrative are reworked in order to question the female role within this plot. But only Sibilla Aleramo, with her transgressive short novel *Trasfigurazione (Lettera non spedita)*, succeeds in creating a text that envisions new epistolary relationships. Although the heroine's story is firmly rooted in an amorous liaison, her correspondent is another woman, rather than her lover. While Aleramo, in this work at least, does not ultimately free her protagonist from traditional bonds, she does endow her with a more liberal articulation of the romantic narrative.

This romantic narrative was secondary to the works examined in chapter 2, which instead took up questions of literary styles and movements. Here, we saw how the epistolary narrative afforded writers an unusual degree of literary experimentation, although, again, their narratives were linked in part to a discussion of female experiences and roles. Although the correspondence in Sibilla Aleramo's *Amo dunque sono* is triggered by the lovers' separation, the female protagonist is as concerned with the exegesis of the creation of a literary text – at the hands of a woman writer. The collection of letters, all written by the heroine, becomes a metatext that comments on and stands for the work of a female artist. Benedetta Cappa Marinetti, in her novel *Astra e il sottomarino*, offered a gendered response to Futurist poetics, which often co-opted the act of creation. The author privileged the letter with a high degree of agency – the female protagonist credits one with saving her life – while also seeing in it a site for explorations of the role of the woman in epistolary novels, Futurism, and romantic narratives. For her part, Gianni Manzini addressed literary matters, questioning in her novel *Lettere all'editore* the role of the epistolary in contemporary cultural debates, such as the neorealist movement. All of these authors challenge issues of canon formation, using as their platform the female-authored letter novel.

The *zeitgeist* of post-war Italy provided a starting point for novels studied in chapter 3, with these authors deploying the epistolary text as a means to examine such issues as the loss of political and personal ideals. The search for a means of communication and connection becomes highlighted in these works. The characters in Alba de Céspedes's *Il rimorso* discover the potential for both personal and social transformations through their correspondences and diary. The author posited an authentic social ethos through her writer-protagonists, conflating art and life in the intersection of epistolary structure and thematic content. Natalia Ginzburg's letter novels, *Caro Michele* and *La città e la casa*, reflect through their narrative framework the disintegration of personal and social connections, an apt theme for a genre whose impetus is one of extending ties.

Female experiences took centre stage in the epistolary texts examined in chapter 4, as feminist authors articulated their socio-political agenda through the forum of the letter novel. Their frank discussions of female sexuality, relationships, and experiences brought the private – the letters – into the public forum. These writers often significantly reworked epistolary tenets, rejecting those harmful to female characters or presenting them in a fresh, more positive light. Isabella Bossi Fedrigotti, in *Amore mio uccidi Garibaldi*, rewrote official history by incorporating the experiences of her female protagonist into the Risorgimento. *Lettera a un bambino mai nato*, by Oriana Fallaci, examined the socio-cultural limitations facing contemporary Italian women, and the importance of taking up an active and committed position in regard to women's rights. Dacia Maraini's novel *Lettere a Marina* also reflected the rhetoric of the feminist movement, as the heroine enacts through her correspondence the practices of *autocoscienza* and *affidamento*. Like Aleramo's *Amo dunque sono*, this novel also created through the intimate record of a female artist a more universal examination of women's contributions to a national literature. Finally, Maraini's novel *Dolce per sé* underscored how a literary text – the epistolary – can engage in a dialogue with its readers through its cultural content, calling them to debate and action.

As fascinating as an examination of these texts, perhaps, is a look at the picture they create when taken together. Just as an epistolary text is more than the sum of its discrete parts – its letters – so this study fashions through a discussion of individual novels a more comprehensive representation of how Italian women made use of the letter text in the nineteenth and twentieth centuries. It is fitting that we look at the connections among these texts, to see what that reveals about this narrative structure. I am struck in particular by two distinct shifts in the epistolary novel, as practised by these women. The first occurs in the post-war period, when de Céspedes and Ginzburg saw in their works a place to observe and perhaps offer a respite from the personal and social alienation they believed supplanted the more authentic and connected ethos existing before and during the Second World War. The works of these two women differ dramatically from those written in the period immediately preceding this moment. Although Alermo, Benedetta, and Manzini were clearly cognizant of the socio-political temperament of the times, their works seem more insular, more concerned with matters literary and artistic. I pass no judgment about the literary merit of these two approaches to the epistolary; rather, I wish to draw attention to the striking transformation of its use. This particular narrative structure can make broad, universal connections with the world beyond its pages, or scrutinize instead issues that pertain more specifically to the genre itself.

A second correspondence among these works links the first and final chapters and their presentation of female experiences. The feminist authors in the latter chapter are connected to those in chapter 1 by their shared concern with the shaping of a literary heroine. But because of the vast social, cultural, political, and legal transformations in Italian society during the twentieth century, these later writers were able to free their protagonists from stifling literary proscriptions that were often coupled with socio-cultural ideology. Their heroines are strong, independent, active, and decidedly not tied to a romantic plot, although amorous relationships abound in these texts. The epistolary practice does not isolate the heroines of these feminist works, but rather creates a community of women.

This community of women is literally visible in the texts; the works by Maraini and Fallaci, for example, emphatically endorse the importance of female friendships. We could read in their novels as well an embrace of their literary foremothers, for I believe these feminist authors deliberately chose to create heroines who were also artists. By featuring protagonist-writers, these women draw attention to a genealogy of female artists, both within their texts and in a larger sense by pointing to a centuries-old tradition of Italian women authors.

My scrutiny of these epistolary texts rests on a reading of the genre as a vehicle for examinations of the female figure, both in the literary work itself and as a representative of larger socio-cultural issues. These authors have taken up and subverted the practice of a narrative form once deemed appropriate exclusively for the female pen, only to rework it with often astonishing results. They have challenged assumptions –

both literary and social – about female behaviours, roles, relationships, and sexuality. Along the way, these authors have refashioned this allegedly stodgy and cautious narrative format to produce more authentic, and occasionally even radical, portrayals of their heroines.

Because of the interplay that lies at the heart of the epistolary novel, the structure itself encourages a response, from both the characters in the text and its readers. The poetics of these epistolary novels, then, is effortlessly extended beyond the borders of their internal correspondences. We, as readers, are invited to share in these exchanges. Readers are cued, by the epistolary correspondences, to read more carefully the critiques of socio-cultural expectations, explicit or not, that underpin so many of these texts. It is as if we are the third correspondent, reading the letters that are seemingly private but, through their relationship to us and through our participation, engender a public discourse.

I believe this narrative strategy played a large part in the decision by Italian women to use this genre, for it allows for – indeed *calls* for – a more active participation in the interpretation of the text. We can go one step further, for these letters, especially those written during the height of the feminist movement, become an invitation to social activism. Just as the intra-textual letters demand a response, so do the authors of these works, asking us to heed the lessons learned and perhaps even to act in concrete and positive ways.

The letter text is not dead; it has not succumbed to a world powered by technology-driven modes of communication. Instead, we can still find in it a means to discover ourselves, to challenge the world and its expectations, to question literary expectations concerning both gender and genre, and, finally, to connect with others.

Notes

Introduction

1 Even as Brown mourns its demise, he notes growing scholarly interest in the letter text and a renaissance of such works in post-war France. Other scholars have discovered a parallel renaissance in other national literatures, often linking the epistolary structure with contemporary literary movements or social issues. Sunka Simon, in her study of recent German epistolary novels, ties the tenets of the epistolary to those of postmodernism, with '[t]heir intersubjectivity and intertextuality, their transgression or subversion of borders.' See *Mail-Orders: The Fiction of Letters in Postmodern Culture* (New York: University of New York Press, 2002), 15. Gail Pool, writing in the introduction to her anthology of contemporary letter stories from around the globe, believes the narrative form speaks in particular to modern concerns: '[T]he struggle to find meaningful stories, relationships, and lives amidst the social and moral disarray of the era; the absence of the omniscient viewpoint and the limitations of the relative perspective – not only in literature but in life; the blurred boundaries between fact and fiction, artist and audience, private and public domain' See *Other People's Mail: An Anthology of Letter Stories* (Columbia: University of Missouri Press, 2000), 3.

2 All translations are mine, unless otherwise noted.

3 One such endeavour speaks to the epistolary structure's capacity for creating connections. *Tra amiche: Epistolari femminili fra Otto e Novecento* [*Between Friends: Female Epistolaries between the Nineteenth and Twentieth Centuries*], ed. Sandra Cammelli and Silvia Porto (Florence: Rivista Nuova, 2005) is a collection of essays examining the letter exchanges of such literary and public figures as Rosa Luxemburg, Emily Dickinson, Janet Flanner,

Hannah Arendt, and others. These letters offer a personal perspective on quotidian life, but also more existential revelations about the authors. The intimate life described in the letters, then, becomes a forum for larger concerns.

4 I am speaking primarily of epistolary fiction, rather than the real correspondences written by medieval women which have garnered much critical attention. See *Dear Sister: Medieval Women and the Epistolary Genre,* ed. Karen Cherewatuk and Ulrike Wiethaus (Philadelphia: University of Pennsylvania Press, 1993). Gabriella Zarri has edited a collection of women's letters from the Renaissance period, in *Per lettera: La scrittura epistolare femminile tra archivio e tipografia secoli XV–XVII* (Rome: Viella, 1999). See as well Meredith K. Ray's important work, *Writing Gender in Women's Letter Collections of the Italian Renaissance* (Toronto: University of Toronto Press, 2009).

5 Few critics have addressed modern Italian epistolary fiction in any systematic manner, although Barbara Zaczek includes illuminating discussions of several such texts in *Censored Sentiments: Letters and Censorship in Epistolary Novels and Conduct Material* (Newark, DE: University of Delaware Press, 1997). Margherita di Fazio includes brief discussions of male and female Italian epistolary texts (along with English, French, American, and German) in *La lettera e il romanzo: Esempi di comunicazione epistolare nella narrativa* [*The Letter and the Novel: Examples of Epistolary Communication in Narrative*] (Rome: Nuova Arnica, 1996).

6 Beebee offers in his text a useful chronology of European epistolary production, including translations, allowing for an examination of a cross-national pollination of this format. See Beebee, *Epistolary Fiction in Europe, 1500–1850* (Cambridge: Cambridge University Press, 1999).

7 Giovanni Ragone has compiled a quantitative study of the novel in Italy during this moment, revealing the emphasis on historical novels. See Ragone, 'Italy, 1815–1870' in *The Novel, Volume I: History, Geography, and Culture,* ed. Franco Moretti (Princeton: Princeton University Press, 2006), 466–78.

8 Critics who focus specifically on the epistolary and women writers include April Alliston, *Virtue's Faults: Correspondences in Eighteenth-Century British and French Women's Fiction* (Stanford: Stanford University Press, 1996); Mary Favret, *Romantic Correspondence: Women, Politics and the Fiction of Letters* (Cambridge: Cambridge University Press, 1993); Amanda Gilroy and W.M. Verhoeven, eds., *Epistolary Histories: Letters, Fiction, Culture* (Charlottesville: University Press of Virginia, 2000); Elizabeth C. Goldsmith, ed., *Writing the Female Voice: Essays on Epistolary Literature* (Boston: Northeast-

ern University Press, 1989); Linda Kauffman, *Special Delivery: Epistolary Modes in Modern Fiction* (Chicago: University of Chicago Press, 1992); and Ruth Perry, *Women, Letters, and the Novel* (New York: AMS Press, 1980).

9 Women's epistolary production could, however, act as a site of rebellion and self-awareness. Olga Kenyon, in her introduction to *800 Years of Women's Letters* (New York: Penguin, 1992), writes that letters 'prove[d] more subtle than talk in strategies for subverting partriarchal limitations. Because letters were the one form of writing which men did not find threatening…they could both explore the sexist devaluation of female values and aid consciousness-raising' (x).

10 *In Love and Struggle: Letters in Contemporary Feminism*, edited by Margaretta Jolly (New York: Columbia University Press, 2008), explicitly highlights the importance of letter writing to the women's movement in the United States and Britain. The text examines letters sent among feminists and writers, epistles that 'suggest feminism's ideals about personal relationship itself as a belief system' (2).

11 See for example *The Cambridge Companion to the Italian Novel*, edited by Peter Bondanella and Andrea Ciccarelli, published in 2003. This comprehensive text comprises fourteen chapters examining the modern novel in Italy. Women's contributions are relegated to one essay – an excellent entry called 'Feminist Writing in the Twentieth Century' by Sharon Wood – although several of the chapters do briefly discuss the works of female authors.

1. Love Letters

1 Sacrati's name is spelled as both Romagnuoli and Romagnoli in various sources; I take my cue from the title page of her novel.

2 Both Lucienne Kroha, in *The Woman Writer in Late-Nineteenth-Century Italy: Gender and the Formation of Literary Identity* (Lewiston, NY: Edwin Mellen, 1992), and Antonia Arslan, in her article on female authors of the same period, 'Ideologia e autorappresentazione,' in *Svelamento: Sibilla Aleramo* (Milan: Feltrinelli, 1988), 172, discuss the 'disagio profondo' (profound uneasiness) of these artists, who had to contend with the expectations of the male literary establishment while at the same time addressing their own dissatisfaction with traditional female archetypes and narrative models. But few women authors risked overtly challenging the entrenched tenets of the canon or alienating a reading public accustomed to these narrative models, and so any subversive action on their part was often deeply encoded within the text.

3 It was not uncommon for authors to participate in both literary and journalistic endeavours at this time, and Donatella Alesi believes this was especially true of women writers. '[L]'idea del giornale come luogo in cui dare voce alle proprie opinioni ed esercitare la capacità di osservare e descrivere il reale è molto diffusa tra le tantissime donne che ... seppero fare del rapporto tra letteratura e giornalismo il centro della propria esistenza professionale,' she writes (206) ['The idea of the newspaper as a place in which to give voice to one's own opinions and to exercise the capacity to observe and describe reality is very widespread among the many women who ... knew how to make the heart of their professional existence the connection between literature and journalism']. See Alesi, 'La Marchesa Colombi e Matilde Serao: due giornaliste a confronto,' in *La Marchesa Colombi: Una scrittrice e il suo tempo*' (Novara: Interlinea, 2001).
   Both Serao and the Marchesa Colombi moved easily between the worlds of fiction and journalism, and both were married to journalists. Serao helped her husband, Edoardo Scarfoglio, launch several newspapers, including *Corriere di Roma*, *Corriere di Napoli*, and *Il Mattino*. She founded her own Neapolitan newspaper, *Il Giorno*, in 1904, overseeing its management and writing a daily column for it until her death in 1927. It subsequently folded. The Marchesa Colombi was married to Eugenio Torelli-Viollier, founder of *Corriere della Sera*, and often wrote essays for various periodicals and newspapers.

4 Gabriella Romani, in her essay on epistolary texts of this era, believes that the sentimental narrative offered 'opportunities for women to access and participate in the national discourse on matters of relevance to women, such as female education or social mores; it was a matter of making reading pertinent to the daily experience of nineteenth-century women's life' (36). See 'Women Writing Letters: Epistolary Practices in Nineteenth-Century Newspapers, Manuels and Fiction,' in *Across Genres, Generations and Borders: Italian Women Writing Lives*, ed. Susanna Scarparo and Rita Wilson (Melbourne: Monash Romance Studies, 2004).

5 Ugo Foscolo's letter novel *Le ultime lettere di Jacopo Ortis* (*The Last Letters of Jacopo Ortis*) was originally published in 1802 and reissued in 1816. By modern, I refer to the period beginning with the 1800s, a period that saw Italy's struggle for national unity. On the literary front, it signalled the moment when the novel began to make its mark on the national canon.

6 The manipulative aunt seems based in part on the scheming Madame de Merteuil of Choderlos de Laclos's 1782 epistolary novel *Dangerous Liaisons*. Both women are driven by greed and a lust for power as they conspire to control the sexual fortunes of their young wards. Both women are rejected

by society at the end of the texts, a fitting punishment for their attempts to ignore social niceties.

7 A conference on the Marchesa Colombi in Novara in 2000, for example, produced an excellent series of articles devoted to all aspects of the author's work.

8 I would prefer to refer to Torriani by her legal name, both because it would create less convoluted phrasing and also to grant her an identity that goes beyond the literary domain. However, the common usage has been to use her literary name, just as critics do with Sibilla Aleramo (born Rina Faccio).

9 With the use of her pseudonym the Marchesa Colombi positioned herself as both a part of the male-dominated establishment and as a disinterested commentator on it. The Marchese Colombi is a foolish but endearing character in Paolo Ferrari's 1856 comedy *La satira e Parini*. The Marchesa Colombi appropriated the name, but made it feminine, assuming 'un esplicito atteggiamento d'ambiguità diretto, sotto la parvenza di obbediente ossequio alle aspettative, ad alterare ed a scompigliare i ferrei schemi imposti alla presenza femminile' (Pierobon, 'Fra questi sí e no son di parer contrario,' *Studi d'italianistica nell'Africa australe* 12 [1999]: 25) ['an explicit attitude of ambiguity directed, under the appearance of an obedient respect for expectations, to change and to upset the ironclad models imposed on the female presence'].

Many women writers used pennames at this time: Neera (Anna Radius Zuccari), Contessa Lara (Evelina Cattermole Mancini), Giovanna Zangrandi (Alma Bevilacqua), and Sibilla Aleramo (Rina Faccio) are only a few examples. Serao used many pseudonyms both in her journalistic and fiction writing, including male names. These authors often used pennames to conceal their own identities or to create a public 'artistic' persona.

10 As Clotilde Barbarulli and Luciana Brandi write in their study of the author's use of these ironic asides, this was a deliberate strategy: 'È l'ironia di chi sa che il proprio genere sta al margine della società, e, riconoscendosi in parte estranea al paradigma dominante, cerca di avanzare un nuovo registro, nella complicità con le lettrici: scarto leggero che tende a spostare il punto di vista sul mondo' ['It is the irony of one who knows that one's own gender rests on the margins of society, and recognizing oneself in part estranged from the dominant paradigm, seeks to advance a new register, in complicity with female readers: a gentle deviation that tends to shift the point of view of the world']. See Barbarulli and Brandi,'La sovversione del sorriso: L'ironia nella Marchesa Colombi,' in *La Marchesa Colombi: Una scrittrice e il suo tempo* (Novara: Interlinea, 2001), 152.

11 An interesting topic that falls outside the parameters of this study is the

close friendship between the two male characters. We learn that long before the events of the novel take place, they both suffered great personal and financial misfortunes. As a result, the two have sworn to be 'onesti, leali, puri e buoni, a costo di sacrificare i nostri interessi e la nostra felicità' (114) ['honest, faithful, pure and good, at the cost of sacrificing our interests and our happiness']. Their personal motto becomes 'Prima morire che macchiarsi' (114) ['Death before dishonour']. At times, the bond between these men seems more intense and heartfelt than those with their respective lovers, and this relationship is underlined by the use of their dictum in the title of the novel.

12 For an examination of how the ideals and rhetoric of the Risorgimento led to the creation of the mythology of a domestic femininity, see Lucienne Kroha in *The Woman Writer in Late Nineteenth-Century Italy*, and Gabriella Romani in her introduction to *Writing to Delight: Italian Short Stories by Nineteenth-Century Women Writers* (Toronto: University of Toronto Press, 2006). These 'angels of the hearth,' as Kroha and Romani note, were to represent the moral centre of the family, and were entrusted with the spiritual upbringing of their children. Their space was clearly delineated as the domestic one, however, and any attempts to cross over into the public arena were seen as major transgressions that could lead to personal dishonour and the degradation of the family.

13 It is telling that a male character is the bearer of this news, for he represents and is charged with upholding the social order.

14 In fact the first letter of the text is a short anonymous note from Augusto to Eva alerting her that her bathroom window is visible from his room.

15 He writes to Leonardo, 'Io mi propongo di sviluppare le facoltà buone che sono latenti nel suo carattere, di risvegliare nell'animo il nobile entusiasmo della virtù, di farle rivolgere la mente a cose serie' (38) ['I propose developing the good qualities that are latent in her character, reawakening in her soul the noble enthusiasm of virtue, turning her mind to serious things'].

16 In fact, Kroha points out that the Marchesa Colombi and Serao 'share a very modern and precocious awareness that literary language and structures are not mimetic and transparent, and that they filter and *construct* images of reality rather than reflecting reality directly: metafiction, parody, pastiche, authorial intrusion all testify to this awareness' (18). She goes on to write that this approach to literature 'makes a search for literary identity through the critical appraisal of those aspects of the tradition experienced as most inauthentic and even as damaging to women' (18).

17 See my *Gendered Genres: Female Experiences and Narrative Patterns in the Works of Matilde Serao* (Madison, NJ: Fairleigh Dickinson University Press,

1999), for an in-depth discussion of the author's sentimental, realist, and
Gothic fiction.

18 While Ursala Fanning examines *Tre donne* in her excellent study of Serao,
she does not specifically address the epistolary nature of the novel.
Because I have dealt at length with this novel in previous writings, I will
only add here that Serao's use of the letters in the second half of *Tre donne*
endows each of the characters with a voice and a presence. The letters
read like diary entries, and are not reciprocated. See Fanning, *Gender Meets
Genre: Woman as Subject in the Fictional Universe of Matilde Serao* (Dublin:
Irish Academic Press, 2002).

19 As Fanning points out, over the course of Serao's life the author became
less and less tied to conventional generic principles, 'ever guided by her
desire to achieve more varied modes of being for her female characters
while reflecting women's position in society' (30).

20 Serao's epistolary works can also be read in relationship with those of
Giovanni Verga, for they are similar in plot. For more on the connection
between these two authors see Gabriella Romani's thorough introduction
to letter fiction, 'From Letter to Literature: Giovanni Verga, Matilde Serao
and Late Nineteenth-Century Epistolary Fiction,' *MLN* 124 (2009) 177–94.

21 To name just a few examples of these contradictions: Serao argued vehe-
mently against the legalization of divorce, yet was herself separated from
her unfaithful husband, and later had a child by her long-term lover, the
lawyer Giuseppe Natale. And despite her insistence that women could
contribute most to society through their work in the domestic sphere,
Serao played an active and public role in the literary and cultural world of
southern Italy. These fundamental contradictions are found in her works
as well, for even her most traditional of narratives often contain a more
subversive subtext.

22 I do not mean to imply that Serao denigrated romantic fiction; she was,
after all, the author of many short stories and novels that were decidedly
sentimental in nature. Some of these texts do indeed read like conventional
examples of romantic fiction, down to their formulaic narratives and their
archetypal male and female characters. But in Serao's more accomplished
romantic fiction, she was also able to subtly subvert these conventions, creating texts that challenge canonic prescriptions. I am thinking in particular
of 'Paolo Spada,' 'O Giovannino o la morte,' *Addio, amore!*, *Fantasia*, *Tre
donne*, and *Cuore infermo*.

23 Can 'La vita è così lunga' also be read as an indictment of romantic fiction? The brief introduction by the anonymous editor – and, of course, the
title of the story – does hint that while love is short-lived, life endures. It

is tempting to interpret this enigmatic assertion as Serao's privileging of realist fiction over romantic literature. I am not sure I want to make that stretch, although it is clear that she is criticizing romantic fiction's expectations of female behaviour.

24 The story recalls the 1899 tale 'Livia Speri,' another text in which the male narrator portrays through correspondence his expectations of how the female character should conduct herself. In 'Livia Speri,' although the title character does not speak a word, a brief coda describing her composed demeanour after receiving her lover's letter ending their relationship reveals that she is the polar opposite of the fragile and emotional woman depicted by him. Serao's strategy in 'Livia Speri' and 'La vita è così lunga' is to allow the female characters their own, albeit indirect, means of self-expression, whether it is contained in the short introduction of 'La vita è così lunga' or in a description of the deliberate and self-contained behaviour of Livia Speri. In both cases, the women do not participate in the actual exchange of letters, just as Mercede in *Prima morire* existed to some degree outside of the novel's correspondence. Instead, Serao's vision of the epistolary text means reading between the letters to tease out the subtext contained in such generic staples as the editor's introduction. In this way the author succeeds in interrogating canonic conventions while questioning, as well, how those strictures govern questions of gender. I discuss 'Livia Speri' in greater depth in *Gendered Genres*.

25 Serao's defence of the love novel in this introduction was perhaps a preemptive strike against critics. One contemporary reviewer, Giuseppe Lipparini, criticized the publication of such light fiction during wartime, when 'milioni di uomini sono in campo o si massacrano spietatmente' (Lipparini, 'Romanzi e novelle,' *Il Marzocco*, Nov. 1914: 5) ['millions of men are on the battlefields or are being piteously massacred']. However, he adds, these sentimental narratives were not completely devoid of plausibility, admitting 's'io leggo le cronache dei giornali, trovo qualcuno che si uccide per amore' (5) ['if I read the news, I will find someone who has killed himself for love']. Serao realized as well that her popularity rested in large part on the many sentimental short stories and novels she wrote throughout her long career, even if most critics preferred her realist works.

26 Diana sings Orfeo's aria from Gluck, a poignant piece in which he laments the death of Euridice. Clearly we are meant to read this allusion as a bit of literary foreshadowing, a strategy underlined by Paolo's frequently referring to Diana as Euridice in his letters. Serao's use of literary allusions in her romantic texts is not uncommon; again in *Ella non rispose*, for example, she compares the couple to Tristan and Isolde, another doomed relationship.

27 Clues to Sir Randolph's character are scattered throughout the text, as Paolo comments on the husband's late-night card playing during his honeymoon, their separate bedrooms, and the lack of physical affection between the couple. He is apparently able to discern the nature of their relationship by his observation of the couple.

28 Aleramo's literary reputation suffered, however, because many could not accept or understand this 'welding together of fiction and reality,' as Bernadette Luciano writes. See 'The Diaries of Sibilla Aleramo: Constructing Female Subjectivity,' in *Italian Women Writers from the Renaissance to the Present*, ed. Maria Ornella Marotti (University ParkPA: Pennsylvania State University Press, 1996), 97. One wonders how much the criticism of autobiographical elements in Aleramo's works was based on a general bias against her as a woman author, writing of female experiences.

29 Rita Guerricchio notes, for example, that by using the epistolary genre, Aleramo could change dates and places to make a fiction of her life. 'Ma nel caso di Sibilla va anche sottolineato il fatto che la sua scrittura epistolare si inserisce in un ambito di scrittura specialmente femminile: si sa del ruolo eminente della donna come scrittrice di epistolari familiari' ['But in the case of Sibilla the fact must also be underlined that her epistolary writing becomes inserted in the sphere of a specifically female writing style: one knows of the important role of women as writers of domestic epistolaries']. See Guerricchio, 'Il romanzo epistolare o l'epistolario romantico di Sibilla Aleramo,' in *Svelamento: Sibilla Aleramo* (Milan: Feltrinelli, 1988), 49.

30 The catalyst for this letter was a brief affair between Aleramo and Papini in 1912. In a fascinating article, Barbara Zaczek examines the actual correspondence between the two lovers to determine how these letters themselves become 'a story with a plot.' Zaczek has reversed, then, one of the staples of the study of epistolary fiction, which often examines how the letters contained in a text influence events and relationships. See Zaczek, 'Plotting Letters,' *Italica* 72 (1995).

31 The characters in this text remain nameless. This is not an uncommon strategy on the part of Aleramo, who used this technique in *Una donna*, for example, to create a portrait of an Everywoman, and in her published diaries, to conflate the narrator with the author herself. In *Trasfigurazione*, however, I suspect Aleramo chose not to name the characters in order to protect their identities. This caused some confusion, however, when the novella was published. According to Zaczek, at least one other former lover of Aleramo's thought *Trasfigurazione* was based on their affair. That particular liaison was depicted in Aleramo's novel *Amo dunque sono*, to be examined in the following chapter. See Zaczek, 'Plotting Letters.'

2. Literary Responses

1 When *The Three Marias* was published in Portugal, the three authors were arrested on charges of indecency for the frank sexuality infusing the text. The charges were dismissed in 1974, but not before generating an international debate on censorship, literary freedom, and the rights of women.

  The authorship of *The Letters of a Portuguese Nun* has been in dispute since its publication, with many maintaining that the epistles were written not by the humble and love-stricken heroine of the title, but rather by Gabriel-Joseph de Lavergne de Guilleragues, in perhaps one of the most successful literary hoaxes. For a thorough discussion of the novel's authorship, see Linda S. Kauffman, *Discourses of Desire: Gender, Genre, and Epistolary Fictions* (Ithaca: Cornell University Press, 1986) and *Special Delivery: Epistolary Modes in Modern Fiction* (Chicago: University of Chicago Press, 1992).

2 Weldon briefly discusses Austen's epistolary texts *Love and Freindship* (sic) and *Lady Susan*, and offers a cogent analysis of the consummate letter novel: 'To accomplish a letter-novel successfully requires a special skill, the skill of a born dramatist – the knack of moving a plot along through the mouths of the protagonists, and laying down plot detail, as it's called, without apparently doing so: the body has to be fleshed, but the bones not allowed to show' (57).

3 See Barbara Zaczek's discussion of these two novels in *Censored Sentiments: Letters and Censorship in Epistolary Novels and Conduct Material* (Newark, DE.: University of Delaware Press, 1997).

4 The events and characters in this novel are apparently based on a relationship between Aleramo and Giulio Parise. As noted in the previous chapter, Aleramo often incorporated her own romantic interludes into her fictional works. She even writes at one point in *Amo dunque sono*, '[T]utto, nella mia vita, si trasforma in cosa d'arte' (46) ['Everything, in my life, is transformed into a thing of art']. For an interesting discussion of autobiography and Aleramo, see Anna Grimaldi Morosoff, *Transfigurations: The Autobiographical Novels of Sibilla Aleramo* (New York: Peter Lang, 1999), and Carole Gallucci, 'The Body and the Letter: Sibilla Aleramo in the Interwar Years,' *Forum Italicum* 33 (1999): 363–91.

  In my examination of *Amo dunque sono*, I use 'Sibilla' when referring to the female protagonist, rather than the author herself.

5 In a fascinating article, Carole Gallucci notes that in the 1947 edition of *Amo dunque sono*, the masturbation episode was deleted, although discussions of homosexuality and lesbianism were not. Those censoring the text,

presumably leftovers from the Fascist regime, were clearly not very atten-
tive readers. See 'The Body and the Letter' for a discussion of the critical
reception awarded Aleramo during the Fascist period.

6 In this citation the use of the word 'letter' refers not to epistolary practices
but to the creation of literary works in general.

7 In an interesting aside, Sibilla asserts that she could have sold her body
'cento volte' ['one hundred times'] in order to have nice things, but was
always stopped by 'una ripugnanza fisica' ['a physical repugnance'] (54). It
is unclear whether she is reassuring Luciano of her faithfulness or pointing
out how desirable she is.

8 The manuscript she refers to is that of *Il passaggio*, published in 1919. She
writes: 'Tu hai letto il libro: l'hai chiamato il libro del tormento. Vorrei
mostrarti come in verità è tormentato questo manoscritto, su fogli di varia
specie ... in inchiostri diversi e matita. ... Non lo rivedevo da anni, mi ha
dato commozione intensa' (73) ['You have read the book: you called it the
book of torment. I would like to show you how truthfully this manuscript
is tormented, on various types of pages ... in different inks and pencils. ...
I haven't seen it for years, it made me intensely emotional'].

9 There has been much work done recently on the relationship between
Futurism and Fascism. I am particularly indebted to Cinzia Sartini Blum,
The Other Modernism: F.T. Marinetti's Futurist Fiction of Power (Berkeley:
University of California Press, 1996), and, for more gendered interpretations of the intersection between the two movements, Clara Orban's
'Women, Futurism, and Fascism,'in *Mothers of Invention: Women, Italian
Fascism, and Culture*, ed. Robin Pickering-Iazzi (Minneapolis: University
of Minnesota Press, 1995), 52–75, and Lucia Re's 'Futurism and Fascism,
1914–1945,' in *A History of Women's Writing in Italy*, ed. Letizia Panizza
and Sharon Wood (Cambridge: Cambridge University Press, 2000),
190–204.

10 The following assessment of Benedetta's novel, written by Bruno Sanzin
on the occasion of her death in 1977, aptly – and explicitly – illustrates the
critical establishment's attitude toward women writers in general: '[È]
impossibile non commentare subito che difficilmente una donna assurge
a sì alto grado di cerebralismo. Normalmente l'animo femminile si lascia
avviluppare e guidare più volentieri dal sentimento che dalla ragione'
(373) ['It is impossible not to comment immediately that a woman rises to
such a high level of intellectualism with difficulty. Normally the female
soul willingly lets itself become enveloped and guided by sentiment rather
than by reason']. He goes on to add that her novel 'va elencato tra I grandi
lavori della letteratura *femminile*' (373; emphasis added) ['will be cited

among the great works of *female-authored* literature']. See 'Omaggio a Benedetta Marinetti,' *Il Ragguaglio librario* 44 (1977).

11 For other analyses of women's role in the Futurist movement, as well as discussions of specific Futurist authors, see Anna Nozzoli, *Tabù e coscienza: La condizione femminile nella letteratura italiana del Novecento* (Florence: La Nuova Italia, 1978), and Lucia Re, 'Futurism and Fascism, 1914–1945.'

12 For an analysis of Saint-Point's manifesto, which echoes Marinetti's martial language and exaltation of virility in both men and women, see Cinzia Sartini Blum, *The Other Modernism*; Lucia Re, 'Futurism and Feminism,' *Annali d'Italianistica: Women's Voices in Italian Literature* 7 (1989): 253–72; Clara Orban, 'Women, Futurism, and Fascism,' in *Mothers of Invention,,* 52–75; and Barbara Spackman, 'Fascist Women and the Rhetoric of Virility,' also in *Mothers of Invention*, 100–20.

13 Benedetta has been credited with softening Marinetti's virulent attitudes toward women, especially after their marriage in 1923. Franca Zoccoli claims that their union marked a 'turnabout' for him: 'from a staunch misogynist, he became an appreciator of the other sex, from a scourger of sentiment, an advocate of feelings' (Bentivoglio and Zoccoli, *The Women Artists of Italian Futurism – Almost Lost to History* [New York: Midmarch Arts Press, 1997] , 108). Although by all accounts Marinetti happily settled into the role of family man, Zoccoli's interpretation pays little attention to the evolution of Futurism in general in the 1920s. For a more subtle reading of Marinetti's development as a political and aesthetic rhetorician see Cinzia Sartini Blum, *The Other Modernism*.

14 Benedetta studied with the Futurist painter Giacomo Balla. Her first solo exhibit, held posthumously in 1998, was sponsored by the Moore College of Art and Design in Philadelphia, and later travelled to the Walker Art Center in Minneapolis. The catalogue from that exhibit includes articles from some of the leading scholars of her life and works.

15 Marinetti's 1910 novel *Mafarka*, in which the hero generates a son without the assistance of a woman, best exemplifies the motif of male procreation in Futurist fiction. See Cinzia Sartini Blum, *The Other Modernism,* and Clara Orban, 'Women, Futurism, and Fascism,' for excellent discussions of this text and others with a similar theme.

16 Simona Cigliana, who wrote the preface for the 1998 reprinting of the novel, points out that there are a number of minor textual discrepancies among the various editions, most involving punctuation. I believe this latest edition remains true to Benedetta's lyrical, if sometimes ungrammatical, style.

17 For a compelling analysis of women's lives during the Fascist regime, see

Victoria De Grazia, *How Fascism Ruled Women: Italy, 1922–1945* (Berkeley: University of California Press, 1992).

18 Blum reads Benedetta's entire *oeuvre* as well as the author's own life as a deliberate challenge to the regime's anti-women positions. She writes, 'Ultimately, the feminine image emerging from Benedetta's work is at odds with the restrictive gender roles prescribed by Fascist propaganda and policies, as well as the characterization of woman as temptress or mother that pervades the writings of male authors in the inter-war years. Benedetta's own experience as avant-garde artist and mother contradicts the regime's model of the New Woman, which excludes intellectual endeavors as symptomatic of, or conducive to, sterility, masculinization, and homosexuality.' See 'Benedetta's Emphatic Journey to Transcendence,' Catalogue for exhibition at the Galleries at Moore, Philadelphia (1998), 29.

19 The English translation of the novel is entitled *Game Plan for a Novel*, emphasizing its work-in-progress structure but also removing it from the epistolarity promised by its original title.

20 Perhaps Cecchi best captured the text's challenging narrative when he wrote: 'Come in uno di quegli scrigni cinesi che contengono, inscatolati uno nell'altro, ordinate e cassettini, casellari, falsi fondi, nicchie, segreti: la ordinate dell'opera è ordinate e disposta su una quantità di piani, perni, sezioni, vuoti, ribalte e strapiombi, tutti in interdipendenza di struttura e movimento' (7) ['Like one of those Chinese boxes that contain, nestled one inside another, small boxes, smaller boxes, false bottoms, nooks, secrets: the work's material is ordered and disposed on a quantity of plans, pivots, sections, lapses, trap doors, and sheer cliffs, all in an interdependence of structure and movement']. See *Di giorno in giorno: Note di letteratura italiana contemporanea (1943–54).*

21 Many critics have examined the Pirandellian aspect in Manzini's work. Others have also traced connections between the author's style and that of such innovative writers as Virginia Woolf and André Gide. See Lia Fava Guzzetta's 'Gianna Manzini e la forma-romanzo,' in *Gianna Manzini tra Letteratura e Vita*, ed. Marco Forti (Milan, Mondadori, 1985), 145–63. Manzini herself, in the 1964 work *Album di ritratti (Photograph Album)*, talked about the influence of Woolf on her writing.

22 It is tempting in an exploration of epistolary fiction to make something of this reference to the mail and its importance in the narrator's life. However, Manzini appears to use this reference merely as a means of setting a scene, rather than highlighting the epistolary properties for the text itself.

23 All translations are taken from Martha King's elegant translation of the novel.

24 This episodic and challenging style is perhaps the reason why few of Manzini's works, many of which have won prestigious literary prizes, have
been translated into English; the idea of faithfully reproducing both her
intricate prose and non-linear structure is indeed daunting.

25 Manzini is one of the few nineteenth- or twentieth-century women writers who succeeded in being critiqued in her own right, rather than being
categorized, and therefore marginalized, as a 'female author.' Giovanna
Miceli-Jeffries points out, however, that critics often pointed to Manzini's
delicate and refined prose, subtly marking her as a 'female' writer. But
overall, she was not as pigeon-holed into the category of 'woman author'
as her contemporaries. It would be encouraging to believe that the critical
establishment was able to evaluate her work on gender-neutral grounds
because of its astonishing complexity, inventiveness, and insight into
contemporary artistic debates, but I suspect these critics were reacting in
part to the lack of emphasis on specifically female-centred themes in her
texts. See Miceli-Jeffries's discussion of this in 'Gianna Manzini,' *Dictionary
of Literary Biography*, vol 177, *Italian Novelists since World War II, 1945–1965*,
ed. Augustus Pallotta (Detroit: Gale Research, 1997).

26 As Geno Pampaloni points out about Manzini's artistry: 'Il suo lavoro
non è frammentistico; ma consiste al contrario nell'aggiungere, depositare
realtà su realtà, piano su piano, rifrazione su rifrazione' (44) ['Her work
is not fragmentary; but it consists on the contrary in adding, deposit-
ing reality on reality, story on story, refraction on refraction']. Pampaloni
does not go so far as to call *Lettere all'editore* a letter text, but clearly he has
recognized its epistolarity. See Pampaloni, 'Per Gianna Manzini,' in *Gianna
Manzini tra Letteratura e Vita*, ed. Marco Forti (Milan: Mondadori, 1985),
39–46.

3. Making Connections

1 For an examination of the relationship between de Céspedes's work with
Radio Bari, *Mercurio*, and her literary production, see Ellen Nerenberg,
'Resistance and Remorse: Alba de Céspedes's Withdrawal from the Public
Sphere,' in *Writing beyond Fascism: Cultural Resistance in the Life and Works of
Alba de Céspedes*, ed. Carole Gallucci and Nerenberg (Madison, NJ: Fair-
leigh Dickinson University Press, 2000), 223–46, and Elena Gagliardi, '*Il
rimorso* di Alba de Céspedes: Ipotesi sul romanzo epistolare del novecento,'
Il lettore di provincia 30 (1999): 3–24.

2 In an interview with Piera Carroli, De Céspedes discussed how narrative
structure took precedence when she began a new work: '[L]o stile è sempre

la prima cosa, lo stile è il taglio del libro' (182) ['Style is always the first thing, style is the cut of the book']. When asked if the structure of a novel should reflect its content, the author answered: 'Questo a un vero scrittore viene naturale' (192) ['To a true writer this comes naturally']. See Carroli, *Esperienza e narrazione nella scrittura di Alba de Céspedes* (Ravenna: Longo, 1993).

3 Despite the success of leftist groups in driving the Germans out of Italy after the armistice of 1943, conservative political parties, supported by the Catholic Church, quickly consolidated power in post-war Italy, forming governments and generally endorsing an ideology that many felt was anti thetical to the values of the partisan movement. In *Il rimorso*, Guglielmo has become a political force in the rightist government, and his newspaper is a leading proponent of its agenda. For more on the politics of the immediate postwar era, see Paul Ginsborg's socio-political histories: *A History of Contemporary Italy: Society and Politics 1943–1988* (London: Penguin, 1990) and *Italy and Its Discontents: Family, Civil Society, State: 1980–2001* (New York: Palgrave Macmillan, 2003).

4 All translations are from William Weaver's translation of the novel.

5 Those expectations are voiced by Rinaldo, Isabella's husband, in two letters to Francesca at the end of the novel. Although it is clear that Isabella committed suicide, Rinaldo does not accept that she would take her own life; she was too pious, he believes, and too devoted a mother and wife to commit that particular religious and familial offence. But there are hints in his letters that despite Rinaldo's devotion to her, he was also patronizing and restrictive. He refused to allow Isabella to drive, or recognize that she might have had interests or needs not met by her family. He blames her recent agitation on hormonal changes, rather than any psychic condition. Finally, Rinaldo did not take his wife seriously, writing: 'Mi domando se Isabella non avesse un segreto che la angustiava. Forse, un sentimento. (Di più no, è da escludere: non ha mai capito niente di certe cose, era una bambina)' (564). ['I wonder if Isabella had some secret that was tormenting her. Perhaps some sentimental thing (no more than that; anything else would be impossible, since she never understood certain matters; she was like a child') (385)].

6 Francesca has asked Isabella to save her letters, and then to send them to Guglielmo after she leaves him; through her letters her husband will understand why she has left. The letters, then, are to act as an intermediary between this couple, who are no longer capable of communicating directly or honestly.

7 Isabella's questionable ethics are documented in an earlier letter to Franc-

esca, when she writes, 'Non è poi tanto importante, la verità: il modo stesso di dirla la trasforma. Importanti sono le intenzioni' (150) ['The truth isn't so important, after all – the very way you tell it changes it. Intentions are important' (98)].

8 Guglielmo is fifty-two years old; the other three protagonists are in their middle to late thirties.

9 The sterility of their marriage is represented by the death of their only child, Lionello, whose upbringing, as appropriate for a family of that social and economic class, was left primarily in the hands of nannies.

Interestingly, Isabella is convinced that her second son was sired by Guglielmo, rather than her husband. She cannot, of course, acknowledge his true parentage, as that would unmask the duplicity on which she has fabricated her life. Her letters to Guglielmo remain the only safe place in which to discuss their son.

10 Francesca's precarious legal and economic situation is underscored in many of the letters. The events of the novel take place before the legalization of divorce in Italy, and Guglielmo is within his legal rights to fight her decision to leave. Over the course of her correspondence, Francesca comes to realize that despite Guglielmo's wealth, she has no money of her own, and any attempt at earning some (her husband wants to set her up in a bookshop) would be subsidized by Guglielmo. In one of her more defiant acts toward the end of the novel, she sells the only thing of value she has: a pair of earrings left to her by her mother. Francesca writes that 'È la prima volta che ho danaro [sic] mio in tasca da quando mi sono sposata. … Mi pare insieme inebriante e disonesto' (495) ['This is the first time I've had money of my own in my purse since I was married … It seems intoxicating to me, and at the same time, dishonest' (337)].

11 It is fitting that the only extended correspondence Guglielmo participates in is with Isabella, for the two share an affinity for and understanding of the conventionality of contemporary society. Like Isabella's, Guglielmo's mask of virtue is also unveiled in his letters; in one, he describes with no sense of irony both his visits to the confessional and his regular trips to brothels, where he prefers younger girls.

A letter also plays a decisive role in their amorous relationship, which occurred years before this current exchange. Isabella recalls how he continued their clandestine meetings only until he was able to get his hands on an incriminating letter; having received it from her, he ripped it up and then told her '"Adesso è finita. Basta. Non potevo troncare finché questa lettera era nella tue mani"' (466) ['"Now it's over. Finished. I couldn't break it off until this letter was in my hands"' (316)].

12 Maria Rosaria Vitti-Alexander convincingly traces the trajectory of de
Céspedes's heroines as they mirror the changes in female expectations,
participating in the 'lotta continua ... per un posto dignitoso nella società
in cui vive' (103) ['continual struggle ... for a dignified place in the society
in which we live']. See 'Il passaggio del ponte: L'evoluzione del personaggio femminile di Alba de Céspedes,' *Campi immaginabili* 3 (1991): 103–12.

13 Like the epistolary genre, the diary novel has traditionally been linked
with female authors, for it emphasizes a personal and intimate mode of
writing. For a discussion of this see Cynthia Huff's '"That Profoundly
Female, and Feminist Genre": The Diary as Feminist Practice,' *Women's
Studies Quarterly* 17 (1989): 6–14. For more general examinations of the
diary text, see Lorna Martens's *The Diary Novel* (Cambridge: Cambridge
University Press, 1985) and Trevor Field's *Form and Function in the Diary
Novel* (Totowa, NJ: Barnes and Noble, 1989), which includes a discussion of
de Céspedes's *Il quaderno proibito*.

14 Other critics, such as Gagliardi and Carroli, have pointed out how the
epistolary structure of *Il rimorso*, with its discrete bits of letters and journal
entries, mirrors the fragmentary nature of contemporary relationships.

15 In Gerardo's case, that means breaking it off with the frivolous Gigliola,
the daughter of a rich industrialist, who represents the corruption of contemporary society.

16 The urgency Francesca feels toward her authorial aspirations is revealed
by the few items that she takes when she finally leaves Guglielmo: paja-
mas, toiletries, and her typewriter.

17 There are a number of excellent studies of Italy in the 1960s and 1970s.
Along with Ginsborg's works, see the collection of essays found in David
Forgacs and Robert Lumley's *Italian Cultural Studies: An Introduction*
(Oxford: Oxford University Press, 1996). Jennifer Burns's *Fragments of
impegno: Interpretations of Commitment in Contemporary Italian Narrative,
1980–2000* (Leeds: Northern University Press, 2001) brings the discussion
up to date with a look at the politics and literature of Italy from 1980 to
2000.

    Ginzburg's 'profound historical pessimism' has been noted by many
critics and reviewers. Although her works rarely comment directly on
specific socio-cultural events or movements unfolding contemporane-
ously with her fictional narratives, they are infused with a general sense
of anxiety about the outside world. As Judith Laurence Pastore writes,
'Ginzburg's career personifies the fusion of political events with artistic
concerns, a fusion found again and again in her writings' (89). See 'The
Personal Is Political: Gender, Generation, and Memory in Natalia Ginz-

burg's *Caro Michele*,' in *Natalia Ginzburg: A Voice of the Twentieth Century*, ed. Angela Jeannet and Giuliana Sanguinetti Katz (Toronto: University of Toronto Press, 2000), 89–98.

18 Ginzburg told one interviewer, '[B]y means of letters in my epistolary novel, *The City and the House*, I am able to get inside more "I"s. In this way I arrive at a sort of panoramic view by using a variety of first persons' (137). See Peg Boyers, 'An Interview with Natalia Ginzburg' *Salmagundi* 96 (1992): 130–56. Multiple narrators fit easily within the epistolary structure; in *Caro Michele*, nine characters write letters, each with a linguistic register particular to its author. *La città e la casa* also features a choral structure.

19 Ginzburg (1916–1991) was born Natalia Levi. Her first husband, Leone Ginzburg, was arrested for his anti-Fascist activities and subsequently died of injuries received under torture by the Nazis. She worked for the Einaudi publishing house, remarried, produced a great number of volumes of prose, and was elected to the Italian parliament in 1983 representing an independent left-wing party. For more on Ginzburg's personal and literary history see Aine O'Healy, 'A Woman Writer in Contemporary Italy: Natalia Ginzburg,' Ph.D. diss., University of Wisconsin-Madison, 1976, and Alan Bullock, *Natalia Ginzburg: Human Relationships in a Changing World* (New York: Berg, 1991).

20 See Rebecca West's illuminating introduction to Angela Jeannet and Giuliana Sanguinetti Katz's collection of essays on Ginzburg. West traces a revision in the often misogynistic attitude toward those (primarily female) writers who focused on the personal and the domestic in their work. Today those very attributes are 'investigated from critical perspectives that validate these areas, not only in and of themselves but also as they are imbricated in greater historical and ideological abstractions' (*Natalia Ginzburg*, 7).

21 *Caro Michele* also contains several chapters of straight narrative and dialogue, presumably to include information not mentioned in the letters themselves.

22 She said very succinctly in 1975, 'È così: io lo penso veramente che viviamo in un tempo dove non c'è futuro' (84) ['That's how it is: I really think that we live in a time that has no future']. See Sandra Bonsanti, 'C'era una volta la famiglia,' *Epoca* 1313 (1975): 83–6.

23 All translations are from Sheila Cudahy's translation of the novel.

24 Osvaldo shows up frequently in the narrated sections of the novel, and is referred to often in the letters of others. He participates actively in the lives of the other characters, and is clearly one of the few in the novel capable of communication and understanding.

25 This is made even more apparent because unlike *Caro Michele* this novel is completely composed of letters. There are no expository chapters with a third-person narrator explaining the connections among the main characters. Here, as Teresa Picarazzi writes, 'the letters themselves carry the stories' (171). See *Maternal Desire: Natalia Ginzburg's Mothers, Daughters, and Sisters* (Madison, NJ: Fairleigh Dickinson University Press, 2002).

26 All translations are from Dick Davis's translation of the novel.

27 Judith Laurence Pastore believes the lack of a parental figure is explicitly linked to the narrative structure. She writes, 'This loss of traditional parental authority is echoed in Ginzburg's style where the narrator simply presents the surface of events, refusing to make any authorial comment – author as parent refusing to take responsibility for her creation' (317). See 'The Sounds of Silence: The Absence of Narrative Presence in Natalia Ginzburg's *La città e la casa*,' *Italian Culture* 11 (1993): 311–22. I would posit instead that while the author may not directly intervene in the work, she certainly shapes the epistolary exchanges in the text, acting as *uber*-parental figure by pulling the threads that bind the characters together.

28 The novel is marked by an alarmingly high number of such untimely deaths; during the two-and-a-half-year time span, we are witness to the loss of Ferruccio, Anne Marie, Nadia, Lucrezia's infant, and Alberico. Ginzburg seems to be underscoring the fragility of human existence against what she saw as the widespread violence of modern society.

29 Alan Bullock notes that Ginzburg 'is plainly still convinced that, as she had already shown in *Dear Michael*, close contact between parents and children is only possible when, paradoxically, they are prevented from meeting face to face and obliged to rely on methods supposedly less intimate but in effect more conducive to genuine communication of emotions and states of mind' (235). See *Natalia Ginzburg: Human Relationships in a Changing World* (New York: Berg, 1991). I agree, and would add that the choice of narrative structure becomes crucial to our understanding of the text.

4. Addressing Women

1 The modern feminist movement in Italy was rooted in the active role many women played in the Resistance during the Second World War, in the formation of the women's group *Unione donne italiane* in 1944, and finally in the 1945 law granting women's suffrage. In the 1960s and 1970s, the feminist movement was part of a period of national transformation, when students, workers, and finally women fought to achieve recognition and reform. The period was marked by a series of legal gains, including

laws guaranteeing the right to birth control information (1971), divorce (legalized in 1970 and upheld by popular referendum in 1974), family law reform (1975), abortion (legalized in 1978 and upheld by popular referendum in 1981), and salary parity (1977). All of these advancements were hard won, as women struggled to challenge centuries of entrenched patriarchy, sustained to a large degree by the Catholic Church.

A number of excellent studies on the Italian women's movement are available. I recommend in particular *La liberazione della donna: Feminism in Italy*, by Lucia Chiavola Birnbaum (Middleton, CT: Wesleyan University Press, 1986) for a historical overview of the movement. For works specifically related to feminist literature, see Adalgisa Giorgio's essay 'The Novel, 1965–2000,' in *A History of Women's Writing in Italy*, ed. Letizia Panizza and Sharon Wood (Cambridge: Cambridge University Press, 2000) and 'Feminist Writing in the Twentieth Century,' by Sharon Wood, in *The Cambridge Companion to the Italian Novel*, ed. Peter Bondanella and Andrea Ciccarelli (Cambridge: Cambridge University Press, 2003). For an examination of the philosophical and theoretical underpinnings of Italian feminism, see *Sexual Difference: A Theory of Social-Symbolic Practice*, by the Milan Women's Bookstore Collective (Bloomington, IN: Indiana University Press, 1990); *Italian Feminist Thought: A Reader*, ed. Paola Bono and Sandra Kemp (Oxford: Basil Blackwell, 1991); and *Italian Feminist Theory and Practice: Equality and Sexual Difference*, ed. Graziella Parati and Rebecca West (Madison, NJ: Fairleigh Dickinson University Press, 2002).

2 See the introduction to Giancarlo Lombardi's *Rooms with a View: Feminist Diary Fiction, 1952–1999* (Madison, NJ: Fairleigh Dickinson University Press, 2002) for a brief overview of the evolution of Italian, European, British, and American women's literature, especially as it pertains to the epistolary novel's literary sister, the diary text.

3 Interestingly, Manzoni himself was the subject of a historical work that borrows from the epistolary, Natalia Ginzburg's *La famiglia Manzoni* (1983) (*The Manzoni Family*). The text is a biography of Manzoni's large family, related through third-person narrative linked together with excerpts from their letters. Ginzburg told one interviewer that the text is an attempt to create a 'fresco of the whole family, a family biography' (148). See Peg Boyers, 'An Interview with Natalia Ginzburg' *Salmagundi* 96 (1992): 130–56. The letters in this work become an important source of information and a means through which the reader can more intimately and thoroughly know the characters.

4 For more on the Italian historical novel, see Cristina Della Coletta's *Plotting the Past: Metamorphoses of Historical Narrative in Modern Italian Fiction* (West

Lafayette, IN: Purdue University Press, 1996), which offers in the introduction a solid analysis of the genre. For an examination of historical novels
by Italian women, see the essays in *Gendering Italian Fiction: Feminist
Revisions of Italian History*, ed. Maria Ornella Marotti and Gabriella Brooke
(Madison, NJ: Fairleigh Dickinson University Press, 1999). Marotti's introduction to *Gendering Italian Fiction* describes in detail how women authors
have re-envisioned the historical novel.

5 Few authors have explored – through the forum of historical fiction, at
least – the female contribution to the period of Italian unification. Rosa
Maria Cutrufelli comes close, with her 1990 novel *La brigante* (*The Brigand*)
(Palermo: La Luna), which describes the exploits of Margherita, a noblewoman who joins up with a group of brigands in southern Italy. Monica
Rossi, in 'Rethinking History: Women's Transgression in Maria Rosa
Cutrufelli's *La brigante*,' provides an interesting discussion of how both
this character and this text present a transgressive vision of Italian history.
She also includes an interview with Cutrufelli, who speaks to the necessity
of re-examining accepted history through a female perspective. See the
essay in *Gendering Italian Fiction*, ed. Marotti and Brooke, 202–2.

6 In his essay 'Rethinking the Risorgimento?' John A. Davis looks in particular at the new social, political, and cultural histories of Italy, concluding that as part of a general 'revisionist enterprise' they have generated
new insights into the role played by social and economic class, gender,
and geographic location in the country's march from unification toward
modernization (27). In *Risorgimento in Modern Italian Culture: Revisiting
the Nineteenth-Century Past in History, Narrative, and Cinema*, ed. Norma
Bouchard (Madison, NJ: Fairleigh Dickinson University Press, 2005), 27–53.
Davis argues that these new explorations may rob the Risorgimento of its
'thematic unity' but in return allow the period of unification to be woven
more thoroughly and successfully into an understanding of the early
modern world (47). Both fictional and non-fictional texts, as Bouchard and
Davis point out, have contributed to a paradigm shift in the way Italian
unification is portrayed and interpreted by exploring and recognizing the
role played by marginalized groups during the Risorgimento.

7 The opportunity to reimagine the world of her ancestors may have been
the impulse behind Bossi Fedrigotti's text; indeed, the first letter in the
text is authentic. In it her great-grandfather writes to his mother about his
upcoming marriage to Leopoldina.

8 Fedrigo's letters also reveal a man unable to fit the mould of masculinity. He is not a natural-born soldier, but timid and cautious, more content
to tend to his estate than fight battles. Indeed, the author notes as she

describes his official portrait that while he bears the uniform and weaponry of the Hussars, behind this garb lies the 'timidezza di chi si sente fuori posto in ogni posto' (10) ['timidity of one who feels out of place everywhere'].

9 This defiance does not extend into a general revolt against all social structures, however, for while Leopoldina may criticize the prescriptions of her world she still wants to preserve the privileges afforded by her social class. Ironically, it is those privileges – title, wealth, and education – that allow her to express her reservations about those limitations on female behaviour.

10 For a discussion of the ideology concerning women in the unification period see Michela De Giorgio, *Le italiane dall'Unità a oggi: Modelli culturali e comportamenti sociali* (Rome: Laterza, 1992). Alberto Mario Banti has an excellent overview of how women (and men) were defined in culturally specific terms. See *Il Risorgimento italiano* (Rome: Laterza, 2004).

11 As Lucia Re writes, women, it was maintained during this period, were to redirect any 'unruly passion' into the 'domestic and respectable feelings of spousal and maternal love.' Unchecked passion was viewed as 'excessive, transgressive, dangerous,' and a threat to the established social order of male primacy (173). See 'Passion and Sexual Difference: The Risorgimento and the Gendering of Writing in Nineteenth Century Italian Culture,' in *Making and Remaking Italy: The Cultivation of National Identity around the Risorgimento*, ed. Alberto Ascoli and Krystyna von Henneberg (Oxford: Berg, 2001), 155–200.

12 It is significant that the novel opens with a letter commending Leopoldina for embodying the traditional tenets of femininity and then goes on to frame the second half of the narrative around her transgression of that ideal. The epistolary format reinforces the thematic content of the novel, a convergence that then returns to the very foundation of a text rooted in correspondence.

13 Luchino Visconti's film *Senso* also subverts unification ideology by casting its romantic hero as an Austrian soldier. See Millicent Marcus's examination of the film in her article 'Visconti's *Senso*: The Risorgimento According to Gramsci or Historical Revisionism Meets Cinematic Innovation,' in *Making and Remaking Italy*, ed. Ascoli and von Henneberg, 277–96.

14 In one letter, written at the outset of the war, Leopoldina writes to her mother of her disgust with all those responsible for the military conflict, 'che mandi al diavolo tutti insieme, Bismarck e Napoleone, Vittorio Emanuele e Garibaldi' (61) ['send Bismarck, Napoleon, Vittorio Emanuele and Garibaldi all to hell']. Despite the privileges of her class, she is as helpless as any other citizen when it comes to the machinations of those in

power. Indeed, perhaps because Leopoldina is privileged, she has more to lose from the unification.

15 To be sure, Bossi Fedrigotti's main characters belong to a advantaged, moneyed class, and are hardly representative of the thousands from the unschooled lower classes who sacrificed their lives fighting for (or against) the unification of Italy. As an officer Fedrigo is granted some degree of protection from the more horrific conditions of war. But the letters do hint of the slow death of this social class, as both Leopoldina and Fedrigo describe the erosion of its traditions and – perhaps more importantly – its financial capital.

16 I argue in an article that through the epistolary structure of *Amore mio uccidi Garibaldi* we can find parallels between the moment in which the text was written – the 1970s, when in Italy many disenfranchised groups struggled to make their stories heard – and the Risorgimento. See 'Rewriting the Risorgimento: Isabella Bossi Fedrigotti's *Amore mio uccidi Garibaldi*,' *Forum Italicum* 42 (2008): 83–98.

17 See John Gatt-Rutter, *Oriana Fallaci: The Rhetoric of Freedom* (Oxford: Berg, 1996) for a discussion of Fallaci's early years.

18 She made this clear in an interview after the publication of *Lettera a un bambino mai nato*. When the interviewer asked Fallaci if she was the mother in the book, she responded by pointing to Flaubert's self-identification with the heroine of *Madame Bovary*. 'Certamente: lo sono. Come sono il dottore e la dottoressa, il padre del bambino, l'amica. ... E comunque sono il bambino. Ma questo è banale e inevitabile'['Certainly: it is me. Just as I am the male and female doctors, the father of the child, the friend ... and I am even the child. But this is trivial and inevitable']. See Patrizia Carrano, *Le signore grandi firme* (Florence: Guaraldi, 1978), 91.

Fallaci said in interviews that the novel's plot was loosely based on her own miscarriages. Although she never had children, she wrote that her books were like offspring to her: 'Io quando scrivo un libro lo fo [*sic*] sempre nella speranza di lasciare un figlio quando morrò. ... Finché vivo, ci sono io che faccio tanto fracasso anche se sto zitta da non aver bisogno di bambini. Ma quando muoio, ecco, quando muoio vorrei proprio lasciare un bambino vivo. Almeno di carta' (91) ['When I write a book I always do it in the hope of leaving an offspring when I die. As long as I'm living, I make a lot of noise even if I'm quiet about not having the need for children. But when I die, there it is, when I die, I would like to leave a living child. At least one made of paper']. See Carrano, *Le signore grandi firme*.

19 Santo Aricò, who has written sensitively on several of Fallaci's other works, seems especially concerned with examining the novel through a

reading of the author's biography. 'She observed, listened, spied, and stole from life to refashion the souvenirs into a new unity,' he writes (171). This reductionist reading overlooks the stylistic and thematic contributions this text made to Italian literature. See *Oriana Fallac:. The Woman and the Myth* (Carbondale, IL: Southern Illinois University Press, 1998).

Claire Marrone's thoughtful examination of this novel, and, coincidentally, of Aleramo's *Una donna*, approaches the text as an autobiographical *bildungsroman*, calling it a 'mélange of fact and fiction' (108). Marrone is careful not to confuse the novel's protagonist with its author, and instead points out its universal appeal, noting that '[r]ather than the autobiographical story of an individual woman, it is a chapter in a potential biography of contemporary female experience' (116). See *Female Journeys: Autobiographical Expressions by French and Italian Women* (Westport, CT: Greenwood Press, 2000).

20 Interestingly, the English translation of the novel does not break the text into numbered entries, or letters, as the Italian edition does. Instead, it uses asterisks and white space to separate the various entries. The effect of this approach is to create a more diaristic narrative structure, removing it to some degree from the epistolary promise of its title.

21 Fallaci knew that both sides of the abortion issue would exploit the novel as a political tool. 'Una cosa è sicura: nel momento stesso in cui lo scrivevo, il libro, sapevo che sarebbe stato usato e sfruttato da tutti e due' (Ferrieri, 62) ['One thing is sure: even while I was writing the book I knew it would be used and exploited by both sides']. See Giuliano Ferrieri, 'Oriana Fallaci spiega il suo libro,' *L'Europeo* (26 Sept., 1975): 58–62.

All translations are from John Shepley's translation of the novel.

22 Robin Pickering-Iazzi, in her examination of motherhood in Aleramo's *Una donna*, Maraini's *Donna in guerra*, and *Lettera a un bambino mai nato*, notes that the texts have in common 'the adoption of the first-person narrator and compositional techniques typical of autobiography, indicating a movement away from the authority of objectivity, and the rejection of refined stylistic and linguistic forms in favor of a more authentic expressiveness' (326). While Pickering-Iazzi does not specifically address epistolarity, these aforementioned techniques are certainly characteristics common to many letter texts. See 'Designing Mothers: Images of Motherhood in Aleramo, Morante, Maraini, and Fallaci,' *Annali d'Italianistica: Women's Voices in Italian Literature* 7 (1989): 325–40.

23 The father's initial response to the narrator's announcement that she is pregnant is 'What would it take [for an abortion]?' (19).

24 John Gatt-Rutter maintains that the 'competing discourses ... tend to

neutralize one another' (*Oriana Fallaci*, 65). But I would argue instead that the plurality of convictions creates a multi-voiced text that points to how deeply complex and subjective these issues are.

25 For a complete list of Maraini's works, along with translations and literary awards, see the invaluable bibliography in Vera Golina's 2004 translation of *Mio marito*: *My Husband* (Waterloo: Wilfrid Laurier University Press, 2004).

26 See in particular Maraini's updated and translated version of the introduction to her 1987 collection *La bionda, la bruna e l'asino: con gli occhi di oggi sugli anni settanta e ottanta*, entitled 'Reflections on the Logical and Illogical Bodies of My Sexual Compatriots,' in *The Pleasure of Writing: Critical Essays on Dacia Maraini*, ed. Rodica Diaconescu-Blumenfeld and Ada Testaferri (West Lafayette, IN: Purdue University Press, 2000). In this essay she points out that critics seem particularly enraged when modern female authors refuse to write with 'the smiling grace, the innate seductive sweetness, the feminine modesty' of previous generations (25).

27 Her forays into generic experimentation include the diary novels *Memorie di una ladra* (*Memories of a Female Thief*) (1973) and *Donna in guerra* (*Women at War*) (1975), the investigative novel *Isolina: la donna tagliata a pezzi* (*Isolina*) (1985), the historical novel *La lunga vita di Mariana Ucrìa* (*The Silent Duchess*) (1990), the autobiographical *Bagheria* (*Bagheria*) (1993), and the detective thriller *Voci* (*Voices*) (1994). Her use of different genres has generated illuminating discussions of generic choice and gender. See, for example, Carol Lazarro-Weis, *From Margins to Mainstream: Feminism and Fictional Modes in Italian Women's Writing, 1968–1990* (Philadelphia: University of Pennsylvania Press, 1993); Ada Testaferri, 'De-tecting *Voci*,' and Giancarlo Lombardi, '*A memoria*: Charting a Cultural Map for Women's Transition from *Preistoria* to *Storia*,' both in *The Pleasure of Writing*, ed. Diaconescu-Blumenfeld and Testaferri.

Throughout her career, Maraini has also woven women into the official strands of history, whether these figures are historical (Mary Stuart or Veronica Franco), mythical (Clytemnestra), literary (Emma Bovary), or simply the scores of fictitious heroines who populate her works. By recording the lives of these characters – both famous and fictional – Maraini challenges both literary and historical narratives.

28 The translation is by Dick Kitto and Elspeth Spottiswood.

29 For an examination of the rise of literature and critical works addressing alternate female sexualities see Beverly Ballaro, 'Making the Lesbian Body: Writing and Desire in Dacia Maraini's *Lettere a Marina*,' in *Gendered Contexts: New Perspectives in Italian Cultural Studies*, ed. Laura Benedetti,

Julia L. Hairston, and Silvia M. Ross (New York: Peter Lang, 1996). For an examination of lesbianism within the Italian feminist movement, see the corresponding essays in *Italian Feminist Thought: A Reader*, ed. Paola Bono and Sandra Kemp (Oxford: Basil Blackwell, 1991).

30 See, for instance, Bianca's relationships with Marco, her perennially unfaithful ex-lover, and Damiano, the young waiter who breaks up with his stepmother (and Bianca) because he has fallen in love with his aunt.

31 For a reassessment of the practice of *affidamento*, including its potentially negative aspects, see Lucia Re's essay entitled 'Diotima's Dilemmas: Authorship, Authority, Authoritariansim,' in *Italian Feminist Theory and Practice: Equality and Sexual Difference*, ed. Graziella Parati and Rebecca West (Madison, NJ: Fairleigh Dickinson University Press, 2002).

32 This passage was cut from the translated text. The 1987 English translation by Dick Kitto and Elspeth Spottiswood restructures some of the novel to include more obvious textual breaks when dialogue is being cited. Some sentences are also reconfigured and other passages are dropped completely, perhaps to make the work easier to read.

33 Maraini herself creates a female literary genealogy with her frequent reflections in this novel on Emily Dickinson and the poet's critical reception. For an excellent discussion of this aspect of *Lettere a Marina*, see Barbara Zaczek, *Censored Sentiments: Letters and Censorship in Epistolary Novels and Conduct Material* (Newark, DE: University of Delaware Press, 1997).

34 For an illuminating study of contemporary texts by Italian women authors see *A Multitude of Women: The Challenges of the Contemporary Italian Novel*, by Stefania Lucamante (Toronto: University of Toronto Press, 2008).

35 Tamaro's forays in epistolary narrative continued with *Cara Mathilda* (*Dear Mathilda*), a 1997 collection of letters and essays she originally published in the Catholic periodical *Famiglia cristiana*.

36 Giancarlo Lombardi, in his fascinating examination of women's diary fiction, sees *Va' dove ti porta il cuore* as a diary text, rather than an epistolary novel. The two narrative structures share many of the same attributes, but I choose instead to read the work as it is plotted: a one-sided correspondence similar to those found in *Lettere a Marina* and *Lettera a un bambino mai nato*. See *Rooms with a View: Feminist Diary Fiction, 1952–1999* (Madison, NJ: Fairleigh Dickinson University Press, 2002).

37 All translations are from John Cullen's translation of the novel.

38 This seemingly innocuous object has been the subject of debate, with Colleen Ryan calling it 'an instrument of creation' (363). See 'In the Heart of the Nineties: Theorizing a Grandmother's Subjectivity in Two Works by Susanna Tamaro,' *Romance Languages Annual* 10 (1999). Lombardi, how-

ever, writes that it 'symbolizes the life of restraint and captivity destined to those women who had willingly embraced their subjection to patriarchy.' He believes Olga's decision to leave the cake mould to her granddaughter 'signifies her desire to perpetuate the same disempowerment to which she once fell victim' (*Rooms with a View*, 165).

39 All translations are from Dick Kitto and Elspeth Spottiswood's translation of the novel.

40 Laura Benedetti, in her excellent study of motherhood in contemporary Italian women's literature, believes the relationship between Vera and Flavia represents a trend in late twentieth-century novels. These works, she writes, 'replicate the emotional ties of a maternal connection, but ... are established by and between individuals who are not necessarily linked biologically' (121). See *The Tigress in the Snow: Motherhood and Literature in Twentieth-Century Italy* (Toronto: University of Toronto Press, 2007).

41 For more on *affidamento* in this novel see Sylvia Setzkorn's 'Geschlechterdifferenzen und Post-Feminismus in Italien: *Dolce per sé* von Dacia Maraini.' In *Geschlecterdiffern-zen*, ed. Katharina Hanau and Volker Rivinius (Bonn: Romanisticher Verlag, 1999).

42 In this poem, Maraini has one male critic saying 'Le poesie delle donne sono spesso / piatte, ingenue, realistiche e ossessive' (28) ['Poetry by women is often / flat, naïve, realistic, and obsessive']. Unlike works by men, he continues, female-authored poems '[m]ancano di leggerezza, di fumo, di vanità' ['lack lightness, fumes, vanity'].

43 This inclusionary politics goes beyond the human sphere to include all living creatures. Vera often refers to the various animals, including bats, cats, mice, and wild boar, that make up Flavia's 'piccole mitologie familiari' (16) ['little family myths' (11)]. An entire letter is devoted to the description of an abused donkey, foregrounding the ideas of ecofeminism, which argues that animals are as deserving of liberation from repressive social, cultural, legal, and political institutions as other oppressed groups. In her novel, Maraini refuses to differentiate between the species, even identifying her protagonist with the abused animal. Flavia clearly inherits these beliefs, for at the end of the text her uncle reports that she 'thinks only about animals' (172). See Lori Gruen, 'Dismantling Oppression: An Analysis of the Connection between Women and Animals,' in *Ecofeminism: Women, Animals, Nature*, ed. Greta Gaard (Philadelphia: Temple University Press, 1993) for a more complete analysis of the connections among feminist theory, environmentalism, and animal rights.

44 For example, Vera reveals to Flavia the language of love, whether it is the nonsensical argot shared by lovers, or the special idioms created by

families. Vera writes that the language she shared with her lover Edoardo included adding 'ero' to the endings of words to make them more fantastical. 'Così, per esempio, lui dice: "Andiamero al cinemero" e io rispondo: "Quale filmero vuoi vederero"' (14). ['So he would say, "Let's go to the cinemero." And I would reply, "Do you want to see that filmero?"' (9)]. The grammatically correct rendition would be 'Andiamo al cinema,' and 'Quale film vuoi vedere.'

45 Even silence has its place in the author's linguistic register. In the novel *La lunga vita di Marianna Ucrìa*, the deaf-mute protagonist learns to voice her subjectivity through non-traditional means of expression. In *Dolce per sé*, silence serves as a weightier motif, for Vera's sister is stricken with a terminal disease affecting her throat, and can only communicate through notes and gestures.

46 Elizabeth MacArthur, whose study focuses on the resolutions of letter texts, believes the epistolary form has been denigrated in part because canonic literature often emphasizes the importance of endings 'in giving shape and meaning to stories' (3). She argues that our definition of narrative must be expanded to accommodate non-traditional literary patterns. See *Extravagant Narratives: Closure and Dynamics in the Epistolary Form* (Princeton: Princeton University Press, 1990).

Works Cited

Abbott, H. Porter, *Diary Fiction: Writing as Action*. Ithaca: Cornell University Press, 1984.

Aleramo, Sibilla. *Amo dunque sono*. Rome: Feltrinelli, 1998.

– *Una donna*. Turin: Sten, 1906.

– *Trasfigurazione (Lettera non spedita)*. With an introduction by Primo Conti. Rome: Riuniti, 1987.

Alesi, Donatella. 'La Marchesa Colombi e Matilde Serao: due giornaliste a confronto.' In *La Marchesa Colombi: Una scrittrice e il suo tempo*, edited by Silvia Benatti and Roberto Cicala. Novara: Interlinea, 2001. 205–14.

Alliston, April. *Virtue's Faults: Correspondences in Eighteenth-Century British and French Women's Fiction*. Stanford: Stanford University Press, 1996.

Altman, Janet Gurkin. *Epistolarity: Approaches to a Form*. Columbus: Ohio State University Press, 1982.

Amatangelo, Susan. *Figuring Women: A Thematic Study of Giovanni Verga's Female Characters*. Madison, NJ: Fairleigh Dickinson University Press, 2004.

Amoia, Alba. *Twentieth-Century Italian Women Writers: The Feminine Experience*. Carbondale, IL: Southern Illinois University Press, 1996.

Aricò, Santo L. *Oriana Fallaci: The Woman and the Myth*. Carbondale, IL: Southern Illinois University Press, 1998.

Arslan, Antonia. 'Ideologia e autorappresentazione: Donne intellettuali fra Ottocento e Novecento.' In *Svelamento: Silbilla Aleramo: una biografia intellettuale*, edited by Annarita Buttafuoco and Marina Zancan. Milan: Feltrinelli, 1988. 164–77.

– 'L'opera della Marchesa Colombi nel panorama della narrativa Italiana fra otto e novecento.' In *La Marchesa Colombi: Una scrittrice e il suo tempo*, edited by Silvia Benatti and Roberto Cicala. Novara: Interlinea, 2001. 11–22.

Ballaro, Beverly. 'Making the Lesbian Body: Writing and Desire in Dacia

Maraini's *Lettere a Marina*.' In *Gendered Contexts: New Perspectives in Italian Cultural Studies*, edited by Laura Benedetti, Julia L. Hairston, Silvia M. Ross. Studies in Italian Culture Literature in History, vol. 10. New York: Peter Lang, 1996. 177–87.

Banti, Alberto Mario. *Il Risorgimento italiano*. Rome: Laterza, 2004.

Barbarulli, Clotilde, Mara Baronti, Sandra Cammelli, Noemi Piccardi, Silvia Porto, Alessandra Vannoni, eds. *La finestra, l'attesa, la scrittura: ragnatele del sé in epistolari femminili dell'800*. Ferrara: Luciana Tufani Editrice, 1997.

Barbarulli, Clotilde, and Luciana Brandi. 'La sovversione del sorriso: L'ironia nella Marchesa Colombi.' In *La Marchese Colombi: Una scrittrice e il suo tempo*, edited by Silvia Benatti and Roberto Cicala. Novara: Interlinea, 2001. 139–55.

Barreno, Maria, Maria Teresa Horta, and Maria Velho da Costa. *New Portuguese Letters*. Translated by Helen R. Lane and Faith Gillespie. London: Readers International, 1994.

Beebee, Thomas O. *Epistolary Fiction in Europe, 1500–1850*. Cambridge: Cambridge University Press, 1999.

Benedetti, Laura. *The Tigress in the Snow: Motherhood and Literature in Twentieth-Century Italy*. Toronto: University of Toronto Press, 2007.

Bentivoglio, Mirella, and Franca Zoccoli. *The Women Artists of Italian Futurism – Almost Lost to History*. New York: Midmarch Arts Press, 1997.

Beverly, Julie. 'I luoghi del cuore e le molte verità: an introduction to the novels of Isabella Bossi Fedrigotti.' *Tuttitalia* 11 (1995): 35–9.

Birnbaum, Lucia Chiavola. *La liberazione della donna: Feminism in Italy*. Middletown, CT: Wesleyan University Press, 1986.

Blum, Cinzia Sartini. 'Benedetta's Emphatic Journey to Transcendence.' Catalogue for exhibition at The Galleries at Moore, Philadelphia, 8 Sept.25 Oct. 1998. 25–30.

– *The Other Modernism: F.T. Marinetti's Futurist Fiction of Power*. Berkeley: University of California Press, 1996.

Bondanella, Peter, and Andrea Ciccarelli, eds. *The Cambridge Companion to the Italian Novel*. Cambridge: Cambridge University Press, 2003.

Bondoc, Anna and Meg Daly, eds. *Letters of Intent: Women Cross the Generations to Talk about Family, Work, Sex, Love and the Future of Feminism*. New York: Free Press, 1999.

Bono, Paola, and Sandra Kemp, eds. *Italian Feminist Thought: A Reader*. Oxford: Basil Blackwell, 1991.

Bonsanti, Sandra. 'C'era una volta la famiglia.' *Epoca* 1313 (1975): 83–6.

Bossi Fedrigotti, Isabella. *Amore mio uccidi Garibaldi*. Milan: Longanesi, 1980.

Bouchard, Norma, ed. *Risorgimento in Modern Italian Culture: Revisiting the Nineteenth-Century Past in History, Narrative, and Cinema*. Madison, NJ: Fairleigh Dickinson University Press, 2005.

Bower, Anne. *Epistolary Responses: The Letter in 20th-Century American Fiction and Criticism*. Tuscaloosa: University of Alabama Press, 1997.

Boyers, Peg. 'An Interview with Natalia Ginzburg.' *Salmagundi* 96 (1992): 130–56.

Brizio-Skov, Flavia. 'Si sta facendo sempre più tardi, *Autobiografie altrui* e *Tristano muore* di Antonio Tabucchi: Dove va il romanzo?' *Italica* 83 (2006): 666–90.

Brown, John L. 'What Ever Happened to Mme de Sévigné? Reflections on the Fate of the Epistolary Art in a Media Age.' *World Literature Today* 64 (1990): 215–20.

Bullock, Alan. *Natalia Ginzburg: Human Relationships in a Changing World*. New York: Berg, 1991.

Burns, Jennifer. *Fragments of impegno: Interpretations of Commitment in Contemporary Italian Narrative, 1980–2000*. Leeds: Northern University Press, 2001.

Cammelli, Sandra, and Silvia Porto, eds. *Tra amiche. Epistolari femminili fra Otto e Novecento*. Florence: Rivista Nuova, 2005.

Campbell, Elizabeth. 'Re-visions, Re-flections, Re-creations: Epistolarity in Novels by Contemporary Women.' *Twentieth Century Literature* 41 (1995): 332–48.

Carrano, Patrizia. *Le signore grandi firme*. Florence: Guaraldi, 1978. 69–102.

Carroli, Piera. *Esperienza e narrazione nella scrittura di Alba de Céspedes*. Ravenna: Longo, 1993.

Cecchi, Emilio. *Di giorno in giorno: Note di letteratura italiana contemporanea (1943–54)*. Rome: Garzanti, 1954. 6–9.

Ceserani, Remo, and Pierluigi Pellini. 'The Belated Development of a Theory of the Novel in Italian Literary Culture.' In *The Cambridge Companion to the Italian Novel*, edited by Peter Bondanella and Andrea Ciccarelli. Cambridge: Cambridge University Press, 2003. 1–19.

Cherewatuk, Karen, and Ulrike Wiethaus, eds. *Dear Sister: Medieval Women and the Epistolary Genre*. Middle Ages Series. Philadelphia: University of Pennsylvania Press, 1993.

Cigliana, Simona. 'Il seme e la rosa: Benedetta o la poesia delle Forze cosmiche.' Introduction to *Le forze umane, Viaggio di Gararà, Astra e il sottomarino*, by Benedetta Cappa Marinetti. Rome: Altana, 1998. 9–42.

Crocenzi, Lilia. *Narratrici d'oggi: De Céspedes, Cialente, Morante, Ginzburg, Salinas-Donghi, Muccini*. Cremona: Mangiarotti, 1966. 5–38.

Cutrufelli, Maria Rosa. *La briganta*. Palermo: La Luna, 1990.

Dagnino, Pauline. 'Fra Madre e Marito: The Mother/Daughter Relationship in Dacia Maraini's *Lettere a Marina*.' In *Visions and Revisions: Women in Italian Culture*, edited by Mirna Cicioni and Nicole Prunster. Oxford: Berg, 1993. 183–97.

Davis, John A. 'Rethinking the Risorgimento?' In *Risorgimento in Modern Italian Culture: Revisiting the Nineteenth-Century Past in History, Narrative, and Cinema*, edited by Norma Bouchard. Madison, NJ: Fairleigh Dickinson University Press, 2005. 27–53.

De Céspedes, Alba. *Il rimorso*. Milan: Mondadori, 1967.

– *Remorse*. Translated by William Weaver. Westport. CT: Greenwood, 1967.

De Giorgio, Michela. *Le italiane dall'Unità a oggi: Modelli culturali e comportamenti sociali*. Rome: Laterza, 1992. 3–38.

De Grazia, Victoria. *How Fascism Ruled Women: Italy, 1922–1945*. Berkeley: University of California Press, 1992.

Della Coletta, Cristina. *Plotting the Past: Metamorphoses of Historical Narrative in Modern Italian Fiction*. West Lafayette, IN: Purdue University Press, 1996.

Diaconescu-Blumenfeld, Rodica. Introduction to *The Pleasure of Writing: Critical Essays on Dacia Maraini*, edited by Rodica Diaconescu-Blumenfeld and Ada Testaferri. West Lafayette, IN: Purdue University Press, 2000. 3–20.

Emilia: Le parole nascoste. Preface by Saverio Tutino. Milan: Rosellina Archinto, 1987.

Fallaci, Oriana. *Lettera a un bambino mai nato*. Milan: BUR, 1997.

– *Letters to a Child Never Born*. Translated by John Shepley. New York: Simon and Schuster, 1975.

Fanning, Ursula. *Gender Meets Genre: Woman as Subject in the Fictional Universe of Matilde Serao*. Dublin: Irish Academic Press, 2002.

Fava Guzzetta, Lia. 'Gianna Manzini e la forma-romanzo.' In *Gianna Manzini tra Letteratura e Vita*, edited by Marco Forti. Milan: Mondadori, 1985. 145–63.

– *Gianna Manzini*. Florence: La Nuova Italia, 1974.

Favret, Mary A. *Romantic Correspondence: Women, Politics and the Fiction of Letters*. Cambridge: Cambridge University Press, 1993.

Fazio, Margherita di. *La lettera e il romanzo: Esempi di comunicazione epistolare nella narrativa*. Rome: Nuova Arnica, 1996.

Ferrieri, Giuliano. 'Oriana Fallaci spiega il suo libro.' *L'Europeo* (26 Sept. 1975): 58–62.

Field, Trevor. *Form and Function in the Diary Novel*. Totowa, NJ: Barnes and Noble, 1989.

Forgacs, David, and Robert Lumley, eds. *Italian Cultural Studies: An Introduction*. Oxford: Oxford University Press, 1996.

Frye, Joanne S. *Living Stories, Telling Lives: Women and the Novel in Contemporary Experience*. Ann Arbor: University of Michigan Press, 1986.

Gabriele, Tommasina. 'From Prostitution to Transsexuality: Gender Identity and Subversive Sexuality in Dacia Maraini.' *MLN* 117 (2002): 241–56.

Gagliardi, Elena. '*Il rimorso* di Alba de Céspedes: Ipotesi sul romanzo epistolare del novecento.' *Il lettore di provincia* 30 (1999): 3–24.

Gallucci, Carole. 'The Body and the Letter: Sibilla Aleramo in the Interwar Years.' *Forum Italicum* 33 (1999): 363–91.

Gatt-Rutter, John. *Oriana Fallaci: The Rhetoric of Freedom*. New Directions in European Writing. Oxford: Berg, 1996.

Gilroy, Amanda, and W.M. Verhoeven, eds. *Epistolary Histories: Letters, Fiction, Culture*. Charlottesville: University Press of Virgina, 2000.

Ginsborg, Paul. *A History of Contemporary Italy. Society and Politics 1943–1988*. London: Penguin, 1990.

– *Italy and Its Discontents. Family, Civil Society, State: 1980–2001*. New York: Palgrave Macmillan, 2003.

Ginzburg, Natalia. *Caro Michele*. Milan: Einaudi: 1973.

– *La città e la casa*. Milan: Einaudi: 1984.

– *The City and the House*. Translated by Dick Davis. New York: Arcade, 1985.

– *Dear Michael*. Translated by Sheila Cudahy. London: Peter Owen, 1975.

Giorgio, Adalgisa. 'The Novel, 1965–2000.' In *A History of Women's Writing in Italy*, edited by Letizia Panizza and Sharon Wood. Cambridge: Cambridge University Press, 2000. 218–37.

Goldsmith, Elizabeth C., ed. *Writing the Female Voice: Essays on Epistolary Literature*. Boston: Northeastern University Press, 1989.

Golina, Vera F. Afterword to *My Husband*, by Dacia Maraini. Waterloo, ON: Wilfrid Laurier University Press, 2004. 145–67.

Gruen, Lori. 'Dismantling Oppression: An Analysis of the Connection between Women and Animals.' In *Ecofeminism: Women, Animals, Nature*, edited by Greta Gaard. Philadelphia: Temple University Press, 1993. 60–90.

Guerricchio, Rita. 'Il romanzo epistolare o l'epistolario romantico di Sibilla Aleramo.' In *Svelamento: Silbilla Aleramo: una biografia intellettuale*, edited by Annarita Buttafuoco and Marina Zancan. Milan: Feltrinelli, 1988. 46–59.

Hallamore Caesar, Ann. 'Proper Behavior: Women, the Novel, and Conduct Books in Nineteenth Century Italy.' In *With a Pen in Her Hand: Women and Writing in Italy in the Nineteenth Century and Beyond*, edited by Verina R. Jones and Anna Laura Lepschy. Society for Italian Studies. Occasional paper no. 5. Leeds, England: Maney Publishing, 2000. 27–36.

Huff, Cynthia. '"That Profoundly Female, and Feminist Genre": The Diary as Feminist Practice.' *Women's Study Quarterly* 17 (1989): 6–14.

Jensen, Katharine Ann. *Writing Love: Letters, Women, and the Novel in France, 1605–1776*. Ad Feminam: Women and Literature Series. Carbondale, IL: Southern Illinois University Press, 1995.

Jewell, Keala J. 'Un furore d'autocreazione: Women and Writing in Sibilla Aleramo.' *Canadian Journal of Italian Studies* 7 (1984): 148–62.

Jolly, Margaretta. *In Love and Struggle: Letters in Contemporary Feminism*. New York: Columbia University Press, 2008.

Kauffman, Linda S. *Discourses of Desire: Gender, Genre, and Epistolary Fictions*. Ithaca: Cornell University Press, 1986.

– *Special Delivery: Epistolary Modes in Modern Fiction*. Women in Culture and Society. Chicago: University of Chicago Press, 1992.

Kenyon, Olga. *800 Years of Women's Letters*. New York: Penguin, 1992.

Kroha, Lucienne. *The Woman Writer in Late-Nineteenth-Century Italy: Gender and the Formation of Literary Identity*. Lewiston, NY: Edwin Mellen, 1992.

Lazzaro-Weis, Carol. *From Margins to Mainstream: Feminism and Fictional Modes in Italian Women's Writing, 1968–1990*. Philadelphia: University of Pennsylvannia Press, 1993.

– 'Stranger Than Life? Autobiography and Historical Fiction.' In *Gendering Italian Fiction: Feminist Revisions of Italian History*, edited by Maria Ornella Marotti and Gabriella Brooke. Madison, NJ: Fairleigh Dickinson University Press, 1999. 31–48.

Lipparini, Giuseppe. 'Romanzi e novelle.' *Il Marzocco* Nov. 1914, 4–5.

Lombardi, Giancarlo. '*A memoria*: Charting a Cultural Map for Women's Transition from *Preistoria* to *Storia*.' In *The Pleasure of Writing: Critical Essays on Dacia Maraini*, edited by Rodica Diaconescu-Blumenfeld and Ada Testaferri. West Lafayette, IN: Purdue University Press, 2000. 149–64.

– *Rooms with a View: Feminist Diary Fiction, 1952–1999*. Madison, NJ: Fairleigh Dickinson University Press, 2002. 13–28.

Lucamante, Stefania. *A Multitude of Women: The Challenges of the Contemporary Italian Novel*. Toronto: University of Toronto Press, 2008.

Luciano, Bernadette. 'The Diaries of Sibilla Aleramo: Constructing Female Subjectivity.' In *Italian Women Writers from the Renaissance to the Present: Revising the Canon*, edited by Maria Ornella Marotti. University Park, PA: Pennsylvania State University Press, 1996. 95–110.

MacArthur, Elizabeth J. *Extravagant Narratives. Closure and Dynamics in the Epistolary Form*. Princeton: Princeton University Press, 1990.

Manzini, Gianna. *Game Plan for a Novel*. Translated by Martha King. New York: Italica, 2008

– *Lettera all'editore*. Florence: Sansoni, 1945.

Maraini, Dacia. *Dolce per sé*. Milan: Rizzoli, 1997.

– 'Le poesie delle donna.' *Donne mie*. Turin: Einaudi, 1974. 28–30.

– *Lettere a Marina*. Milan: Bompiani, 1981.

– *Letters to Marina*. Translated by Dick Kitto and Elspeth Spottiswood. Freedom, CA: Crossing Press, 1987.

– 'Reflections on the Logical and Illogical Bodies of My Sexual Compatriots.' In *The Pleasure of Writing: Critical Essays on Dacia Maraini*, edited by Rodica Diaconescu-Blumenfeld and Ada Testaferri. Translated by Rodica Diaconescu-Blumenfeld. West Lafayette, IN: Purdue University Press, 2000. 21–38.

– *The Violin*. Translated by Dick Kitto and Elspeth Spottiswood. London: Arcadia, 2001.

Marchesa Colombi. *Prima morire*. Rome: Lucarini, 1988.

Marcus, Millicent. 'Viconti's *Senso*: The Risorgimento According to Gramsci or Historical Revisionism Meets Cinematic Innovation.' In *Making and Remaking Italy: The Cultivation of National Identity around the Risorgimento*, edited by Albert R. Ascoli and Krystyna von Henneberg. Oxford: Berg, 2001. 277–96.

Marinetti, Benedetta Cappa. *Astra e il sottomarino: Vita trasognata*. Rome: Altana, 1998.

Marotti, Maria Ornella, and Gabriella Brooke, eds. *Gendering Italian Fiction: Feminist Revisions of Italian History*. Madison, NJ: Fairleigh Dickinson University Press, 1999.

Marrone, Claire. *Female Journeys: Autobiographical Expressions by French and Italian Women*. Contributions in Women's Studies no. 180. Westport, CT: Greenwood Press, 2000.

Martens, Lorna. *The Diary Novel*. Cambridge: Cambridge University Press, 1985.

Meda, Anna. 'Lui, lei, e l'altra: Trasfigurazione di Sibilla Aleramo e l'identità femminile.' *Studi d'italianistica nell'Africa australe* 12 (1999): 47–67.

Merry, Bruce. *Dacia Maraini and the Written Dream of Women in Modern Italian Literature*. North Queensland: James Cook University, 1997.

Miceli-Jeffries, Giovanna. 'Gianna Manzini.' In *Dictionary of Literary Biography* 177. *Italian Novelists since World War II, 1945–1965*, edited by Augustus Pallotta. Detroit: Gale Research, 1977. 171–9.

– 'Gianna Manzini's Poetics of Verbal Visualization.' In *Contemporary Women Writers in Italy: A Modern Renaissance*, edited by Santo L. Aricò. Amherst: University of Massachusetts Press, 1990. 91–106.

Milan Women's Bookstore Collective. *Sexual Difference: A Theory of Social-Symbolic Practice*. Bloomington, IN: Indiana University Press, 1990.

Morosoff, Anna Grimaldi. *Transfigurations: The Autobiographical Novels of Sibilla Aleramo*. Writing about Women: Feminist Literary Studies Series vol. 23. New York: Peter Lang, 1999.

Nerenberg, Ellen. 'Resistance and Remorse: Alba de Céspedes's Withdrawal from the Public Sphere.' In *Writing beyond Fascism: Cultural Resistance in the Life and Works of Alba de Céspedes*, edited by Carole C. Gallucci and Ellen Nerenberg. Madison, NJ: Fairleigh Dickinson University Press, 2000. 223–46.

Nozzoli, Anna. *Tabù e coscienza: La condizione femminile nella letteratura italiana del Novecento*. Florence: La Nuova Italia, 1978.

– 'I "ritratti" di Gianna Manzini.' *Gianna Manzini tra Letteratura e Vita*. Atti di Convegno. Ed. Marco Forti. Milan: Mondadori, 1985. 131–44.

O'Healy, Anne-Marie. 'Natalia Ginzburg and the Family.' *Canadian Journal of Italian Studies* 9 (1986): 21–36.

– 'A Woman Writer in Contemporary Italy: Natalia Ginzburg.' PhD. diss., University of Wisconsin-Madison, 1976.

Orban, Clara. 'Women, Futurism, and Fascism.' In *Mothers of Invention: Women, Italian Fascism, and Culture*, edited by Robin Pickering-Iazzi. Minneapolis: University of Minnesota Press, 1995. 52–75.

Pampaloni, Geno. 'Per Gianna Manzini.' In *Gianna Manzini tra Letteratura e Vita*, edited by Marco Forti. Milan: Mondadori, 1985. 39–46.

Panareo, Enzo. *Invito alla lettura di Gianna Manzini*. Milan: Mursia, 1977.

Panzera, Lisa. 'La Futurista: Benedetta Cappa Marinetti.' Catalogue for exhibition at the Galleries at Moore, Philadelphia, PA, 8 Sept.-25 Oct. 1998. 6–16.

Pappas, Rita Signorelli. Review of *Caro Michele*, by Natalia Ginzburg. *Italian Quarterly*, 28 (1987): 88–90.

Parati, Graziella, and Rebecca West, eds. *Italian Feminist Theory and Practice: Equality and Sexual Difference*. Madison, NJ: Fairleigh Dickinson University Press, 2002.

Parsani, M. Assunta, and Neria De Giovanni. *Femminile a Confronto: Tre realtà della narrativa contemporanea: Alba de Céspedes, Fausta Cialente, Gianna Manzini*. Rome: Lacaita, 1984.

Pastore, Judith Laurence. 'The Personal Is Political: Gender, Generation, and Memory in Natalia Ginzburg's *Caro Michele*.' In *Natalia Ginzburg: A Voice of the Twentieth Century*, edited by Angela M. Jeannet and Giuliana Sanguinetti Katz. Toronto: University of Toronto Press, 2002. 89–98.

– 'The Sounds of Silence: The Absence of Narrative Presence in Natalia Ginzburg's *La città e la casa*.' *Italian Culture* 11 (1993): 311–22.

Perry, Ruth. *Women, Letters, and the Novel*. New York: AMS Press, 1980.

Picarazzi, Teresa. *Maternal Desire: Natalia Ginzburg's Mothers, Daughters, and Sisters*. Madison, NJ: Fairleigh Dickinson University Press, 2002.

Picchietti, Virginia. *Relational Spaces: Daughterhood, Motherhood, and Sisterhood in Dacia Maraini's Writings and Films*. Madison, NJ: Fairleigh Dickinson University Press, 2002.

– 'Symbolic Mediation and Female Community in Dacia Maraini's Fiction.'

In *The Pleasure of Writing: Critical Essays on Dacia Maraini*, edited by Rodica Diaconescu-Blumenfeld and Ada Testaferri. West Lafayette, IN: Purdue University Press, 2000. 103–20.

Pickering-Iazzi, Robin. 'Designing Mothers: Images of Motherhood in Aleramo, Morante, Maraini, and Fallaci.' *Annali d'Italianistica: Women's Voices in Italian Literature* 7 (1989): 325–40.

Pierobon, Ermenegilda. '"Fra questi sí e no son di parer contrario": affermazione di sé e nome d'arte nella Marchesa Colombi.' *Studi d'italianistica nell'Africa australe* 12 (1999): 22–46.

Pomata, Gianna. 'Premiss: A Figure of Power and an Invitation to History. Epilogue: to Room Nineteen.' In *The Lonely Mirror: Italian Perspectives on Feminist Theory*, edited by Sandra Kemp and Paola Bono. London: Rutledge, 1993. 155–69.

Pool, Gail, ed. and intro. *Other People's Mail: An Anthology of Letter Stories*. Columbia: University of Missouri Press, 2000.

Ragone, Giovanni. 'Italy, 1815–1870.' In *The Novel, Volume I: History, Geography, and Culture*, edited by Franco Moretti. Princeton: Princeton University Press, 2006. 466–78.

Ray, Meredith K. *Writing Gender in Women's Letter Collections of the Italian Renaissance*. Toronto: University of Toronto Press, 2009.

Re, Lucia. 'Diotima's Dilemmas: Authorship, Authority, Authoritarianism.' In *Italian Feminist Theory and Practice: Equality and Sexual Difference*, edited by Graziella Parati and Rebecca West. Madison, NJ: Fairleigh Dickinson University Press, 2002. 50–74.

– 'Fascist Theories of "Woman" and the Construction of Gender.' In *Mothers of Invention: Women, Italian Fascism, and Culture*, edited by Robin Pickering-Iazzi. Minneapolis: University of Minnesota Press, 1995. 76–99.

– 'Futurism and Feminism.' *Annali d'Italianistica: Women's Voices in Italian Literature* 7 (1989): 253–72.

– 'Futurism and Fascism, 1914–1945.' In *A History of Women's Writing in Italy*, edited by Letizia Panizza and Sharon Wood. Cambridge: Cambridge University Press, 2000. 190–204.

– 'Impure Abstraction: Benedetta as Visual Artist and Novelist.' Catalogue for exhibition at the Galleries at Moore, Philadelphia, PA, 8 Sept.–25 Oct. 1998. 31–47.

– 'Passion and Sexual Difference: The Risorgimento and the Gendering of Writing in Nineteenth-Century Italian Culture.' In *Making and Remaking Italy: The Cultivation of National Identity around the Risorgimento*, edited by Alberto R. Ascoli and Krystyna von Henneberg. Oxford: Berg, 2001. 155–200.

Romani, Gabriella. 'From Letter to Literature: Giovanni Verga, Matilde

Serao and Late Nineteenth-Century Epistolary Fiction.' *MLN* 124 (2009): 177–94.

– Introduction. In *Writing to Delight: Italian Short Stories by Nineteenth-Century Women Writers*, edited by Antonia Arslan and Gabriella Romani. Toronto: University of Toronto Press, 2006.

– 'Women Writing Letters: Epistolary Practices in Nineteenth-Century Newspapers, Manuals and Fiction.' In *Across Genres, Generations and Borders: Italian Women Writing Lives*, edited by Susanna Scarparo and Rita Wilson. Melbourne: Monash Romance Studies, 2004. 24–37.

Rorato, Laura. 'Childhood Prisons: Denied Dreams and Denied Realities: The Ritualization of Pain in the Novels of Susanna Tamaro.' *Romance Studies* (Fall 1996): 61–78.

Rosbottom, Ronald C. 'Motifs in Epistolary Fiction: Analysis of a Narrative Sub-genre.' *L'Esprit Créateur* 17 (1977): 279–301.

Rossi, Monica. 'Rethinking History: Women's Transgression in Maria Rosa Cutrufelli's *La briganta.*' In *Gendering Italian Fiction: Feminist Revisions of Italian History*, edited by Maria Ornella Marotti and Gabriella Brooke. Madison, NJ: Fairleigh Dickinson University Press, 1999. 202–22.

Ryan, Colleen Marie. 'In the Heart of the Nineties: Theorizing a Grandmother's Subjectivity in Two Works by Susanna Tamaro.' *Romance Languages Annual* 10 (1999): 360–7.

Sacrati, Orintia Romagnuoli. *Lettere di Giulia Willet.* Rome: Stamparia de Romanis, 1818.

Salaris, Claudia. *Le futuriste: Donne e letterature d'avanguardia in Italia (1909–1944).* Milan: Edizione delle donne, 1982.

Salsini, Laura A. *Gendered Genres: Female Experiences and Narrative Patterns in the Works of Matilde Serao.* Madison, NJ: Fairleigh Dickinson University Press, 1999.

– 'Rewriting the Risorgimento: Isabella Bossi Fedrigotti's *Amore mio uccidi Garibaldi.*' *Forum Italicum* 42 (2008): 83–98.

Santoro, Anna. *Narratrici italiane dell'ottocento.* Naples: Federico & Ardia, 1987.

Sanzin, Bruno. 'Omaggio a Benedetta Marinetti.' *Il Ragguaglio librario* 44 (1977): 371–4.

Senardi, Fulvio. 'Nonne e Giardini: la narrativa di Susanna Tamaro, ovvero come si costruisce il successo letterario.' *Problemi: Periodico Quadrimenstrale di Cultura* 102 (1995): 180–99.

Serao, Matilde. *Ella non rispose.* Milan: Treves, 1914.

– 'Falso in scrittura.' In *Fior di passione.* Milan: Baldini, Castoldi, 1899. 197–204.

– 'La vita è così lunga.' In *La vita è così lunga.* Milan: Treves, 1918. 33–41.

– 'Livia Speri.' In *La vita è così lunga.* Milan: Treves, 1918. 45–54.

Setzkorn, Sylvia. 'Geschlechterdifferenzen und Post-Feminismus in Italien: *Dolce per sé* von Dacia Maraini.' In *Geschlechterdifferenzen*, edited by Katharina Hanau and Volker Rivinius. Bonn: Romanisticher Verlag, 1999. 205–18.

Simon, Sunka. *Mail-Orders: The Fiction of Letters in Postmodern Culture.* New York: State University of New York Press, 2002.

Spackman, Barbara. 'Fascist Women and the Rhetoric of Virility.' In *Mothers of Invention: Women, Italian Fascism, and Culture*, edited by Robin Pickering-Iazzi. Minneapolis: University of Minnesota Press, 1995. 100–20.

Sumeli Weinberg, Grazia. *Invito alla lettura di Dacia Maraini.* Pretoria: University of South Africa Press, 1993.

Tamaro, Susanna. *Follow Your Heart.* Translated by John Cullen. New York: Delta, 1996.

– *Va' dove ti porta il cuore.* Milan: Baldini & Castoldi, 1994.

Testaferri, Ada. 'De-tecting *Voci.*' In *The Pleasure of Writing: Critical Essays on Dacia Maraini*, edited by Rodica Diaconescu-Blumenfeld and Ada Testaferri. West Lafayette, IN: Purdue University Press, 2000. 41–60.

Vitti-Alexander, Maria Rosaria. 'Il passaggio del ponte: L'evoluzione del personaggio femminile di Alba de Céspedes.' *Campi immaginabili* 3 (1991): 103–12.

Weldon, Fay. *Letters to Alice on First Reading Jane Austen.* New York: Carroll & Graf, 1984.

West, Rebecca. Introduction to *Natalia Ginzburg: A Voice of the Twentieth Century*, edited by Angela M. Jeannet and Guiliana Sanguinetti Katz. Toronto: University of Toronto Press, 2000. 3–9.

Wood, Sharon. 'Feminist Writing in the Twentieth Century.' In *The Cambridge Companion to the Italian Novel*, edited by Peter Bondanella and Andrea Ciccarelli. Cambridge: Cambridge University Press, 2003. 151–67.

– *Italian Women's Writing: 1860–1994.* Women's Writing 1850–1990s. London: Athlone, 1995.

Zaczek, Barbara Maria. *Censored Sentiments: Letters and Censorship in Epistolary Novels and Conduct Material.* Newark, DE: University of Delaware Press, 1997.

– 'Plotting Letters: Narrative Dynamics in the Correspondence of Giovanni Papini and Sibilla Aleramo and in *La Trasfigurazione.*' *Italica* 72 (1995): 54–69.

Zancan, Marina. 'Una biografia intellettuale: Sibilla Aleramo.' In *Svelamento: Silbilla Aleramo: una biografia intellettuale*, edited by Annarita Buttafuoco and Marina Zancan. Milan: Feltrinelli, 1988. 13–28.

Zarri, Gabriella, ed. *Per lettera: La scrittura epistolare femminile tra archivio e tipografia secoli XV-XVII.* Rome: Viella, 1999.

Index

Lightning Source UK Ltd.
Milton Keynes UK
UKHW010034120322
399939UK00001B/93